Secrets Need Words

This series of publications on Africa, Latin America, and Southeast Asia is designed to present significant research, translation, and opinion to area specialists and to a wide community of persons interested in world affairs. The editor seeks manuscripts of quality on any subject and can generally make a decision regarding publication within three months of receipt of the original work. Production methods generally permit a work to appear within one year of acceptance. The editor works closely with authors to produce a high-quality book. The series appears in a paperback format and is distributed worldwide. For more information, contact the executive editor at Ohio University Press, Scott Quadrangle, University Terrace, Athens, Ohio 45701.

EXECUTIVE EDITOR
Gillian Berchowitz

AREA CONSULTANTS
Africa: Diane Ciekawy
Latin America: Thomas Walker
Southeast Asia: William H. Frederick

The Ohio University Research in International Studies series is published for the Center for International Studies by the Ohio University Press. The views expressed in individual volumes are those of the authors and should not be considered to represent the policies or beliefs of the Center for International Studies, the Ohio University Press, or Ohio University.

Secrets Need Words

Indonesian Poetry 1966–1998

EDITED AND TRANSLATED BY

Harry Aveling

OHIO UNIVERSITY CENTER FOR INTERNATIONAL STUDIES
RESEARCH IN INTERNATIONAL STUDIES
SOUTHEAST ASIA SERIES NO. 105
ATHENS

The books in the Ohio University Research in International Studies Series
are printed on acid-free paper ∞ ™

Library of Congress Cataloging-in-Publication Data

Secrets need words : Indonesian poetry, 1966–1998 /
edited and translated by Harry Aveling.
p. cm. — (Research in international studies.
Southest Asia series ; no. 105)
ISBN 0-89680-216-7 (pbk. : alk. paper)
1. Indonesian poetry—20th century—Translations into English.
2. Politics and literature—Indonesia—History—20th century.
3. Politics in literature. I. Aveling, Harry. II. Series

PL5086.5.E5 S43 2001
899'.2211208—dc21

00-069558

This project has been assisted by the Government
of the Commonwealth of Australia,
through the Australia Council,
its Arts funding and advisory body.

SUBAGIO SASTROWARDOYO

Nada Awal

Tugasku hanya menterjemah
gerak daun yang bergantung
di ranting yang letih. Rahasia
membutuhkan kata yang terucap
di puncak sepi. Ketika daun
jatuh takada titik darah. Tapi
di ruang kelam ada yang merasa
kehilangan dan mengaduh pedih.

The first sound

My task is to translate
the movement of the leaves, hanging
on tired branches. Secrets
need words, spoken
in silence. When a leaf
falls, there is no blood. But
in a dark room, someone
feels grief and cries out
in pain.

*1989

Contents

Acknowledgments

THE DISTANT ROOTS of this book are to be found in my two volumes of literary translation, *Contemporary Indonesian Poetry* (first published by the University of Queensland Press, St. Lucia, Brisbane, in 1975) and *Arjuna in Meditation: Three Young Indonesian Poets* (Calcutta: Writers Workshop, 1976). Both were undertaken during the heady days of the first decade of the "New Order" period of Suharto's presidency of Indonesia.

The present work represents an attempt to come to terms with the development of Indonesian poetry throughout the whole era, now ended with Suharto's resignation on May 21, 1998. Although this volume necessarily includes some of the writers, and indeed some of the poems (often in a revised form) to be found in those earlier books, this is a completely new work. In this volume, I have traced the further development of those earlier writers, presented newer writers from the succeeding three decades, and sought to conceptualize the dynamic of the complete cultural period. Whereas the short time-span of those earlier volumes allowed the works of each author to be grouped together in the one place, one writer after the other, the present work follows a sequence that is primarily thematic and historical.

The initial financial support for the collection and translation of the writing represented here was received in the form of a Translation Grant from the Australia Council, the arts funding and advisory body of the Government of the Commonwealth of Australia. My work in Indonesia was made possible through the good offices of the Indonesian Ambassador to Australia, His Excellency Mr. Wiryono Sastrohandoyo, and the Dean of the Faculty of Letters,

University of Indonesia, Dr. Sapardi Djoko Damono. It was immeasurably enriched by the friendship of so many of the poets and by their willingness to see their work made available to an audience beyond the Republic of Indonesia. Dorothea Rosa Herliany graciously helped with obtaining appropriate permission from the various writers to use their works in this book.

At the University of Technology, Sydney, I have been blessed by the ongoing trust and encouragement shown by Dr. Paul Gillen, Associate Professor Glenda Adams, and Mr. Martin Harrison, of the Faculty of Humanities and Social Sciences. Professor Stephen Muecke has provided the constant and appropriate administrative support necessary for this project. I am also grateful for the kind hospitality shown to me during my period as visiting professor in the Creative Writing Program at the University of Maryland, College Park, during the Fall Semester of 1999, most especially by Professors Thomas Moser, Michael Collier (who kindly shared his office with me), Joyce Kornblatt, Phillis Levin, Stanley Plumly, and Mr. Don Berger. Thanks to Ann Beth Kantar, also of the University of Maryland, and Lucy Thomason, of the University of Texas, for sharing their enthusiasm about literature. At Ohio University, I am indebted to Professors Elizabeth Collins and William Frederick, Ms. Gillian Berchowitz, and the staff of Ohio University Press and Inari Information Services, whose committment to detail is of the highest order.

Sara Aveling and Claire Horsley first typed the English translations and the Indonesian originals, respectively. Marian Quartly patiently guided me through the mysteries of word-processing. Phillip Thomas and Pat Afable were gracious hosts and wonderful friends in Maryland.

Preface

Apabila kita berbicara tentang susastra, kita masuk ke dalam wilayah kontemplasi.

    —Y. B. Mangunwijaya[1]

The Setting

THE PERIOD 1966 to 1998 represents a distinct era in Indonesian history. The "New Order" carefully defined itself against the aims and failures of the "Old Order" of Sukarno, Indonesia's first president, whom it had forcibly rejected.[2] The new era followed the widespread economic crisis and clear political discord of the period of Sukarno's "Guided Democracy" (1959–1965), in which the president, the Armed Forces, and the Communist Party had existed in constant, but shifting, alliances and opposition. The beginnings of the New Order were marked by widespread civil violence, student demonstrations, and the toppling of a leader considered to have grown corrupt and contemptuous of his people. Throughout the following three decades, "the longest period of one-man rule in modern Southeast Asian history,"[3] Suharto ruled with a firm hand over the twin policies of economic development and political stability.[4]

David Bourchier has suggested that these policies were closely related. He has argued that: "If there has been a leitmotif in the ideology of the Suharto regime, it has been the concept of 'order' (*ketertiban*). Suharto has described stability, order and security 'as an object of development itself, namely, to make [people] . . . feel physically secure and have peace of mind, free from fear of threats from without and from worrying over disturbance from within.'"[5] There can be little doubt that in the pursuit of 'order' over these years, many freedoms were lost. Suharto's leadership steadily became more autocratic; the political system became more and more inflexible; the military sought to establish themselves as the dominant political power in the country, unchallenged by other sociopolitical forces; and the public expression of personal opinion was consistently under suspicion and, indeed, threat of punishment by arrest and even imprisonment.[6]

Suharto's unexpected decision to step down on May 21, 1998, was received with great enthusiasm by Indonesian society. Ironically, the pattern that marked the end of the era—economic crisis, political discord, student demonstrations, and growing public violence—was remarkably similar to its beginning.

The Poetry

The tradition of modern Indonesian literature is conventionally dated from the 1920s.[7] Throughout most of this time, critics have been fairly well agreed on who counted as major authors and what their significant works were. This was again the case after 1966, when a distinct new group of writers came into prominence and steadily developed their craft throughout the seventies. Focusing at first on the social and political issues raised by the change in government, the "Generation of 1966"[8] soon began to explore the existential significance of the world of nature, the difficulties of human relationships, and a wide range of personal experience. Although there were growing penalties for direct criticism of the policies of the New Order, a few well-known writers also sought to make their opinions known widely.

By the beginning of the eighties, the development of literature in general, and poetry in particular, had become increasingly obscure, in both senses of the term. On the one hand, volumes of poetry were obscure, because they were difficult to find. They were published in small editions, occasionally outside Jakarta, and often writing appeared in newspapers and periodicals without being collected at all for long periods. As a consequence, it was harder to see what was being written. On the other hand, what was written itself seemed obscure to many. Henk Maier, Professor of Malay at Leiden University in the Netherlands, has argued, with particular reference to the prose writing of the period, "Rejecting realism and strict moralism, the tales of the seventies and eighties were preoccupied with an experimental freedom and playfulness that confused the critics, alienated those who thought that 'literature' still had a role to play in the New Order, and discouraged new and young readers who subsequently turned away from *sastra* as a crucial manifestation of national culture." It was Maier's opinion that "Suharto and his administrative apparatus have castrated a generation of writers, robbing them of their generative power, the power of being historical witnesses who could tell others about what is happening before their very eyes."[9]

In this volume, I hope to show not the failure of Indonesian poetry during the New Order but its great diversity and richness. I seek to do this by presenting a broad selection of poetry written during the period of 1966 to 1998, both in the original Indonesian and in English translation. Believing that literature moves within its own normative structures as a way of expressing the thoughts, emotions, and insights of its authors in the most intense language available to them, the selection aims to map the changing norms of the whole period in a positive manner. The introductions to the various sections of the volume are intended to outline briefly the political changes that were taking place at the time in which these poems were written.[10] More importantly, they are also meant to prepare the reader for the poems that follow, presenting alternative criteria to "realism and strict morality," and encouraging an appreciation of the "experimental freedom and playfulness," which are indeed abundantly in evidence throughout the entire period. In this way, some of the shifts in style and subject matter may also be understood as successful strategic responses on the part of writers to the power of a "strong state" intent on controlling any diversity of opinions.[11]

The anthology is divided into two parts. The first covers the period from 1966 to the mid-eighties, and the writers there are simply described as "The Generation of 1966." The second part begins in the mid-eighties and continues through to the resignation of Suharto from the presidency in 1998. As most of the poets in this second part were born after the Declaration of Indonesian Independence on August 17, 1945, and indeed had scarcely known any other president besides Suharto, I have entitled this second part "The Post-Indonesian Generation."[12]

The date shown after each translation indicates the date of composition as given by the poet. If this is not available, I have provided a date with an asterisk (e.g., *1968) to indicate the date of publication of the volume in which the poem first appeared.

In a survey of "Recent Developments in Indonesian Literature" written over a decade ago, I argued that "It is more difficult in 1990 than it was ten years ago to discern tendencies and designate rising stars. The Polish theatre director Jerzy Grotowski has argued for 'an extreme confrontation, sincere, disciplined, precise and total—not only with our thoughts, but a confrontation including our instincts and subconscious, through to our most lucid states.' There can be no doubt that this confrontation has continued to take place over the past twenty-five years in Indonesian literature and that it has produced great diversity and profound uncertainty. If the situation today appears to be confused, that is the result, let us sincerely hope, of certain tendencies that are still working themselves out. We are awaiting the appearance of that fabulous creature, the new generation."[13] The commitment to "extreme confrontation" of the new generation of the nineties is as genuine and as powerful as that of their elders, who have continued to write alongside them. The proof is clearly evident in this anthology.

PART ONE

The Generation of 1966

Chapter 1

THE BEGINNING
OF THE NEW ORDER

Coup and Counter-Coup

In a landmark essay entitled "The Generation of 1966: The Emergence of a Generation," the doyen of Indonesian literary critics, the late H. B. Jassin, wrote:

> Now, in the year 1966, in Indonesia, an important event has taken place. The event has given birth to a generation which calls itself "The Generation of '66." The event was the shattering of the degenerate condition brought about by corruptness of the wider state, a corruption which brought the nation to the very edge of total collapse. Just as Chairil Anwar expressed his opposition to Japanese oppression in 1943 through the words: "*Aku ini binatang jalang dari kumpulannya terbuang*" ("I am a wild beast, cast out from its group"), so we too have seen a rebellious outburst on the part of the poets, writers and intellectuals, who have been so long oppressed by unnatural slogans which are alien to the nature of our people. We have our heroes too, heroes who have come to maturity in this present struggle.[1]

The "event" to which Jassin refers, of course, was the Coup of September 30, 1965. On that night, six generals of the Indonesian Army were killed by members of the palace guard, the Cakrabirawa, under the leadership of Lt. Col. Untung. Members of the unit also captured the state radio station and the postal exchange. On the morning of October first, and then regularly throughout the day, communiqués were broadcast explaining the latest developments. Later in the same day, the establishment of an "Indonesian Revolutionary Council" was announced. The daily newspaper of the Indonesian Communist Party (PKI), *Harian Rakyat,* described the Movement's actions as "patriotic and revolutionary," while also indicating that what had happened was purely "an internal Army affair."[2]

Two senior generals, Major General Suharto and General Nasution, escaped the massacre. By that evening of October 1, they had used battalions in Jakarta to recapture the radio station and control the city. For about a week, there was intermittent fighting in Central Java, involving members of the communist youth organization, Pemuda Rakyat. The fighting was put down by Army para-commandos, also dispatched by Suharto. Justifiably or not, the Communist Party had been well and truly implicated in the coup by the support shown for the plotters in their newspaper and by the apparent eagerness of their young men to fight an old enemy, the Indonesian Army. In response to this perceived betrayal, a form of civil war broke out on a large scale across Sumatra, Java, and Bali as young Muslim men, in particular, engaged in attacks on those believed to be members of the Communist Party or at least sympathetic to its aims. The estimates of the numbers killed have varied between 78,000 and one million persons.[3]

Untung had not included Sukarno in the "Revolutionary Council," but neither did "the President/Supreme Commander/Great Leader of the Revolution/Mandatory of the MPRS"[4] come out clearly against the plotters or the Communist Party. Inflation continued to rise during the next few months, and was exacerbated by increases in the costs of petrol, kerosene, and public transport. At the beginning of January, high school and university students in Jakarta and Bandung organized themselves into "action fronts," and launched an extensive series of street demonstrations demanding the disbanding of the PKI, the restructuring of the cabinet, and a lowering of the prices of basic necessities. During these demonstrations, a number of students were shot.[5] On March 11, 1966, Sukarno finally requested Lieutenant General Suharto to "guarantee the security, calm and stability of the government and the revolution," and his own "personal safety and authority."[6] This action effectively marked the transition of power from the one man to the other.[7] Bernard Dahm has concluded that it was "the student movement, with the silent approval of the new army leadership under General Suharto, [which] brought about the collapse of the Sukarno regime."[8] Suharto was appointed Acting President by the MPRS on March 11, 1967, during a week-long special session, and became the second president of the Republic of Indonesia on March 27, 1968.

The Generation of 1966

The year 1966 marked the passing of the power of the literary "Generation of 1945," many of whom still held important positions in the various writers associations formed to apply Sukarno's ideals to literature. The works of a number of those clearly identified with what were now considered extreme left-wing positions were also banned, whatever their actual content.[9] This cleared a space for their successors, the so-called "Generation of 1966," to emerge as the unchallenged champions of a new literature.

The support of non-socialist students and intellectuals for the New Order was evident in Jassin's literary anthology *Angkatan 66, Prosa dan Puisi* (The generation of 1966, poetry and prose), first published in 1968. The motto of Jassin's book was *"Sastra demi Keadilan dan Kebenaran"* (Literature for the sake of justice and truth), and it had a clear political aim. The work prominently featured a large number of poems which Jassin describes as *"sajak demonstrasi"* (protest poems), poems which had been read to encourage students and the wider public during the public protests of early 1966. The volumes in which these verses first appeared themselves carried such committed titles as *Tirani* (Tyranny) and *Benteng* (Fortress), by Taufiq Ismail; *Mereka telah bangkit* (They have risen up), by Bur Rusuanto; *Perlawan* (Resistance), by Mansur

Samin; *Pembebasan* (Liberation), by Abd. Wahid Situmeang; and *Kebangkitan* (Uprising), by students of the Faculty of Letters of the University of Indonesia.[10]

The protest poetry of Taufiq Ismail, the first poet included here (and almost the last, too), was typical of those volumes. His poems were simply written and heavily didactic, so as to be readily understood by the student groups who heard them read aloud. Their descriptions were simple and related to certain immediate scenes, including the funeral procession of Arief Rachman Hakim, the Salemba campus of the University of Indonesia, the soldiers and their weapons, and the changing sky above the city of Jakarta (misty when the mood was intended to be sad, hot when it was angry).

The poems relied on certain rhetorical assumptions about good and evil, in relation to the nature of the state. Clifford Geertz has noted the forceful emergence in Indonesia after 1960 of the traditional Javanese doctrine that "the welfare of the nation proceeds from the excellence of its capital, the excellence of the capital from the brilliance of its elite, and the brilliance of its elite from the spirituality of its ruler."[11] By claiming that this situation had now been reversed, that the decadence of the capital and the corruption of the elite was the reason for the terrible hardships being experienced by the masses, Taufiq was able to attack Sukarno's leadership and that of his closest associates. He was also able to suggest that the students' struggle was just, because it was committed to restoring the well-being of the people. In "Kita adalah pemilik syah republik ini" (The republic is ours), the suffering people were shown to reassert their legitimate right to ownership of the Republic, which had been taken from them by the murderous and hypocritical henchmen of the great leader, who had no hesitation in supporting his every tyrannical action. The inclusive pronoun "we" (*kita*), spoken in the title by all who were presented as the rightful owners of the Republic, began with the students but reached out to include the whole nation.

There was a second traditional metaphysical belief which was also crucial to these poems. This asserted that each age is self-contained and had its own characteristics. Those who are able to attune themselves to those characteristics, and to take advantage of the opportunities they offer, will advance; those who do not, will be left behind.

At a number of points in these poems, the framework provided by time was extended in order to take on a major cyclical historical significance. Many poems in Taufiq's two volumes asserted that the demonstrations of 1966 were a way of properly continuing the original Revolution of 1945, a favorite theme of Sukarno's, and were thus aimed at setting the nation back onto the earlier path dedicated to "Justice and Truth." Sometimes this repetition was symbolized by the parents of one generation sending their children off to fight in the new struggle to restore Indonesia to its full integrity.

The poems also show what some have considered questionable about much of this writing: it could not allow for real social change. The rhetoric blamed "the moral turpitude of the political leaders," seeking to replace them with better leaders (those of the rising middle class itself), but had no criticism to make of "factors integral to the structure of the system itself."[12] In fact, despite Jassin's claim that the work of the "generation of 66" was distinctive, a number of Indonesian writers and critics were quick to point out that there were great similarities between the "socialist" poetry of the preceding period and that of the "Generation of 1966." Goenawan Mohamad, for example, has written that the first half of the sixties was:

> a period which reflected the strength of social realism on both its adherents and its enemies. The period began with the writing of "struggle" poetry by almost anyone at all and ended with the verse of the 1966 conflict. In both phases "heroism," "social destiny," "great principles," praise of the fatherland and of the masses, as well as historical optimism, formed a single storehouse of mutual themes.[13]

Similarly, Subagio Sastrowardoyo commented on what seemed to him to be the paradox of enemies writing the same style of verse, comparing the work of the left-wing poet Klara Akustia with that of Taufiq Ismail. Subagio suggested that both authors wrote verse filled with conviction and spirit; both relied on a common range of catch-phrases and slogans to express readily apprehensible political ideals, while neither, in his opinion, produced "genuine verse."[14] (Such an assessment depends of course on how one judges the quality of socially committed writing. Certainly subtlety and interior personal exploration do not necessarily count for much in these situations. On the other hand, if one wanted to motivate large groups of people to undertake direct action, they were, no doubt, effective enough.)[15]

A New Avant-garde

After their support was no longer needed by the Armed Forces, the students and intellectuals were encouraged to step back from the political stage. Some found positions with the government, the corporations, or the press. In time, later student generations were to become one of the few ongoing sources of opposition to the perceived corruption and social equality of the New Order throughout the rest of its existence.[16] (The other major source was Islam.) The narrow type of verse which Jassin championed ceased to matter somewhere between 1967 and 1968.[17] Out of the politically motivated "chaotic diversity of 1966"[18] there burst, as Goenawan Mohamad noted, "a new sense of freedom and widespread experimentation in prose, poetry and the theater." He continued: "it was as if we were watching the beginnings of a new avant-garde movement, similar to that which developed after 1945. Writers came as individuals, bowing to no common artistic creed, clearly aware (and many of them were new writers) of the rediscovery of a creative elan."[19]

Some of the writers who made their greatest impact after 1967 were new writers; others had been writing for over a decade but had always been overshadowed by more established writers of the generation of the Revolution. Taufiq Ismail may indeed be considered a newer poet. Although he had begun publishing in the early 1960s, the earliest poem he now wishes to have remembered is the first one in this volume, "Bukit biru, bukit kelu" (The silent hills), dated 1965.[20] Two of his later poems, both written in 1971—"Bagaimana Kalau" (What if) and "Kembalikan Indonesia Padaku"

(Give Indonesia back to me)—show how he continued to develop his writing after 1966. The poems refine and deepen the strong nationalist commitments and social protest he had displayed through the use of longer, more complex lines, in the service of unexpected conjunctions of objects and a sardonic humor. The first of these later poems already showed a keen awareness of the contradictions and difficulties of New Order Indonesia. The second was a renewed demand for Indonesia to be returned to those to whom it rightly belongs. Interestingly, in this second poem Taufiq never actually defined whom he was addressing, whom exactly he wanted to give Indonesia back to its people. At the time the poem was written, those who read the poem may have thought that the poem was still directed against the forces of the Old Order who had impoverished their nation. Or they may have cast it in wider terms, as an attack on economic forces beyond the republic. My own recollection is that no one then considered it to be an outright criticism of the new government.

Other, older authors, who emerged as major figures after 1968, had begun writing in the early fifties and then deliberately moved away from poetry under the pressures of Guided Democracy. Ajip Rosidi, for example, had published his first volume of poetry in the Indonesian language in 1956 and then two further volumes in 1959 and 1960, before retreating into writing in the Sundanese language of West Java during the early sixties. There were those, including Subagio Sastrowardoyo and Goenawan Mohamad, who had gone abroad for further studies, Subagio to Yale, Goenawan to the Collège d'Europe in Belgium. Many of the genuinely younger writers had been forced into virtual silence by the controversy that surrounded the non-socialist "Cultural Manifesto" of 1963, banned by Sukarno in May of the next year.[21]

Undoubtedly, the boldest of the more mature writers was W. S. Rendra. Rendra had published his first volume of poetry, *Ballada Orang-orang Tercinta,* in 1957, and later volumes of love poetry, *Empat Kumpulan Sajak,* in 1961. From 1964 to 1967, however, he too had lived abroad, undertaking the two-year Professional Training

Program of the American Academy of Dramatic Arts in New York. When he returned to Indonesia, his impact was enormous. In the theatre, instead of the conventional realist plays, he staged dance dramas, using a bare minimum of words in favor of an emphasis on pure sounds. These were usually described simply as "bip-bop" theatre. In poetry, Rendra wrote both personal and social verse. The long and highly theatrical poem "Pelacur-pelacur kota Jakarta" (Prostitutes of Jakarta—Unite!), presented here, shows how Rendra was able to adapt to the current conventions of satirizing the upper classes for their lust, dishonesty and corruption, and praise the working classes for their capacity to survive in an immoral world.

In their earliest works, both Ajip Rosidi and Rendra had claimed to be turning away from the heavily Europeanized concerns of the older members of the "Generation of 1945" toward local, regional concerns.[22] Rendra's first poetry had dealt with Central Javanese themes and was from the start written on a large scale. Ajip Rosidi's poetry dealt with West Java and was more understated. It tended, as he suggested in "Hanya dalam puisi" (Only in poetry), to prefer the "clear and definite." The world Ajip observed in this poem framed the hard-working farmer from the window of the passing train. The farmers were seen as lonely, romantic figures, their brows covered with sweat, caught in the wider setting of rice-fields and the exquisitely beautiful mountains of West Java. The description of the farmer was probably not meant to be particularly heroic, except by necessity. Instead, Ajip set human labor in the context of an implicitly Islamic religious submission to the fate decreed by God, and contrasted the farmers with the primal hubris of the poet. Humanity is born to struggle and suffer. The person of the poet, however, tries to reach out beyond everyday work, to shape another world. In this attempt to go beyond, to knock on every door, Ajip suggested, the author must ultimately fail in comparison with the natural poetry of the created world and the simple surrender of the farmer.

It was this same religious surrender which also characterized the following two poems, written in a style which is characteristic of traditional verse in Malay, rhymed four-line verses. In these poems there can be no doubt that the "you" addressed was Allah, God, and that the condition which the poem sought was one of stillness and union with that loving and changeless God. The return to simple piety was characteristic of the faith of regional society; it was not a quality prominent in Indonesian poetry of the highly secularized and modern Generation of 1945.

Bukit biru, bukit kelu

Adalah hujan dalam kabut yang ungu
Turun sepanjang gunung dan bukit biru
Ketika kota cahaya dan di mana bertemu
Awan putih yang menghinggapi cemaraku

Adalah kemarau dalam sengangar berdebu
Turun sepanjang gunung dan bukit kelu
Ketika kota tak bicara dan terpaku
Gunung api dan hama di ladang-ladangku

Lereng-lereng senja
Pernah menyinar merah kesumba
Padang hilalang dan bukit membatu
Tanah airku.

Kita adalah pemilik syah republik ini

Tidak ada lagi pilihan lain. Kita harus
Berjalan terus
Karena berhenti atau mundur
Bererti hancur

Apakah akan kita jual keyakinan kita
Dalam pengabdian tanpa harga
Akan maukah kita duduk satu meja
Dengan para pembunuh tahun yang lalu
Dalam setiap kalimat yang berakhiran:
"Duli Tuanku"?

Taufiq Ismail

The silent hills

There is rain in the violet mist
Falling along the mountains and blue hills
As the city shines and meets with
The white clouds which rest on my pines

There is drought in the lightning dust
Falling along the mountains and silent hills
As the city lies speechless, nailed down
By volcano and scourge in my fields

The valleys of twilight
Shine like red coral
The grassy fields and hills of stone
Are my home.

1965

The republic is ours

There is no other choice. We must
Go on,
Because to stop or withdraw
Would mean destruction.

Should we sell our certainty
For meaningless slavery,
Or sit at a table
With last year's murderers
Who end each sentence
"As Your Majesty wishes"?

Tidak ada lagi pilihan lain. Kita harus
Berjalan terus
Kita adalah manusia bermata sayu, yang di tepi jalan
Mengacungkan tangan untuk oplet dan bus yang
                                        penuh
Kita adalah berpuluh juta yang bertahun hidup
                                        sengsara
Dipukul banjir, gunung api, kutuk dan hama
Dan bertanya-tanya diam inikah yang namanya
                                        merdeka
Kita yang tak punya kepentingan dengan seribu slogan
Dan seribu pengeras suara yang hampa suara

Tidak ada lagi pilihan lain. Kita harus
berjalan terus.

Bagaimana kalau

Bagaimana kalau dulu bukan buah khuldi yang
    dimakan Adam, tapi buah alpukat.
Bagaimana kalau bumi bukan bulat, tapi segi empat.
Bagaimana kalau lagu "Indonesia Raya" kita rubah,
    dan kepada Kus Plus kita beri mandat.
Bagaimana kalau ibukota Amerika Hanoi dan ibukota
    Indonesia Monaco.
Bagaimana kalau malam nanti jam sebelas, salju turun
    di Gunung Sahari.
Bagaimana kalau bisa dibuktikan bahwa Ali Murtopo,
    Ali Sadikin dan Ali Wardhana ternyata pengarang-
    pengarang lagu pop.
Bagaimana kalau hutang-hutang Indonesia dibayar
    dengan pementasan Rendra.

There is no other choice. We must
Go on.
We are the people with the sad eyes, at the edge of the
                                                    road

Waving at vans and crowded buses.
We are the tens of millions who have lived in misery
Beaten about by flood, volcano, curses and pestilence,
Who silently ask for freedom
But are ignored in a thousand slogans
And meaningless loudspeaker voices.

There is no other choice. We must
Go on.

                                        1966

What if

What if it were not an apple Adam ate but an avocado.
What if the earth were not round but square.
What if we changed the national anthem and gave the
    mandate for a new one to the Kus Plus group.
What if the capital of America were Hanoi and the
    capital of Indonesia Monaco.
What if precisely at eleven o'clock tonight snow began
    to fall in Sahara Row, Jakarta.
What if it could be definitely proven that the
    technocrats wrote all the pop songs.
What if our national debts could be paid off with
    Rendra's plays.

Bagaimana kalau segala yang kita angankan terjadi,
  dan segala yang terjadi pernah kita rancangkan.
Bagaimana kalau akustik dunia menjadi demikian
  sempurna sehingga di kamar tidur kau sampai deru
  bom Vietnam, gemerisik sejuta kaki pengungsi,
  gemuruh banjir dan gempa bumi serta suara-suara
  percintaan anak muda, juga bunyi industri presisi
  dan margsatwa Afrika.
Bagaimana kalau pemerintah diizinkan protes dan
  rakyat kecil mempertimbangkan protes itu.
Bagaimana kalau kesenian dihentikan saja sampai di
  sini, dan kita pelihara ternak sebagai pengganti.
Bagaimana kalau sampai waktunya kita tidak perlu
  bertanya bagaimana lagi.

Kembalikan Indonesia padaku

Hari depan Indonesia adalah duaratus juta mulut yang
  menganga.
Hari depan Indonesia adalah bola-bola lampu 15 wat,
  sebagian berwarna putih dan sebagian hitam, yang
  menyala bergantian.
Hari depan Indonesia adalah pertandingan pingpong
  siang-malam, dengan bola yang bentuknya seperti
  telur angsa.
Hari depan Indonesia adalah pulau Jawa yang
  tenggelam karena seratus juta penduduknya.
          Kembalikan
          Indonesia
          padaku.

What if all that we planned happened and all that
     happened had been planned by us.
What if the world's acoustics were so good that you
     hear, in your own bedroom, the fall of bombs in
     Vietnam, the rustle of a million refugee feet, the
     thunder of flood and earthquake and the gentle
     voices of young people making love, as well as the
     roar of factories and of animals in Africa.
What if the government were allowed to protest and
     the people had to pass judgment on their case.
What if art stopped right where it was and we turned to
     keeping animals instead.
What if the time came when we no longer needed to
     ever again ask what if.

1971

Give Indonesia back to me

Indonesia's future is two hundred million gaping
     mouths.
Indonesia's future is 15-watt light globes, some white
     and some black, lighting alternately.
Indonesia's future is a game of Ping-Pong, going on all
     day and all night with a ball shaped like a goose egg.
Indonesia's future is the island of Java sinking under its
     population of one hundred million people.
Give
Indonesia
back
to me.

Hari depan Indonesia adalah satu juta orang main
    pingpong siang malam dengan bola telur angsa di
    bawah sinar lampu 15 wat.
Hari depan Indonesia adalah pulau Jawa yang pelan-
    pelan tenggelam lantaran berat bebannya kemudian
    angsa-angsa berenang-renang di atasnya.
Hari depan Indonesia adalah duaratus juta mulut yang
    menganga, dan di dalam mulut itu ada bola-bola
    lampu 15 wat, sebagian putih dan sebagian hitam,
    yang menyala bergantian.
Hari depan Indonesia adalah angsa-angsa putih yang
    berenang-renang sambil main pingpong di atas
    pulau Jawa yang tenggelam dan membawa seratus
    juta bolalampu 15 wat ke dasar lautan.
                    Kembalikan
                    Indonesia
                    padaku.
Hari depan Indonesia adalah pertandingan pingpong
    siang malam dengan bola yang bentuknya seperti
    telur angsa.
Hari depan Indonesia adalah pulau Jawa yang
    tenggelam karena seratus juta penduduknya.
Hari depan Indonesia adalah bola-bola lampu 15 wat,
    sebagian berwarna putih dan sebagian hitam, yang
    menyala bergantian.
Hari depan Indonesia adalah dua ratus juta mulut yang
    menganga.
                    Kembalikan
                    Indonesia
                    padaku.

Indonesia's future is one million people playing Ping-
    Pong night and day with a goose-egg under the 15-
    watt light globes.
Indonesia's future is Java sinking slowly because of the
    weight of its burden and then the geese swimming
    on top of it.
Indonesia's future is two hundred million gaping
    mouths, with 15-watt light globes in them, some
    white and some black, lighting alternately.
Indonesia's future is white geese swimming as they play
    Ping-pong on top of the sinking island of Java and
    taking the hundred million 15-watt light globes to
    the bottom of the sea.
            Give
            Indonesia
            back
            to me.
Indonesia's future is a game of Ping-Pong going on all
    day and all night with a ball shaped like a goose-egg.
Indonesia's future is the island of Java sinking under its
    population of one hundred million people.
Indonesia's future is 15-watt globes, some white and
    some black, lighting alternately.
Indonesia's future is two hundred million gaping
    mouths.
            Give
            Indonesia
            back
            to me.

                    1971

Bersatulah pelacur-pelacur kota Jakarta

Pelacur-pelacur kota Jakarta
dari kelas tinggi dan kelas rendah
telah diganyang
telah diharu-biru.
Mereka kecut
keder
terhina dan tersipu-sipu.

Sesalkan mana yang mesti kau sesalkan.
Tapi jangan kau klewat putus asa.
Dan kau relakan dirimu dibikin korban

Wahai, pelacur-pelacur kota Jakarta.
Sekarang bangkitlah.
Sanggul kembali rambutmu.
Kerna setelah menyesal
datanglah kini giliranmu
bukan untuk membela diri melulu
tapi untuk lancarkan serangan.
Kerna:
Sesalkan mana yang mesti kau sesalkan
tapi jangan kau rela dibikin korban.

Sarinah.
Katakan kepada mereka
bagaimana kau dipanggil ke kantor mentri
bagaimana ia bicara panjanglebar kepadamu
tentang perjuangan nusa bangsa
dan tiba-tiba tanpa ujung pangkal
ia sebut kau inspirasi revolusi
sambil ia buka kutangmu.

W. S. Rendra

Prostitutes of Jakarta—Unite!

The prostitutes of Jakarta
the greatest and the least
have been crushed
hunted
They are frightened
lost
offended and embarrassed.

Regret as you may
But don't despair
Or allow yourselves to be sacrificed.

Prostitutes of Jakarta
Arise now
Comb your hair
Having sorrowed
it is now your turn
—not just to defend yourselves—
but to attack
So
Regret as you may
but do not allow yourselves to be sacrificed.

Sarinah!
Tell them
how you were called to the ministerial suite
and how he spoke long and deeply to you
about the national struggle
then suddenly—without even finishing what he was
    saying,
calling you the inspiration of the revolution,
undid your bra.

Dan kau, Dasima
Kabarkan kepada rakyat
bagaimana pemimpin revolusi
secara bergiliran memelukmu
bicara tentang kemakmuran rakyat dan api revolusi
sambil celananya basah
dan tubuhnya lemas
terkapai di sampingmu.
Ototnya keburu tak berdaya.

Politisi dan pegawai tinggi
adalah caluk yang rapi.
Konggres-konggres dan konperensi
tak pernah berjalan tanpa kalian.
Kalian tak pernah bisa bilang "tidak"
lantaran kelaparan yang menakutkan
kemiskinan yang mengekang
dan telah lama sia-sia mencari kerja.
Ijizah sekolah tanpa guna.
Para kepala jawatan
akan membuka kesempatan
kalau kau buka paha.
Sedang di luar pemerintahan
perusahaan-perusahaan macet
lapangan kerja tak ada.
Revolusi para pemimpin
adalah revolusi dewa-dewa.
Mereka berjuang untuk surga
dan tidak untuk bumi.
Revolusi dewa-dewa
tak pernah menghasilkan
lebih banyak lapangan kerja
bagi rakyatnya.
Kalian adalah sebahagian kaum penganggur
yang mereka ciptakan.

And you, Dasima
Tell the people
how all the leaders of the revolution
embraced you in turn
speaking of the prosperity of the masses and the flame
    of the revolution
while their trousers were wet and bodies sprawled
    beside you
their bolts too rapidly shot.

The politicians and senior civil-servants
are a tight bunch of rogues
Their congresses and conferences
wouldn't go without you
You who must never say "no"
because of the terror of hunger
the yoke of poverty
and your long futile search for work
School diplomas were useless
The section heads
could only open the door of opportunity
if you would open your legs
And outside government
were only run-down businesses
with no vacancies—
The leader's revolution
was a revolution of gods
they fought for heaven
and not for their earth
A revolution by gods
has never produced
more jobs
for the ordinary people—
You are a part of the proletariat
they have created.

Namun
sesalkan mana yang mesti kau sesalkan
tapi jangan kau klewat putus asa
dan kau rela dibikin korban.

Pelacur-pelacur kota Jakarta
berhentilah tersipu-sipu.
Ketika kubaca di koran
bagaimana badut-badut mengganyang kalian
menuduh kalian sumbur bencana negara
aku jadi murka.
Kalian adalah temanku.
Ini tak bisa dibiarkan.
Astaga.
Mulut-mulut badut.
Mulut-mulut yang latah.
Bahkan seks mereka perpolitikkan.

Saudara-saudariku.
Membubarkan kalian
tidak semudah membubarkan partai politik.
Mereka harus beri kalian kerja.
Mereka harus pulihkan darjat kalian.
Mereka harus ikut memikul kesalahan.

Saudari-saudariku. Bersatulah.
Ambillah galah.
Kibarkan kutang-kutangmu di ujungnya.
Araklah keliling kota
sebagai panji-panji yang telah mereka nodai.
Kini giliranmu menuntut.
Katakanlah kepada mereka:
Menganjurkan mengganyang pelacuran
tanpa menganjurkan
mengawini para bekas pelacur
adalah omong kosong.

Still
Regret as you may
But don't despair
or allow yourselves to be sacrificed.

Prostitutes of Jakarta
Stop being ashamed
When I read in the papers
how those clowns persecute you
accuse you of being the source of all the nation's
      disasters
I am enraged.
You are my friends
I can't have this
God
What clownmouths
What foulmouths
They have even politicized sex.

My sisters
It is harder to put you down
than a political party
They must give you work
They must return your standing
They too must bear the weight of their mistakes.

My sisters. Unite.
Take up sticks
Wave your bras about on the ends of them
Carry them around the town in procession
waving them like flags they have disgraced.
Now it is your turn to demand
Tell them:
That recommending the persecution of prostitutes
without also recommending
marrying them
is nonsense.

Pelacur-pelacur kota Jakarta.
Saudari-saudariku.
Jangan melulu keder pada lelaki.
Dengan mudah
kalian bisa telanjangi kaum palsu.
Naikkan taripmu dua kali
dan mereka akan klabakan.
Mogoklah satu bulan
dan mereka akan puyeng
lalu mereka akan berjina
dengan isteri saudaranya.

Prostitutes of Jakarta
My sisters
Do not tremble before men
When quite easily
you can strip the fakes
Double your prices
let them flounder
Strike for a month
soon they will be committing adultery
with their brothers' wives.

*1967

Hanya dalam puisi

Dalam karetaapi
Kubaca puisi: Willy dan Mayakowsky
Namun kata-katamu yang kudengar
Mengatasi derak-derik deresi.
Kulempar pandang ke luar:
Sawah-sawah dan gunung-gunung
Lalu sajak-sajak tumbuh
Dari setiap bulir peluh
Para petani yang terbungkuk sejak pagi
Melalui hari-hari keras dan sunyi.

Kutahu kaupun tahu
Hidup terumbang-ambing antara langit dan bumi
Adam terlempar dari surga
Lalu kian ke mari mencari Hawa.

Tidakkah telah menjadi takdir penyair
Mengetuk pintu demi pintu
Dan tak juga ditemuinya: Ragu hati
Yang tak mau
Menyerah pada situasi?

Dalam lembah menataplah wajahmu yang sabar.
Dari lembah mengulurlah tanganmu yang gemetar.

A JIP R OSIDI

Only in poetry

In the train
I read poetry: Rendra and Mayakovsky,[†]
Yet above the rhythm of the wheels
The words I hear are yours.
I look outside:
Rice fields and mountains
And a poem rises
From each bead of sweat
On the brows of the farmers
Throughout their long and lonely day.

I know you know
That life drifts between heaven and earth
Adam was expelled from Paradise
Then searched for Eve.

The poet's fate
Is to knock on door after door
And never to find: Restlessly
Refusing
To surrender to his situation.

In the valley I see your calm face.
From the valley your hand stretches out.

---

† *Rendra:* major Indonesian poet (see elsewhere in this volume).
Vladimir Vladimirovich Mayakovsky (1883–1930) was a major Russian
socialist poet.

Dalam karetaapi
Kubaca puisi : turihan-turihan hati
Yang dengan jari-jari besi sang Waktu
Menentukan langkah-langkah Takdir: Menjulur
Ke ruang yang kuatur
        sia-sia.

Aku tahu.
Kau pun tahu.
Dalam puisi
Semuanya jelas dan pasti.

Di sini segalanya tak mengenal dimensi waktu

Di sini segalanya tak mengenal dimensi waktu.
Tiada lagi mendua-arti : antara kau dengan aku!
Dalam cahaya yang abadi kasihmu mengalir abadi
Sedangkan mati tak lagi punya arti.

Doa

Tuhan. Beri aku kekuatan
Menguasai diri sendiri, kesunyian
dan keserakan. Beri aku petunjuk selalu
untuk memilih jalanMu, keridoanMu. Amin

In the train
I read poetry: submission to emotion
Which through the iron fingers of Time
Determines the path of Fate: reaching out
Into the realm of dreams which I shape
        to no avail.

I know.
You know.
In poetry
Everything is clear and definite.

1968

Here time's dimensions are unknown

Here time's dimensions are unknown
Ambiguity is absent: between you and me
Your eternal love flows in eternal light
And death has no meaning

1970

Prayer

God. Give me the strength
To master myself, loneliness
and greed. Guide me
in your path, to obey your will. Amen.

*1970

Chapter 2

NATURE AND IRONY

A New Framework for the Arts

THE EXPLOSION OF creative activity by the Generation of 66 was supported by the rapid development of excellent facilities for the cultivation of art and literature. The literary magazine *Horison* was founded in July 1966, with eventual support from the Congress for Cultural Freedom. *Horison* immediately "set the standards for 'serious' literature, providing models that writers all over Indonesia attempted to emulate, and its critical essays defined the dominant literary issues of the time."[1] It was joined in 1968 by *Budaja Djaja,* a literary and cultural magazine published by Dewan Kesenian Jakarta and edited by Ajip Rosidi, whose publishing house Pustaka Jaya, established in 1971, was itself a major publisher of contemporary writing. *Budaja Djaja* occasionally published a whole issue devoted to a particular poet—e.g., Subagio Sastrowardoyo's *Daerah Perbatasan* appeared in April 1970, while Taufiq Ismail's *Sajak Ladang Jagung* formed a self-contained issue in 1973.

The arts center, Taman Ismail Marzuki, also founded in 1968, provided an excellent venue in central Jakarta for regular theatrical presentations, poetry readings, and seminars, and was an ideal setting for writers to "hang out" together in a free and unconstrained environment. TIM was not only well located, it was also well funded by the city of Jakarta itself, and was administered by a board of artists with little outside interference.[2] With these various resources, Jakarta became the perceived center of artistic excellence and renewal for the whole nation.[3]

Neo-Romanticism

Once the focus on confrontational politics began to recede, two major trends emerged in contemporary Indonesian poetry.[4] The first was a return to a certain type of romanticism. Subagio Sastrowardoyo has argued that romanticism is "the main stream" that runs throughout modern Indonesian poetry. Romanticism in Indonesian poetry was not the world of untroubled spiritual significances sometimes met with in Europe.[5] Rather, it placed a major stress on the lyrical projection of a melancholy and rather lonely personal emotion onto an imagined external landscape. Thematically, such poems have often shown the artist as an alien voyager, passing through a landscape that was barren and empty of people, usually during the darkest hours of the night. The major proponents of this neo-romanticism in the early New Order were Goenawan Mohamad, Sapardji Djoko Damono, and the younger writer Abdul Hadi.

Goenawan's earliest verse was written between 1961 and 1964. Burton Raffel has commented that these works showed "[an] ability to coin swift-moving passionate phrases," which sometimes led him, however, to "too many words saying too little."[6] The verses written while he was travelling in Europe after completing his studies there were less obscure and more contemplative than his first work. These newer poems used the somewhat stricter form of the quatrain, and their imagery was more focused than in his earlier work. "Senja pun jadi kecil, kota pun jadi putih" (Twilight fades the city white) is notable for its concrete yet allusive settings, its cold, lonely imagery, and the sense of travel and uncertainty.

The following prose poems, "Asmaradana" and "Di kota itu, kata orang, gerimis telah jadi logam" (It is a town, so they say, in which the rain has become lead), marked a third phase in Goenawan's writing. A major theme in Goenawan's cultural essays of the late sixties related to the tension between the village and the new, confusing realm of the city. Ajip had presented the poet as belonging to a region outside of Jakarta, but also as unable to transcend personal identity. Goenawan sensed that, as a writer, the very quest for personal freedom, individuality, and the desire to experiment had alienated him from the emotional, social, spiritual, and even linguistic support of past surroundings. As a result, his fate was "to be alone and doubt."[7] The poem "Di kota itu" showed a profound mistrust of the city and its effect on human relationships, which were here condemned to end in the death of the lovers. In "Asmaradana" Goenawan explicitly turned back toward Javanese tradition and in so doing suggested a way of revitalizing the modern tradition through the redevelopment of the old. The themes of the passing of time and the separation of lovers took on deeply tragic dimensions in this poem, as they were woven around characters with whom the Javanese reader (at least) might be assumed to be intimately familiar.

Like Taufiq Ismail and Goenawan Mohamad, Sapardi Djoko Damono too had begun writing in the early sixties. His verse reached an astonishing maturity with the volume *dukaMu abadi* (The eternal sorrow of God), published in 1969. The volume moved on two distinct levels. The first level was ambiguously religious. Sapardi used a framework of myths provided by the Koran (and, before it, the Bible) to enclose the more personal verse of the two sections, "1967" and "1968." The religious symbolism dealt with the story of Adam and Eve, expelled from Paradise by the arbitrary and unjust whim of God. The love of Adam and Eve for each other, and their yearning for God, were linked with the poet's own marriage; the power of death and personal extinction emphasized fears concerning the severe illness of his father-in-law.

The opening poems, "Prologue" and "Sajak putih" (White poem), in accordance with the title of the volume itself, were highly paradoxical. They suggested that God's action had not only left mankind alone, but that in His haste God had also condemned Himself to grieve the absence of an other. In "Ziarah" (Pilgrimage), the very existence of God passes into the realm of clever tales, told by the old to reassure the young and help them endure the suffering of the world. Sapardi seemed to suggest simultaneously that only the myths of religion could give life meaning, yet they were also untrue, and even unworthy of human adulthood. Sapardi further used the myths of the death of Abel and the crucifixion of Jesus in these poems to present these figures as powerful symbols of the human condition, of self-affirmation in a world without compassion. In "Prologue," they signified the increasingly small space left for human action, as the divine Letters of the scriptures are written in the black soot of human mortality. "Dua sajak di bawah satu kata" (Two poems with the one title) affirmed the justness of Cain's human self-assertion in an empty, desolate world, where the only true principle is "*kesunyian*," non-being, desolation and meaninglessness.

These poems gained much of their strength by the use of a subtle and systematic pattern of contrastive imagery. "Here" is the world of work, pain and death; "there" is the comfort of heaven which may have existed but probably did not. The sun represented the harsh reality of human suffering; night and the mists of dawn suggested the force of death toward which all mankind is inevitably moving. Using this symbolic pattern, Sapardi was able, on the more personal level of his writing, to place his contemporary actors at the point of tension between various extremes, as time inevitably brings them too closer to their own extinction. The wonderfully lyrical "Sebuah taman sore hari" (A park in the afternoon), for example, was set at twilight, in a park (where no one, of course, lives), and the "waiting" of the main character was marked by simple but intensely poignant details of the flight of a small bird, the falling of leaves, and the relentless chime of a clock indicating the passing of day and light.

Sapardi's poetry often carried an imminent sense of violence beneath the surface beauty of its imaginary nature. In "Variasi pada suatu pagi" (Morning variations), written after *dukaMu abadi,* the pleasant images of butterflies, dragonflies, and flowers are enclosed in a cruel arena where the dragonfly is taken by a bird, the butterflies fall to the earth fighting, and the sun burns an old leaf, "leaving no trace."

Abdul Hadi was younger than Goenawan Mohamad and Sapardi Djoko Damono by about six years. His earliest verse dated from 1967; his first book was not published until 1971, the second and third in 1975. The difference in the date of his publications tended to place Hadi as a member of a somewhat younger generation. Like his seniors, Hadi's writing was precise in its form, but it was also notable for the gentle self-assurance with which it dealt with the small details of everyday life. His poetry lacked their bite and irony. "Prelude," for example, lovingly described the work of two fishermen in Abdul Hadi's own region, Madura, as they prepared to set out for the night's work. The setting contained mystery but no real menace. The action was, if anything, almost coquettish: the moon trembles, the blue sky whispers, the tempting voice of the north wind is soft, lyrical. Other poems carried overtones of the work of his mentors: "En Soi" reminds one strongly of Goenawan's writing, "Sajak samar" (Obscure poem) used the same imagery as Sapardi's work. Yet he was also searching for new directions, freed from the urban landscape of individual alienation without redemption. The Platonic dictum, "Know Thyself" (*gnoti seauton*), led him in a religious direction that was far more open and definite than Sapardi's; while affirming human freedom, his work was also conscious of the choice between "prophets and holy men" and the painful intensity of daily human existence. He also explored other cultures. "Meditasi" (Meditation), for example, has the delicacy of a Chinese painting on porcelain; again, there is a sensuousness to the scene described, and a certain pathos as individuals move comfortably in the realm of what is possible for them in their particular situations.

Masks of Irony

The second trend in post-Coup poetry was to be found in the work of Subagio Sastrowardoyo and Toeti Heraty. Both were far more intellectual and detached in their outlook than the writers of Neo-Romanticism. Instead, their work emphasized a critical observation of the world and personal experience, always the less popular option in Indonesian writing in Subagio's own opinion.[8] These university-based authors were not interested in any possible relationship between the environment and the issues of life and death, meaning and alienation. On the contrary, they almost seemed to mock any attempt to establish deep meanings or assert some ultimate conception of self-worth. Their work involved the objectification of reality and relied on a subtle, sophisticated psychological analysis of personal experience, rather than on the mythologization of shadowy doubts and yearnings.

Sapardi's poetry longed for a God whom he knew did not exist. Toeti Heraty's work set itself a similarly difficult task: the finding of a relationship in which a woman might participate as an equal partner to her lover. Her writing used an apparently free line with great precision, in order to work out the presentation of thoughts and emotions fully and precisely. Toeti's poetry presented love as a totally consuming physical, emotional and intellectual act, capable of offering both persons complete self-transcendence (as in "Saat-saat gelap" [Dark moments of meeting]). It was something to be hoped for, often earnestly, yet also sometimes humorously, as in "Cintaku tiga" (I have three loves). However, the basic images in many of her poems also made frequent reference to costumes, masks, social rituals, and hypocritical language, used as ways of justifying the sexual exploitation of woman by man, and thus rendering any true meeting of male and female impossible.

A key-word in "Pria" is *"pretensi,"* pretensions, pretendings, or "subterfuges." The poem questioned conventional social assertions of masculine power and the sacred blessing conferred on a woman by marriage. Pretty ideological statements were laid out in a way which already seemed to qualify them through the use of question marks. The mocking tone was particularly evident in the exaggerated phrase "almost a god" (*"semacam dewa"* literally suggests "some sort of a god, not necessarily a good one"). Interwoven into the text were two quotations from D. H. Lawrence's *Lady Chatterley's Lover,* which, in the original novel especially, actually presented the masculine partner in a position of weakness. The first quotation was a comment made by Lady Chatterley as she held her lover's penis in her hand after they have made love. The second adapted a mocking statement by Lawrence to further parody the claims for the masculine superiority of reason. The source of the statements is barely identified in the Indonesian text; this, combined with the non-gendered nature of the Indonesian third-person pronoun, rendered them more ambiguous and perhaps less threatening. The sense of female helplessness, however, is made clear in the middle of the poem, and reinforced in the conclusion where the image of the garden is used to indicate that, in her future marriage, deceit and pain will be a "natural" part of woman's life.

The neo-romantics had emphasized loneliness *(sepi)* as the consequence of a metaphysical abandonment in the world. Toeti's work dwelt on real physical abandonment. Disappointment of a more concrete type was, therefore, an integral part of her writing too. Man, being imperfect and interested only in his own pleasure, must one day leave woman, in his pursuit of his own social success. In "Suatu departemen" (The department), his final message wishes her the impossible, that she always be "as young and beautiful as she is today." Obviously she cannot be; his leaving closes her off from other possibilities of love in a world where youth and beauty are indeed primary qualities for a woman to be attractive to men. Disappointment also marked the long poem "Cyclus," which analyzed the various stages of an affair. It is an affair the speaker has encouraged, and although the seeds of its destruction are presented from the beginning, her response to his leaving is still one of bitterness.

Female voices are few in Indonesian poetry. Toeti Heraty's writing spoke with an honesty, range of emotion, and even directness which few other writers could match. Subagio's earliest work, published in 1957, had been rough and assertive, prefaced as it was by a quotation from Beethoven: "I do not play for pigs!" *Daerah Perbatasan,* published in 1970, was a far softer work, which ranged widely over traditional and contemporary subject matter. In his more mature work, Subagio tended to deal with situations outside himself. "Genesis" is an unusual affirmation of human immortality (even if the creator does live "far from the village"). For the voice of a middle-aged man, aware of his own limitations in a way that matches Toeti Heraty's awareness, we must wait another decade for Subagio's consideration of the complexities of the role of husband and lover in the poem "Hotel."

Senja pun jadi kecil, kota pun jadi putih

Senja pun jadi kecil
Kota pun jadi putih
Di subway
Aku tak tahu saat pun sampai

Ketika berayun musim
Dari sayap langit yang beku
Ketika burung-burung di rumput
Terhenti mempermainkan waktu

Ketika kita berdiri sunyi
Pada dinding biru ini
Menghitung ketidak-pastian dan bahagia
Menunggu seluruh usia

Twilight fades the city white

Twilight fades
the city white
In the subway
I cannot tell when
we will arrive

As the season falls
from the frozen wings of the sky
As birds on the cold grass
Cease their game with time

As we stand alone
Against the blue wall
Balancing uncertainty and happiness
Waiting for death

1966

Dingin tak tercatat

Dingin tak tercatat
pada termometer

Kota hanya basah

Angin sepanjang sungai
mengusir, tapi kita tetap saja

di sana. Seakan-akan

gerimis raib
dan cahaya berenang

mempermainkan warna.

Tuhan, kenapa kita bisa
bahagia?

Cold unregistered

Cold unregistered
on the thermometer

The city lost
in the dampness

Along the river the wind
drives us away, yet we stay

there. As if

the light swimming
through the invisible rain

is playing with the colors.

God, how can we be
so happy?

1971

Asmaradana

Ia dengar kepak sayap kelelawar dan gugur sisa hujan
dari daun, karena angin pada kemuning. Ia dengar
resah kuda serta langkah pedati ketika langit bersih
kembali menampakkan bimasakti, yang jauh. Tapi di
antara mereka berdua, tidak ada yang berkata-kata.

Lalu ia ucapkan perpisahan itu, kematian itu. Ia
melihat peta, nasib, perjalanan dan sebuah peperangan
yang tak semuanya disebutkan.

Lalu ia tahu perempuan itu tak akan menangis. Sebab
bila esok pagi pada rumput halaman ada tapak yang
menjauh ke utara, ia tak akan mencatat yang telah
lewat dan yang akan tiba, karena ia tak berani lagi.

Anjasmara, adikku, tinggallah, seperti dulu.
Bulan pun lamban dalam angin, abai dalam waktu.
Lewat remang dan kunang-kunang, kaulupakan
        wajahku, kulupakan wajahmu.

Asmaradana[†]

He heard the beat of the wings of the bats and the fall of
the rest of the rain, the wind against the teak trees. He
heard the restlessness of the horses and the tug of the
chariot as the sky cleared of cloud, revealing the pole star
in the distance. Between them words were unnecessary.

Then he spoke of the separation, the death. He saw the
map, fate, the journey and a war indistinctly.

He realized she would not cry. In the morning there
would be footprints on the grass in the yard, to the
north. She would refuse to consider what had passed or
what was to come, no longer daring to do so.

Anjasmara, my love, stay, again.
The moon is covered by the wind, time ignores it.
Passing cloud and ember, you forget my face, I forget
    yours.

1971

---

† Damarwulan is here taking leave of Anjasmara before he goes to battle
the invincible Menakjingga in defense of his queen. *Asmaradana* is a tra-
ditional Javanese form used for love songs. One of the most popular
includes the two beautiful lines: *Karia mukti, wong ayu/ Kakangmas
pamit palestra* (Stay and be faithful, beautiful one, I leave to meet death).

Di kota itu, kata orang, gerimis telah jadi logam

Di kota itu, kata orang, gerimis telah jadi logam. Di
bawah cahaya hari pun bercadar, tapi aku tahu kita
akan sampai ke sana.

Dan kita bercinta tanpa batuk yang tersimpan,
membiarkan gumpal darah di gelas itu menghijau.
Dan engkau bertanya mengapa udara berserbuk di
antara kita?

Lalu pagi selesai, burung lerai dan sisa bulan tertinggal
di luar, di atas cakrawala aspal.

Jika samsu pun berdebu, kekasihku, juga pelupukmu.
Tapi tutupkan matamu, dan bayangkan aku
    menjemputmu, mautmu.

It is a town, so they say, in which the rain has become lead

It is a town, so they say, in which the rain has become lead.
Beneath the covering light of day, only I know our
destination.

And we will cough as we love, allowing the globules of
blood in the glass to turn green. And you will wonder
why the air fills with pollen in the space between us.

Then the morning will finish, the birds separate and the
remains of the moon hang outside, above the asphalt sky.

As the sun gathers dust, my love, so shall your eyelids.
But close your eyes and imagine me coming to meet you,
your death.

1971

Nature and Irony   47

Prologue

masih terdengar sampai di sini
dukaMu abadi. Malam pun sesaat terhenti
sewaktu dingin pun terdiam, di luar
langit yang membayang samar

kueja setia, semua pun yang sempat tiba
sehabis menempuh ladang Qain dan bukit Golgota
sehabis menyekap beribu kata, di sini
di rongga-rongga yang mengecil ini

kusapa dukaMu jua, yang dahulu
yang meniupkan zarah ruang dan waktu
yang capai menyusun Huruf. Dan terbaca
sepi manusia, jelaga

Sajak putih

beribu saat dalam kenangan
surut pelahan
kita dengarkan bumi menerima tanpa mengaduh
sewaktu detik pun jatuh

kita dengar bumi yang tua dalam setia
Kasih tanpa suara
sewaktu bayang-bayang kita memanjang
mengabur batas ruang

kita pun bisu tersekat dalam pesona
sewaktu Ia pun memanggil-manggil
sewaktu Kata membuat kita begitu terpencil
di luar cuaca

Prologue

even now we hear
the eternity of Your sadness. Night stopping a moment
when cold grows quiet, outside
the sky casting dark shadows

I faithfully record all that happened
after the field of Cain and the hill of Golgotha
after a thousand words ripen, here
in these narrowing spaces

I address Your sadness too, of old
which blew particles of space and time,
finally forming the Sacred Script. And I read:
the loneliness of man, dust

1967

White poem

a thousand remembered seconds
ebb slowly
we hear the earth receive without complaint
the final seconds fall

we hear the earth grown old in faithfulness
silent Love
as our shadows lengthen
blackening the borders of space

we are dumb, stuck fast in enchantment
as He calls
as the Word isolates us
outside its warmth

1967

Sebuah taman sore hari

dari sayap-sayap burung kecil itu
berguguran sepi, sepiku
saat terhenti di sebuah taman kota ini
daun jatuh di atas bangku, bagai mimpi

di antara datang dan suatu kali pergi
beribu lonceng berbunyi
kekal sewaktu bercakap kepada hati
lalu kepada bumi. Di sini aku menanti

Ziarah

Kita berjingkat lewat
jalan kecil ini
dengan kaki telanjang; kita berziarah
ke kubur orang-orang yang telah melahirkan kita.
Jangan sampai terjaga mereka!
Kita tak membawa apa-apa. Kita
tak membawa kemenyan atau pun bunga-bunga;
kecuali seberkas rencana-rencana kecil
(yang senantiasa tertunda-tunda) untuk
kita sombongkan kepada mereka.
Apakah akan kita jumpai wajah-wajah bengis,
atau tulang-belulang, atau sisa-sisa jasad mereka
di sana? Tidak, mereka hanya kenangan.
Hanya batang-batang cemara yang menusuk langit
yang akar-akarnya pada bumi keras.
Sebenarnya kita belum pernah mengenal mereka;

A park in the afternoon

from the wings of this small bird
silence scatters, my silence
as I sit in a park in this town
leaves fall on my bench, like dreams

between coming and once going
a thousand bells ring
eternity speaks to my heart
then to the earth. Here I wait

1967

Pilgrimage

We tiptoe along
a tiny road
with bare feet; we are pilgrims
to the graves of those who have given us birth.
Do not wake them up!
We bring nothing. Neither
incense nor even flowers;
only a small bundle of plans
(continually postponed) to
boast of.
Will we find cruel faces
or bones, or the remains of their bodies
there? No. They are only memories.
Only casuarina stems stabbing the sky
with their roots in the hard earth.
In fact, we never knew them;

ibu-bapa kita yang mendongeng
tentang tokoh-tokoh itu, nenek-moyang kita itu,
tanpa menyebut-nyebut nama.
Mereka hanyalah mimpi-mimpi kita,
kenangan yang membuat kita merasa
pernah ada.
Kita berziarah; berjingkatlah sesampai
di ujung jalan kecil ini:
sebuah lapangan terbuka
        batang-batang cemara
                angin.
Takada bau kemenyan takada bunga-bunga;
mereka telah tidur sejak abad pertama
semenjak Hari Pertama itu.
Takada tulang-belulang takada sisa-sisa
jasad mereka.
Ibu-bapa kita sungguh bijaksana, terjebak
kita dalam dongengan nina-bobok.
Di tangan kita berkas-berkas rencana
di atas kepala
        sang Surya.

our parents told us fairy stories
about them, our ancestors,
without mentioning their names.
They are only figures in our dreams,
memories which make us think
that we might be.
We are pilgrims; tiptoeing to
the end of this tiny road:
an open field
          casuarina stems
                    the wind.
There is no fragrance of incense, there are no flowers;
they have slept since the first century
since the First Day.
There are no bones, there are no remains
of their bodies.
Our parents were wise, they tricked us
with their lullaby legends.
In our hands are bundles of plans,
above our head
          is the Sun.

1967

Dua sajak di bawah satu nama

I

darah tercecer di ladang itu. Siapa pula
binatang-korban kali ini, saudara
lalu senyap pula. Berapa jaman telah menderita
semenjak Ia pun mengusir kita dari Sana

awan-awan kecil mengenalnya kembali, serunya:
telah terbantai Abel, darah merintih kepada Bapa
(aku pada pihakmu, saudara, pandang ke muka
masih tajam bau darah itu. Kita ke dunia)

2

kalau Kau pun bernama Kesunyian, baiklah
tengah-hari kita bertemu kembali: sehabis
kubunuh anak itu. Di tengah ladang aku tinggal sendiri
bertahan menghadapi Matahari

dan Kau pun di sini. Pandanglah dua belah tanganku
berlumur darah saudaraku sendiri
pohon-pohon masih tegak, mereka pasti mengerti
dendam manusia yang setia tetapi tersisih ke tepi

benar. Telah kubunuh Abel, kepada siapa
tertumpu sakit-hati alam, dendam pertama
kemanusiaan
awan-awan di langit tetap berarak, angin senantiasa
menggugurkan daunan; segala atas namamu:
Kesunyian

Two poems under the one name

1

the blood spills in the field. Who
is the sacrificial animal this time, brother?
Then silence. How many ages have suffered
since He drove us out of There

the small clouds recognize it, they shout:
Abel has been butchered, his blood cries out to God
(I am on your side, brother, look ahead
though sharp the smell of the blood. We go to the world)

2

if You are Non-being, it is well
that we meet in the middle of the day: after I have killed
him. In the middle of the plain I remain alone
enduring beneath the Sun

and You are here too. Look at my hands
stained with the blood of my brother
the trees stand stiff, they understand
the bitterness of a faithful man who has been ignored

it's true. I killed Abel, the recipient
of nature's bitterness, of humanity's first hatred
the clouds in the sky still move, the wind
still fells the leaves, all in your name: Non-being

1968

Variasi pada suatu pagi

(i)

sebermula adalah kabut; dan dalam kabut
senandung lonceng, ketika selembar daun luruh,
setengah bermimpi, menepi ke bumi, luput
(kaudengarkan juga seperti Suara mengaduh)

(ii)

dan cahaya (yang membasuhmu pertama-tama)
bernyanyi bagi capung, kupu-kupu dan bunga; Cahaya
(yang menawarkan kicau burung) susut tiba-tiba
pada selembar daun tua, pelan terbakar, tanpa sisa

(iii)

menjelma bayang-bayang. Bayang-bayang yang tiba
   tersentak
ketika seekor burung menyambar capung
(selamat pagi pertama bagi matahari), risau bergerak-
                     gerak
ketika sepasang kupu-kupu merendah ke bumi basah,
                     bertarung

Morning variations

(i)

in the beginning was fog; and in the fog
echoes of a bell, as a single leaf falls,
and, half-asleep, edging to the sea, vanishes
(can you hear it sighing, like a Voice)

(ii)

and the light (which first bathed you)
singing for a dragonfly, flowers, and two butterflies;
the Light (offered in the song of a bird) suddenly
    retreating
onto an old leaf, slowly burning, leaving no trace

(iii)

turning into shadows. Shadows which suddenly stir
as the bird swoops on the dragonfly
(good morning sun), shivering restlessly
as the butterflies fall to the wet earth, fighting

1970

Abdul Hadi W. M.

Prelude

I

Di atas laut. Bulan perak bergetar
Suhu pun melompat
Di bandar kecil itu. Aku pun dapat
menerka. Seorang pelaut mengurusi jangkar

II

Siapakah bertolak bersama pelaut-pelaut itu?
Angin senja dari benua. Sesekali suara sauh
Siapakah yang berseru bersama pelaut-pelaut itu?
Langit yang biru, bisik-bisik. Sesekali bayang-bayang
                                        negeri jauh

III

Dua nelayan Madura terjun ke sampannya
Angin tak menyuruh mereka, dingin yang baja
Seperti kata nenekmoyangnya, mereka lepaskan
                                        mantera
Seperti kata nenekmoyangnya, engkau hanya
                            menawarkan angin utara

IV

Angin akan kembali dari bukit-bukit, menyongsong
                                        malam hari
angin yang tidur siang hari, yang kedengaran
                            membetulkan kemarau
Angin yang tahu, seperti engkau, ke mana arah musim
                                        ini mati
ke laut: membujuk nelayan. Suara yang lirih sesekali

Abdul Hadi W. M.

Prelude

I

At sea. The silver moon trembles
The anchor leaps
It is a small town. I can
guess. Somewhere a sailor winds a rope.

II

Who voyages with them?
The twilight wind from the land. The occasional splash
                                        of an anchor,
Who calls?
The whispering blue sky. The occasional shadow of a
                                        far-off land.

III

Two Madurese sailors going down to their ships
not sent by the wind, the cold as hard as iron,
praying, as their ancestors taught
a bribe to the north wind, as their ancestors taught

IV

The wind returns from the hills, bringing night
the wind, asleep all day, soothes the drought
the wind knows, as you do, where the season ends
tempts the sailors to the sea. Its voice is lyrical.

1967

Sajak samar

Ada yang memisahkan kita, jam dinding ini
ada yang mengisahkan kita, bumi bisik-bisik ini
ada. Tapi tak ada kucium wangi kainmu sebelum pergi
tak ada. Tapi langkah gerimis bukan sendiri

En soi

Suara malam, hanya daun-daunan
Gugur diusir ke beranda
Dari jauh kemarau. Almanak lepas lagi
Melemparkan bumi yang mati

Dan di manakah kau sekarang? Berdiri
Setelah sibuk mengurus matahari
Setelah sibuk membuat abstraksi
(dari jauh laut Merah yang pasang abadi)

Di Qur'an kini hanya aljabar
Beratus persamaan-persamaan tersamar
Soal-soal ujian yang belum selesai
Kini terjamah lusuh helai-helai

Aku tak mengurusnya lagi
Jemu. Cahaya sebentar datang, lalu hilang kembali

Obscure poem

Something divides us, the clock on the wall.
Something talks to us, the earth
whispering of life. But the smell of departing death
is in the air. It is raining.

1967

En soi

The sound of leaves at night
Driven to the verandah by the wind
By distant summer. The calendar falls
Against the dead earth

Where are you now?
Now that you've finished organizing the sun
Now that you've finished with your abstractions
(The Red Sea rises in the distance)

Algebraic formulations in the Koran
Hundreds of confused metaphors
Unsolved examination questions
Tired, dirty pages

I don't organize anything any more
I'm bored. The light comes for a moment, then

vanishes.
1968

Engkau menunggu kemarau

Di Guest House
Engkau menunggu kemarau
Hari hampir malam
Membersihkan pelabuhan

Sebelum engkau berdiri
Pergi
Di langit lembayung terdengar suara awan
Bahwa rawa sudah kausiapkan
Bahwa kesal sudah kau diamkan

Waiting for the dry season

In the Guest House
You wait for the dry season
Day is almost night
and washes over the harbor

You hear, before you go
alone
the clouds in the crimson sky
announcing that sorrow is ready
and so is regret.

1968

Meditasi

Itulah bidadari Cina itu, dengan seekor lilin
dan menyeret kainnya basah; menggigil dalam kuil
(daun-daun salam berguguran dan di beranda
masih terdengar suara hujan, hujan pasir) Ia
menunjukkan yin-yang yang kabur di atas pintu
dan di mataku terasa hembusan angin yang
                                    merabunkan
(lihat, ujarmu, ia mengajak kita ke tempat sepi
di mana berdiri sebuah makam kaisar yang mati
dalam terpemuran merebut kota dari desa) Angin
berlarian menghamburkan bau-bauan dari tangan
perempuan-perempuan yang wangi dan kedinginan
di atas gapura yin-yang yang mulai memuat lumut
dengan tulisan-tulisan tua yang tak terbaca sudah
(langit adalah bayang-bayang, kau menyesal
telah mengimpikannya; dan di sebelahnya
berdiri gedung, beribu sungai dan tebing gunung
yang terbuat dari batu, anggur dan lempung
yang kini menampakkan bintang kemukus yang
                                    panjang)

Itulah bidadari Cina itu dan mendekat ke arahmu
memandang dinding dan bertelanjang di sofa, tapi tak
mengerti (ia membeku jadi arca, waktu tentara kaisar
mulai membangun kota di langit) dan beribu mantra
memenuhi telinganya yang tuli

Meditation

The one with the candle, lifting her wet skirt,
is a princess: look at her shivering in the temple
(The leaves bow to each other, on the verandah
you can hear the sound of the rain on the sand)
She pointed to an obscure *yin-yang* over the door
and my eyes felt the incense burn in the wind
(Look, you said, she is inviting us to a lonely place,
the grave of an emperor who died fighting the peasants
to save a city) The running wind scatters the smell of the
          hands
of cold, fragrant women. Above the door
the *yin-yang* gathers moss, the writing is illegible:
(the sky casts shadows, you are sad
because it is only a dream: next to the temple
stands a building, a thousand rivers and tall mountains
made of rock, clay and grapes, here is the extended
          polestar)

The princess comes closer. She turns toward you
and undresses next to the couch (She is as stiff as an arc,
the emperor's army is building castles in the air)
Uncomprehendingly, a thousand spells fall on her deaf
          ears

1972

Pria

siapa yang mengatakan:
     "bagai kuncup terkulai di tangan"
     (yang menyanjungnya)

dasar wanita
     berterima kasih dalam-dalam
     karena takdir telah menyentuhnya
takdir? bahwa dunia merekah dan
     dupa keramat melingkari dengan mantera
     mantera abadi?
dengan senyum pada pandang karena
sendiri tidak berjaya, pada pergelangan tangan
     mesra dihela ke taman hakiki
hati padat-penuh kekaguman akan
manusia jantan, semacam dewa!
siapa pula yang mengatakan:
     "ikatan restu antara dua
     insan dewata . . . . . ."

lazim,
sebagai halnya tanda rahasia timbulkan
pretensi-pretensi sewajarnya—
kuncup, berduri, geli dan kesal
—taman hakiki . . .

Man

who says:
    "like a little bud in my hand"[†]
    the woman holding him

a woman
    should be grateful
    for her good fortune
fortune? The world divided into two,
    wrapped in holy incense
    and everlasting spells?
smiling at him,
powerless as he takes her by the hand
    and leads her into the garden of life,
her heart full of wonder
at this man, almost a god!
who says:
    "a sacred bond
    between two divine beings"[‡]

it is nothing new
soon, the secrets
lead to natural
subterfuges.

in the garden of life
the buds have thorns,
they laugh
and cry.

    *1970

[†] D. H. Lawrence: *Lady Chatterley's Lover,* Penguin, 1982 reprint, p. 219.

[‡] Compare *Lady Chatterley's Lover,* p. 38, "blessed be the tie that binds
our hearts in kindred something-or-other."

Saat-saat gelap

saat-saat gelap pertemuan
   —yang keramat—
membenam dalam pangkuan
senyap sunyi, titian yang harus dilewati
curam sunyi, semesta yang menjadi saksi
hari cipta terulangi

bukan, ini bukannya pertemuan lagi
tetapi
iba tergetar menyingkirkan diri dari kesaksian

manusia yang menyerah pada keangkuhan tunggal
tetapi diam-diam menikmati
jari membelai, meneguk—
dari sumber kehidupan

Cintaku tiga

cintaku tiga, secara kanak-kanak
   menghitung jari
kusebut satu per satu kini
yang pertama serius dan dalam hatinya
   tidak terduga
bertahun-tahun ku jadi idaman
mesraku membuat pandangnya sayu mungkin
   ia merasa iba padaku
ingin aku membenam diri, melebur
   dalam mesra rayu, iba dan sayu

Dark moments of meeting

dark moments of meeting
        sacredly seeding
in the lap of silence
        razor's edge to be surpassed
        lonely space to signify
recurrence of creation day

no, this is
not a meeting,
but
pathos trembling, withdrawing from witnesses,

man surrendering to a single arrogance

secretly enjoying, caressing fingers,

greedily drinking
        from thc well of life

*1970

I have three loves

I have three loves, like a child
        counting on her fingers
I'll recite them one by one:
the first is serious
        deep in his heart he has loved me for years
loving me makes his sadness possible
        or perhaps he merely pities me
I want to dive down and dissolve
        in his sad love and sorrow

pandangnya begitu sepi, tapi ia
paling mudah dikelabui—
yang lain, berfilsafat ringan dan kesabaran
tak pernah kulepas ia dari pandangan
petuah orang —lidah tak bertulang—
        tak kuperduli karena ia
kata-katanya tepat untuk setiap peristiwa
sesudah akhirnya mengecap bibirnya
        ia tinggalkan aku dan sesudah itu?
ah, biasa saja, tak ada sesuatu terjadi
memang ia tidak begitu perduli
perlu pula kusebut yang ketiga, bukannya
        lebih baik dirahasiakan saja, karena
ia datang hanya malam hari, engsel pintu pun
telah diminyaki
suaranya tegang, berat, menghela
        ke sorga tirai-ranjang
pandang pesona tajam memaksa, akhirnya
        menghitung hari setiap bulan
meskipun itu urusan nanti
ketiga cinta yang kumiliki
        kapan kujumpai pada satu orang?

Suatu departemen

kau katakan pada ku
pesan terakhir:
        bawakan keindahan dan
        kemudaan selalu

ruang menyesak, karena
keusangan debu membiak

he looks so lonely, but
it is too easy to deceive him
The next is a clever philosopher and
        endlessly patient
I can never let him out of my sight
"mind his easy words"
        people say, but why
        should I worry
when he has the right words for every occasion
        but he'll go away, finally,
        after the taste of his lips
and there'll be the usual nothing again
he doesn't care that much anyway
Should I mention the third, rather
        than be secretive now, for
he comes at night when the hinges of the door are oiled
his voice is virile, his look is forceful
hauling me to that secluded heaven
but then I'll be counting the days again
        for each month to come, yet
I know I shouldn't worry, but where
and when will I meet my three loves
        in the one man?

*1970

The department

in your last letter
you said:
        may you always be
        as young and as beautiful
        as you are today.

the office closes in around me.
thick dust spreads across

map-map, berkas dan kertas dengan
ujung-ujung layu dan harapan-harapan
telah ditumpuk, diperam
        membisu dalam debu

gairah, semula menggetar
bangunkan nyala-nyala jingga pada
hidup yang hijau muda,
jadi coretan-coretan
secarik kertas dengan ketikan pemohonan
        yang dibiarkan saja

jendela terbuka dan tirai menyisi
lewatkan matahari menghangati
jam-jam kerja yang semakin pendek
disobek sana-sini—karena
meja-meja lengang, asbak mengkilat
dan telpon berdering berkali-kali
suara hilang dalam iseng
        yang berlipat ganda ini

ah, manusia hidup kukuh-tenang
dengan akar dalam-dalam mencekam bumi
        dan rapat-rapat, seminar, laporan
        serta prasaran, naskah-naskah kerja
wejangan oleh bapak-bapak atau wakilnya?
hidup manusia terlalu membara
dan tanpa isyarat akan menganggap sepi
tumpukan debu yang berkumandang
        menyentuh anak-anak penjual koran
        di depan pintu, mobil-mobil dinas
        berderetan datang dan lalu

memang,
jauh dari hidup
dan pesan akhirmu

the files, folders, and pieces of paper
with ragged corners, full of holes
left in a heap, to ripen
        and die in the dust.

passion, once alive,
burning bright orange
in light-green lives,
is eventually reduced
to a few notes on a scrap of paper,
        initialed and ignored.

through the windows and open curtains
the sunlight warms the working hours.
the days grow shorter,
shredded by empty desks, shining ashtrays,
telephones ringing from time to time,
voices lost
        in the ever expanding emptiness.

proud man moves calmly,
his roots sunk deep in the earth
        and meetings, seminars, reports
        working papers, preliminary statements
        who makes the final decisions?
life is too intense.
it is easy to dismiss
the echoing dust
        which brushes across the paperboys
        outside the office, as official cars
        come and go.

far from life
and your last letter

                        *1970

Cyclus

Penundaan

karena usia yang lebih tua, dari dia
    tak lebih dari itu saja
kesabaran, kuharapkan
    suatu kemustahilan?
karena lebih menimang-nimang waktu
jadi malahan lebih terburu-buru
    siapa tahu, perhitungan
hanya beda satu-dua minggu

suata saat kota baja dengan dinding
dinding logika akan menyerah dan arus
    akan deras menyambar,
membawa ke mata air di mana hidup
lebih penuh dengan degup yang lebih nyata
    syaraf dan serat
digenangi oleh getar bianglala

meskipun satu per satu, batu dan nisan
endapan dari sekian peran dan laku
ditumpuk-tumpuk —
    untuk menghalangi jalan
tidak, ini kali akan tenang dan bijaksana
mempertimbangkan segala kemungkinan:

bahwa hati kita rapuh, dan kehilangan itu
terlalu melanda, suatu cengkeram hampa
    sudah kuketahui sejak lama

bahwa angan selalu timbul, menganyam
pola-pola gemilang, susul-menyusul disulam
dengan khayal, diwarnai oleh isyarat, ini
    pula tak asing lagi

Cyclus

Postponement

being older
      I asked no more of him
than patience
      is that impossible?
because he has considered more
done more
      who knows, perhaps
a few weeks' difference at most

sometime the iron city
walled in logic
will fall and the mighty current
      swoop down
bringing us to the well
where life is fuller, emotion stronger,
      flooded in the vibration of the rainbow

although one by one, stone and tombstone
precipitated from numerous roles and actions
will stack
      to stop the path
no, this time we must consider calmly
weigh the possibilities:

that our lives are brittle, the loss
may be too awful, murder made meaningless
      this I have long known

that hopes continually arise, weaving
bright patterns, threading desires
with dreams, coloring with promises,
      this too is no longer strange

dinding akan rapuh hancur
oleh deras arus melingkar karena bendungan
        akhirnya kita buka juga

karena itu kau, karena usia dan karena
memang lebih tahu tentang dunia, tinggalkan
        perhitungan dengan waktu, biar
kulepas permainan laut dan bulan, kini
menikmati kota untuk jangka tidak terlalu lama
        untuk segera, toh meninggalkannya

Sekali-sekali

setelah tiga hari bercinta, sudah kuduga
        kata-kata tegas terang
tak akan menjelaskan
        oasis di tengah padang
dan bahwa hidup dijelajahi dalam-dalam
sehingga mereka enggan kembali

dari dunia, dibatasi oleh tirai
bulu-mata berkedip dan lingkar cahaya
        yang tak lebih
hanya boleh menerangi bagian pipi
kesegaran mata air, kepenuhan
        madu hangat-tungku
tiada lain adalah kecupanmu

siapa dia, siapa aku bila kulit
        pemisah dengan ruang menghantu
hanya jadi lembab selubung karena
        belai merah lembayung
mendekap muka pada dada
membenam dalam bayang sana sini
tersingkap rahasia dan gelap

lalu terdiam temukan kata-kata kembali
        terucap, tanpa ujung pangkal

the walls will gently break
in the force of the encircling flood because
        we will open the dam

because of you, because of age, and because
you know more of the world, leave
        the reckoning with time, allow
me to commence the sea-moon game, now
enjoy the city for a brief space
        then quickly,
        go

Repetition

After three days and nights of love, I realize
        words
will never explain
        the oasis in the desert
setting out to explore life
they are reluctant to return

separated from the world by curtains
eyelashes and a circle of light
        just strong enough
to color part of the cheek
and the freshness of tears, full
        of heart-warm honey
your kiss

which is he, which me, when skin alone
        separates ghosted spaces
a moist cover as
        crimson red caresses
press face to breast
merging in the shadow of here and there
revealing secrets and darkness
then silently finding words again
        spoken pointlessly

sebelum lingkungan mengambil wujud lagi
        betapa kejam
perpisahan setelah sama-sama mendiami
liang semesta penuh ilham

dan saingan pertanyaan :
        bila bertemu kembali—
        akan seperti ini?
jadi kesenyapan tanya-jawab, saat akrab
yang telah lenyap hanya didambakan
        samar-samar nanti :

bunga berkelopak hitam
berkembang mendadak dalam gelap
untung, tak ada yang menyaksikan

Cocktail party

meluruskan kain-baju dahulu
meletakkan lekat sanggul rapi
lembut ikal rambut di dahi
        pertarungan dapat dimulai
berlomba dengan waktu
dengan kebosanan, apa lagi
        pertaruhan ilusi
seutas benang dalam taufan
amuk badai antara insan

taufan? ah, siapa
yang masih peduli
tertawa kecil, mengigit jari adalah
        perasaan yang dikebiri
kedahsyatan hanya untuk dewa-dewa
tapi deru api unggun atas
        tanah tandus kering
angin liar, cambukan halilintar
        mengiringi

before the world reforms.
        how cruel
the separation after both living in
the perfect mandala

both asking:
        will the next time
        be like this time
a silence of question and answer, a moment of intimacy
gone once coveted
        followed by darkness:

black flowers
suddenly unfold in the dark
fortunately no one sees them

Cocktail party

formal-wear straight
hair immaculate
a curl on the forehead
        let the competition begin
racing with time
and boredom,
        the stakes illusions
threads in the hurricane
storms raging among men

storms? no one
notices
laugh gently, bite your finger
        castrate feelings
intensity is for gods
to be followed by the roar of ashen fire
        in the dry wasteland
wild wind, lightning whip

Nature and Irony   79

perempuan serem yang kuhadapi, dengan
garis alis dan cemooh tajam
        tertawa lantang —
aku terjebak, gelas anggur di tangan
tersenyum sabar pengecut menyamar —
        ruang menggema
dengan guman hormat, sapa-menyapa
dengan mengibas pelangi perempuan
itu pergi, hadirin mengagumi

mengapa tergoncang oleh cemas
dalam-dalam menghela nafas, lemas
        hadapi saingan dalam arena?
kata orang hanya maut pisahkan cinta
tapi hidup merenggut, malahan maut
        harapan semu tempat bertemu
itu pun hanya kalau kau setuju

keasingan yang mempesona, segala
tersayang yang telah hilang —
        penenggelaman
dalam akrab dan lelap
kepanjangan mimpi tanpa derita
dan amuk badai antara insan?
gumam, senyum, dan berjabatan tangan.

Cyclus

sejenak pun tak akan kubiarkan
hiruk-pikuk pikir dan getir
        merasuki
hutan belalang yang tak terseberangi lagi
karena kau telah resmi minta diri

resmi bersikap menunggu memberi waktu
        untuk berkemas
melemparkan diri dalam api, ah janda

I talk to a terrible woman, with
eyebrows and sharp ridicule
        piercing laughter
and am trapped, a glass of wine in my hand
smiling patiently as I try to hide—
        the room echoes
with mumbled politeness, greetings
the rainbow-colored woman flaps her tail
as she goes, the guests gape

why do I tremble with fear
breathe deeply, choke
        as if fighting in a pit?
They say only death can kill love
but life too pulls at it, death
        deceives us with hope of meeting again
if you like, that is

such sparkling alienation, all
that we love is gone—
        torpedoed
in friendship and sleep
a long dream in which no one suffers
and the storm which rages among men?
mumbles, smiles and handshakes

Cyclus

not for a moment shall I allow
confusion of thought and bitterness
        invade
the uncrossable forest
now that you have gone

gone—decently—allowing me time
        to pack
no one expects me to hurl myself into the flames,

setia dan perawan suci
        tidak diharapkan
hanya ketulusan untuk berjabat tangan
tersenyum ringan

harapan dahulu, penyesalan kini
merupakan larangan, hanya menghela nafas
        karena berlomba dengan waktu
menghitung bulan dan hari, pula
membuang kesempatan, karena terlalu segera
        sudah sampai di sini saja

menghilang dari hidupku, melepaskan
depakan bersyarat di atas pulau
terdampar oleh gerak harapan akhir
        bertumpu erat
dengan pertimbangan-pertimbangan getir

di perbatasan, lambaian tangan dan
diam-diam mulai menanggapi tanda-tanda
        penuh arti, suatu bukti
bahwa telah kau redakan pencarian peran
yang enggan menambatkan diri pada usia
        antara manusia

karena kaubelai dengan kata, hangati
        dengan berahi, membuahi
hati dengan nikmat madu dan pelangi
lembut jari mencari, menjelajahi
bukankah segala ingin kau ketahui?
        segala ingin kau ketahui
karena asing, mungkin tersayang
seperti maut tampak demikian, tidur
        membawa mimpi di peraduan
paduan, dengan yang mesra, dengan kedasyatan
yang masih asing, yang baru lampau
        yang telah hilang

a faithful widow and pure maiden
        I hoped for more
at least an honest handshake
        and a faint smile

past hopes, present sorrows
form barriers, breathe deeply
        in the race with time
count the months and days, time
wasted, we arrived too soon

lost from my life, free
from conditional embrace, run aground
on an island in the final shift of hope
        balanced tight
in bitter reckoning

at the border, wave and
listen silently for a sound
        a sign, proof
that you are ready for the role
reluctantly tethered to age
        among men

because you caressed with words, warmed
        with desire, budded
the heart with honeyed pleasure and the rainbow
softly the fingers sought, pierced
didn't you want to know it all?
        you wanted it all
being strange, perhaps love and
death are the same, a sleep
        bringing dreams to the bed
wed, intimately and cruelly,
still strange, still recent
        gone

                                    *1970

Genesis

pembuat boneka
yang jarang bicara
dan yang tinggal agak jauh dari kampung
telah membuat patung
dari lilin
serupa dia sendiri
dengan tubuh, tangan dan kaki dua
ketika dihembusnya napas di ubun
telah menyala api
tidak di kepala
tapi di dada
—aku cinta—kata pembuat boneka
baru itu ia mengeluarkan kata
dan api itu
telah membikin ciptaan itu abadi
ketika habis terbakar lilin
lihat, api itu terus menyala

Genesis

The puppet maker
who seldom speaks
and lives far from the village
made a puppet
of wax
which looked exactly like himself
with a body, hands and two legs.
When he blew
on the crown of the puppet's head
a candleflame burned
not in the head
but in the heart.
"I love you," said the puppet maker
and as soon as he spoke
the candle caught alight and
the work of his hands was immortal.
Look! The wax has melted,
the flame still burns.

*1975

Petunjuk sutradara

Waktu adalah faktor penting dalam permainan
Waktu menguasai irama pada gerak, pada pertemuan
    dan percakapan
Waktu menetukan beberapa lama pelaku tampil,
    undur dan hilang dari panggung
Waktu membagi cerita dalam adegan yang seimbang:
    kapan akan membuka tabir dan menutup pada
    akhir
Waktu membatasi kelangsungan peran: mereka yang
    bunuh diri hendak mengatasi kadar kemungkinan
Nah, di sudut panggung ini Bima akan tertusuk
    pedang dan mati
di puncak cerita: itu adalah pemecahan yang wajar dari
perhitungan waktu.

The producer's directions

Time is an important part of the play
Time controls the rhythm of the actions, the meetings
    and the conversations
Time determines when an actor enters, when he leaves,
    and how long he is absent from the stage
Time divides the story into equal parts: tells when to
    open the curtains
and when to close them at the end
Time limits the extent of each role: those who commit
    suicide must overcome the limitations of what is
    possible
Now, in this corner here, Bima[†] is stabbed with a sword
    and dies,
at the climax of the story: a natural solution
to the problem of time.

*1970

[†] Bima is the largest and most aggressive of the five Pandawa brothers, the heroes of the traditional Javanese shadow-play. According to legend, he dies a natural death while he is on a pilgrimage in the Himalayas. Although he is indestructible, he cannot overcome time.

Chapter 3

THE WORLD BECOME ABSURD

The Consolidation of the New Order in the 1970s

BY THE EARLY 1970s, the New Order had established patterns of economic policy and governmental procedures which were to persist until well into the 1990s, with important consequences for literary creativity.[1]

There was, firstly, the shift toward an open market economy that was carefully overseen by the government. This new capitalism was heavily reliant on overseas investment and international funding agencies. It was justified by an ideology of "development" *(pembangunan)* and later reinforced by the obligatory framework of *Pancasila,*[2] the five principles enunciated in the Preamble to the 1945 Constitution—Belief in God, humanitarianism, nationalism, democracy, and social justice. Criticism of the distribution of economic rewards could readily be blocked in the name of higher principles.

Secondly, Indonesia moved toward becoming "a state operating above politics."[3] The first general elections, held on July 5, 1971, saw the "state party,"[4] Golkar, win two-thirds of the popular vote, taking 236 of the 360 elected seats in the People's Representative Assembly (DPR), together with an absolute majority of 23 of the 26 provinces of Indonesia.[5] The other parties were allowed only a very limited opportunity to represent competing class, ethnic, religious or other sectional interests, and were within a few years reduced to two large groupings, the United Development Party (Partai Persatuan Pembangunan, PPP), and the Indonesian Democratic Party (Partai Demokrasi Indonesia, PDI). Political activity at village level, except by Golkar, was discouraged on the principle that the people were still uneducated in such matters. The parties were forbidden to "intimidate opponents, offend the dignity of the government and its officials, disrupt national unity, or criticize national policy."[6] Direct social comment, thus, also had the potential to be considered illegal political action.

Thirdly, the authority structures in both the military and the civil realms were dominated by military personnel operating under the policy of *dwifungsi* (dual functionality). As Crouch summarizes: "During the first 15 years of the New Order, military officers were placed in senior bureaucratic positions in almost all government departments, nearly all provinces were headed by governors with military backgrounds, most *kabupaten* (area under a regent, or *bupati*) were headed by military *bupati,* many key diplomatic posts were held by military officers, and military officers were made directors of state corporations. During the 1980s and 1990s, the number of such appointments declined sharply, but military officers—whether active or retired—still made up about half of the provincial governors and around 40 percent of *bupati*. Altogether about 6,000 officers were serving in civilian positions in the late 1990s."[7] Military training encouraged quick, firm decision-making and had little place for the ambiguity or sentiment that the writers and readers of literature valued.

Finally, the increasingly small space for social commentary was formalized by legal restrictions placed on the public expression of personal opinion, particularly opinion unfavorable to the president and the state. While Article 28 of the 1945 Constitution declared that "the freedom of association, thought, expression, and so on, should be laid down by law," this was understood by the government to mean that these rights could *only* be determined by the

law.[8] This legalization of the right to criticize had two final conse-
quences for writers. One was retrospective: there was henceforth
an extensive refusal to address memories of socialism, left-wing
ideology, and the massacres of 1965.[9] The other was more immedi-
ate: there were clear barriers between the literary and the political,
which were reinforced by the government's powers to ban writ-
ings, and arrest and detain individuals.[10]

By 1969 Arif Budiman had already pointed out that, although
there still was some social comment in modern Indonesian litera-
ture, it no longer made any impact on the wider society.[11] For the
reasons outlined above, this situation was not likely to improve in
the coming years.

The World Become Absurd

We have already seen the use of humor in the poetry of Rendra and
Taufiq Ismail in the late sixties. Humor was also a prominent fea-
ture of contemporary prose writing, especially in the works of Iwan
Simatupang, Danarto, Putu Wijaya, and Budi Darma, which were
variously categorized as "non-realist," "absurd," "surreal," or "fan-
tastic." A playful, non-serious attitude to the self, language, and so-
ciety was to become a major characteristic of the poetry of Sutardji
Calzoum Bachri, Darmanto Jatman, and Yudhistira, written dur-
ing the early 1970s. As another poet, Remy Sylado, insisted in re-
sponse to the formality of writers he particularly associated with
Horison: "Poetry is not a sacred object; poems are easy to make and
can be used for all sorts of purposes, including ridicule, surprise and
jokes."[12]

Sutardji explained his approach to poetry in his "Poetic Credo,"
dated March 30, 1973. "Words," Sutardji insisted, "are not tools
which convey meaning. They are not like a pipe which carries wa-
ter. They are free." Meaning is a form of oppression of language,
and ideas are a burden. He claimed to have liberated his language
from the shackles of dictionaries, grammar, and morality. In doing
so, words were free to be creative once more, to play and determine
their own desires. As a result of their excitement in discovering

their own independence, "words can jump about and dance on the page, get drunk, take their clothes off, wander backwards and forwards, sometimes show their faces and their backs, which may be the same or not, divide at will, unite with other words in order to gain new strength, turn around or upside down as they wish, fight with each other in their freedom to do as they want or if necessary kill themselves in order to show that they are capable of rejecting and rebelling against the meanings which others seek to impose upon them." The only duty of the poet is to allow words to form their own meanings and receive *"aksentuasi yang maksimal,"* the greatest possible stress.

Sutardji concluded: "Writing, for me, is a way of freeing words, which means returning them to their origin. In the beginning was The Word. And the first word was a mantra. For me, writing poetry means returning words to the status of the mantra."[13]

In Muslim theology, the first word was indeed a creative act: *kun fayakun,* "Let it Be!" called the whole world into existence. Sutardji's early poems sometimes dealt with God, often with less exalted subjects. The concrete poem, *"Pot,"* may refer to a flower pot, a chamber pot, an illegal drug (often used as an herb for cooking in some parts of Indonesia and not illegal at all). The bubbling sound creating by the repetition of the word "pot . . . pot . . . pot" may lead listeners to decide on a coffee pot as the "true subject" of the poem, but that meaning is surely as arbitrary as any other. The poem "Daun" (Leaf) presented a kaleidoscope of natural features — leaves, rivers, birds, the sky; colors; and rhyming objects (*dada,* the chest, *dadu,* dice). In addressing the world through the intimacy of the second-person pronoun *kau,* you, the same word in capitals, *KAU,* is both contained and yet highlighted. The YOU may be God, but it need not be. God, as the obscure "Q" indicates, is a mystery Who can be gestured at but not named. The exclamation marks may be expressions of wonder at His greatness, or they may be anything.

Human sexuality was also a subject that interested him. Rather than serve as a means of increasing intimacy, the poems seemed to suggest that love could move toward aggression or even violence. "Mesin kawin" (Marriage machine) and "A Gift of love from an Indonesian Gentleman . . ." both have a showy, voyeuristic tone, which emphasized the desire to shock his audience. His poems published later in the seventies in the collection *Amuk* (Amok) are filled with blood and various degrees and types of pain: "Berdarah" (Bleeding) is typical of those works.

Sutardji experimented with sounds and patterns of words, but wrote a rather Malay form of Indonesian. Darmanto Jatman's poetry was more sprawling in the length of its lines and frequently mingled words together from Indonesian, Javanese, English, Dutch, and later Hawaiian and Chinese in a pastiche that was, perhaps, typical of the Indonesian spoken by the young urban sophisticates of the new nation state. Darmanto's concern in his first volume of poetry, *Bangsat!* (You Bastard!), was focused on himself and the problems of early adulthood: work, love, morality, and religion of the Roman Catholic variety. Despite the despair of being "almost 27" years of age and "still nothing yet," Darmanto's narrator presented himself as comfortable with his modern persona, which included not only the world of *wayang* shadow theater but also the literary works of T. S. Eliot, Yevgeny Yevtushenko, the beat poet Allen Ginsberg, and the music of Bob Dylan. Darmanto's writing no longer pitted East and West against each other but blended them in one new Indonesian culture.

Yudhistira was the least serious of these three not very serious poets. (Potentially, even his name was a joke. Yudhistira, whose name the poet deliberately borrowed, was the oldest of the five Pandawa brothers of the world of *wayang,* the son of Indra, the god of *dharma,* duty and righteousness.) His poems often seem little more than brazen jokes. Beneath this veneer, however, was a "bitterness at the injustices rampant in Indonesian society at present," aimed at "the symbols and slogans which enable the privileged to present an altruistic public image while actually promoting their own selfish interests with impunity."[14]

Judging an Absurd World

Not all critics (especially foreign critics, who had the least to lose by such comments) approved of the literary frivolity of the seventies, although their major comments were more often directed toward prose writings than poetry. David Hill, for example, has argued that the "fantastical and bizarre styles" which developed throughout this decade were unrelated to contemporary social problems and issues. Rather they were concessions made in response to the official suppression of political organization and analysis, which writers could make without difficulty because of their "universalist, ahistorical literary perspectives" and their "lack of social commitment."[15]

Others have been less skeptical. Paul Tickell has provided an interesting argument that contrasts realism and fantasy. Tickell argued that the dominant position of realism in Indonesian literature was closely linked, by both the right and the left, with "the ideology of the modern." Modernism is dominated by a worldview that is assumed to be rational, logical, scientific, and positivistic. It therefore emphasizes "seeing and depicting the world *as it really is,* unfettered by superstition and moribund tradition."[16] With the growth of "an increasingly powerful, effective, centralized state . . . all pervasive and omniscient,"[17] modern Indonesian literature became increasingly uncertain of the role of "the active, animate and human agent in the world," and slowly came, instead, to see the self as victim.[18] The fantastic, however, communicated through symbol and metaphor rather than through the conventions of realist representation. It relied on association and the subconscious, rather than making use of the conventional linearity of realist narrative.[19] "Surrealism," therefore, had "the power to interrogate and at times undermine conventions of literary representation and, indeed, often give some insight into the 'true' nature of the world—the relationships between human consciousness, social forces, language and so on."[20]

Marshall Clark has taken Tickell's argument several steps further. Fantasy, Clark argued, was not only an expression of resistance to dominant literary and social conventions. It was also, specifically, a way of resisting the New Order hegemony which had become increasingly preoccupied with defining cultural identity in terms of "unity,"[21] at the expense of diversity, particularly diversity of a challenging or subversive kind. Clark insisted that fantasy was consistently used in Indonesian literature throughout the New Order to open up the collective consciousness to the disorder which lurks just outside the dominant literary and cultural system. It challenged hegemonic assumptions of what the world is and the way it should be. Further, it even revealed the hidden realities of the undercurrents of Indonesian society: the massacres, the murders, the disappearances . . . attitudes to women, the poor, the youth, the colonized, the ghosts. Literature, thus, had the power to document the missing gaps of contemporary society when other forms of political expression necessarily remained somewhat less outspoken.[22]

Pot

pot apa pot itu pot kaukah pot aku
pot pot pot
yang jawab pot pot pot pot kaukah pot itu
yang jawab pot pot pot pot kaukah pot aku
pot pot pot
potapa potitu potkaukah potaku?
POT

Daun

daun
                              burung
             sungai
               kelepak
mau sampai   langit
               siapa   tahu
      buah   rumput   selimut
               dada   biru
               langit   dadu
                       mari!
      rumput   pisau   batu kau
kau   kau   kau   kau   kau   kau   kau
      kau   kau   kau   KAU   kau   kau   kau
      kau   kau   kau   kau   kau   kau   kau
               kau

Pot

what pot is that pot pot are you my pot
pot pot pot
it answers me pot pot pot are you that pot
it answers me pot pot pot are you my pot
whose pot is that pot is it my pot
POT

1970

Leaf

leaf
bird
river
flutter
climbing to the sky
who can tell
fruit   grass   blanket
blue   breast
sky dice
come
knife of grass
you are a rock
you you you you you you you
you you you YOU you you you
you you you you you you you
you

*1973

Mesin kawin

burung membuat sarang di luar bunga menjadi buah di
taman dua seksolog membikin mesinkawin dari
kotakkotakkotak daging di atas ranjang baut itu
telungkup sekrup telentang per ingin berdenyut busi
telanjang tiktaktiktak tiktaktiktak baut mengangkang
sekrup telungkup seksolog saling memasukkan per mulai
berdenyut dan busi mengerang tujuh enam lima empat
tiga dua satu zero wau!   motor menderam roda
menggelindingkan daging di atas daging di atas pelamin
di atas daging seksolog senyum laju bahtera laju
tiktaktiktaktiktak cecak dan aku tersipu seksolog senyum
laju bahtera laju tiktaktiktaktiktak mau kau mencoba
mesinkawin? tiktaktiktaktiktaktik taktiktak no no no no
no no no no no no no mulut menjemput mulut daging
menjemput daging sekrup baut menangkup hati dan
kelamin tiktaktiktaktiktaktiktak tiktak seksolog senyum
laju bahtera laju mau kau mencoba mesinkawin? tik
taktiktaktiktak aku tak mau dikotak tak mau disekrup
aku mau daging di padang aku mau burung terbang aku
mau buah yang lapang tiktaktiktaktiktaktiktaktiktak
seksolog   senyum laju bahtera laju mau kau memakai
mesinkawin stainless steel tahan goyang ditanggung sedap
menggeliat sendiri bebas dari penat? tiktaktiktaktiktak
tiktaktiktak   no no no no no no no no no no no
zzzzzzzzzzz zzzzzzzzzzz zzzzzzzzzzz zzzzzzzzzzz
zzzzzzzzzzzz no

Marriage machine

birds nest outside flowers seed fruit in the garden two
sexologists make a marriage machine with boxes of
flesh on a bed   bolt down nut up naked throbbing
sparkplug flame tiktaktiktaktiktaktiktaktik bolt up
nut over final check sexologists in and out timing firing
seven six five four three two one zero go! the motor
roars the wheels turn flesh on flesh on the bed on flesh
the sexologists smile the boat sails tiktaktiktaktiktak
the boat sails tiktaktiktaktiktak hold your nose   I am
embarrassed the sexologists smile would you like to try
our marriage machine?   tiktaktiktaktiktaktik prick
prick prick prick prick mouth on mouth flesh on flesh
bolt down heart and body tiktaktiktaktiktaktiktak the
sexologists smile the boat sails would you like to try our
marriage machine? tiktaktiktaktiktak no I don't want
to be put in a box I don't want to be screwed I want
flesh in the field and the bird to fly and fruit to grow
tiktaktiktaktiktaktiktaktiktak the sexologists smile the
boat sails do you want to use our marriage machine
stainless steel shockproof water resistant guaranteed
fresh would you like to shake yourself free from pain?
tiktaktiktak tiktaktiktaktiktak prick prick prick pri
zzzzzzzzzzzzz   zzzzzzzzzzzzz   zzzzzzzzzzzzz
zzzzzzzzzzzzz zzzzzzzzzzzzz prick

1973

Q†

                !   !
                  !   !   !
                      !   ! !   ! !   !
                                !

                !   a
                        lif !   !
                    l
                    l   a
                l   a   m
                          !   !

        mmmmmmmmmmmmmmmmmmmmmmmmmmmmmmmmmmmmmm
                    iiiiiiiiiiiiiiiiiiiiiii
        mmmmmmmmmmmmmmmmmmmmmmmmmmmmmmmmmmmmmm

                                    *1973

---

† The mysterious letters *alif* (a), *lam* (1), and *mim* (m) appear at the
  beginning of a number of chapters of the Koran without explanation.
  In themselves, they may be taken to stand for Allah and the prophet,
  Muhammad, and are often used this way in Indonesian and Malay
  spells.

**A gift of love from an Indonesian gentleman in Iowa City, USA,
to a young Indonesian maiden in Jakarta**[†]

some lovers send gifts of flowers
some lovers send gifts of blood
some lovers send gifts of tears
I send you my penis

may it grow longer and longer
may it stretch thirteen thousand miles
from me to you, ignoring US postal regulations
against parcels longer than 3'6"

my lady, my love, don't cry, relax
open your soul, your mind, be naked
let us hope that my almighty penis
can stand tall and straight
as magnificent as the flagpoles outside the United Nations,
soaring into the air, offering you peace,
amen.

*1975

[†] An earlier English version of this poem first appeared in *Writing from the World,* edited by Paul Engle and Hualing Nieh Engle (University of Iowa, Iowa City 1976). The Indonesian text has never been published. (Trans.)

Kucing

ngiau! kucing dalam darah dia menderas lewat dia
mengalir ngilu ngiau dia bergegas lewat dalam aortaku
dalam rimba darahku dia besar dia bukan harimau
bukan singa bukan hiena bukan leopar dia macam
kucing bukan kucing tapi kucing ngiau dia lapar dia
merambah rimba afrikaku dengan cakarnya dengan
amuknya dia meraung dia mengerang jangan beri
daging dia tak mau daging jesus jangan beri roti dia tak
mau roti ngiau kucing meronta dalam darahku
meraung merambah barah darahku dia lapar O
alangkah lapar ngiau berapa juta hari dia tak makan
berapa ribu waktu dia tak kenyang berapa juta lapar
lapar kucingku berapa abad dia mencari mencakar
menunggu tuhan mencipta kucingku tanpa mauku dan
sekarang dia meraung mencariMu dia lapar jangan beri
daging jangan beri nasi tuhan menciptanya tanpa
setahuku dan kini dia minta tuhan sejemput saja untuk
tenang sehari untuk kenyang sewaktu untuk tenang di
bumi ngiau! dia meraung dia mengerang hei berapa
tuhan yang kalian punya beri aku satu sekedar pemuas
kucingku hari ini ngiau huss puss diamlah aku pasang
perangkap di afrika aku pasang perangkap di amazon
aku pasang perangkap di riau aku pasang perangkap di
kota kota siapa tahu nanti ada satu tuhan yang kena
lumayan kita bisa berbagi sekerat untuk kau sekerat
untuk aku ngiau huss puss diamlah

Cat

Meow! there is a cat in my blood he roars he runs he
flows Meow! painfully through the aorta of my heart in
the forest of my blood he is enormous but he is not a
tiger and not a lion not a hyena not a leopard not a cat
but a cat Meow! he is hungry he levels the forests of
Africa with his claws and his madness he roars he howls
don't feed him meat he doesn't like meat Jesus don't
feed him bread he doesn't want bread Meow! a cat
fighting in my blood roaring punching his way through
the coals in my heart he is hungry very hungry Meow!
he has not eaten for millions of days thousands of
centuries he has been hungry for millions of ages for
endless eons he has been searching scratching waiting
God created my cat I didn't ask Him to and now he
roars in search of God he is hungry don't give him meat
or rice God created him I didn't ask God to do that but
now my cat wants God however briefly so that he can be
at peace for a day at rest for a while and live in
tranquility Meow! he roars he screams Hey! how many
gods are there? give me one to keep my cat quiet for at
least one day Meow! shush pussy shush I fix traps in
Africa in the Amazon in Riau in cities all over the world
who knows perhaps I'll catch me a god not bad a slice
for you and a slice for me shush pussy shush Meow!

1973

Satu

kuterjemahkan tubuhku ke dalam tubuhmu
ke dalam rambutmu kuterjemahkan rambutku
jika tanganmu tak bisa bilang tanganku
kuterjemahkan tanganku ke dalam tanganmu
jika lidahmu tak bisa mengucap lidahku
kuterjemahkan lidahku ke dalam lidahmu
aku terjemahkan jemariku ke dalam jemarimu
jika jari jemarimu tak bisa memetikku
ke dalam darahmu kuterjemahkan darahku
kalau darahmu tak bisa mengucap darahku
jika ususmu belum bisa mencernakan ususku
kuterjemahkan ususku ke dalam ususmu
kalau kelaminmu belum bilang kelaminku
aku terjemahkan kelaminku ke dalam kelaminmu

daging kita satu arwah kita satu
walau masing jauh
yang tertusuk padamu berdarah padaku

Berdarah

hari ini aku berdarah. kapak hitam menakik almanakku.
pecahlah rabuku mengalirlah pecahlah seninku
    mengalirlah pecahlah selasaku mengalirlah pecahlah
    jumatku mengalirlah darah mengalir dalam denyut
    dalam debar. darah nyerbu dalam kamus diriku
    dalam rongga pustakaku. segalanya terdedah untuk
    darah segalanya terbuka untuk luka.

One

I will translate my body into your body
I will translate my hair into your hair
if your hand cannot be my hand
I will translate my hand into your hand
if your tongue cannot speak my tongue
I will translate my tongue into your tongue
I will translate my fingers into your fingers
if your fingers cannot touch me
I will translate your blood into my blood
if your blood follows a separate rhythm
if your stomach cannot swallow my stomach
I will translate my stomach into your stomach
if your genitals are not my genitals
I will translate my genitals into your genitals

our flesh will be one, our souls one
even when they are far apart
what pierces you will make me bleed

1979

Bleeding

I am bleeding today, a black ax lies buried deep in my
    diary.
breaking open my Wednesday blood flows my Monday
    blood flows my Tuesday blood flows my Friday
    blood flows blood flows and throbs rushing through
    my dictionary my library everything is covered in
    blood scarred with deep wounds

badan tangan jalan bintang zarah kalian berdarah.
hari ini aku berdarah tapi tak satu pun sampai tahu
    nyeriku.
aku berteriak lengang yang menjawab aku bercakap
    sepi yang mengucap aku bertanya duri yang
    menganga aku bernyanyi sunyi yang menari.
kau kirim anakanak ke sekolah kau kirim mereka
    bertahun tahun dalam kelas sampai tumbuh
    janggutnya sampai panjang misainya sampai
    tumbuh jembutnya.
siapa dapat menerjemahkan peri?
siapa kamus yang tahu arus?
tak hijau tak kuning tak biru tak merah tak warna
    darah mencemplung dalam diriku membikin laut
    dan aku ikan dari pedih lautan.
karang kerang tripang udang penyelam kita dari dalam
    yang sama dari pedih yang sama. apa yang tersayat
    dalam diriku ada dalam kalian.
hari ini aku berjalan lewat almanakku. aku berteriak
    koyak aku menggumam demam aku mengigau risau.
    aku begitu darah! bahkan kalau hanya bayangku
    menyentuh tanah tanah kan menggumpal darah!
pedihku pedih kalian pedih kita
kita dari pedih yang sama. apa yang tersayat dalamku
    ada dalam kalian. tapi mungkin kalian tak tau.
    masih tak. tak.

my hand body road stars atoms all bleed
I am bleeding today but no one knows the extent of my
    pain
I shout desolation replies I call silence speaks I ask
    thorns reply I sing melancholy dances
you send your children to school you send them year
    after year they sprout pubic hair moustaches long
    hair
who can translate my pain?
who knows the right words?
not green not yellow not blue not red no color the blood
    splashing inside me is a sea and I am a fish in a sea of
    pain
we dive for coral, prawns, cockles and tripang the way
    we dive for pain. the wounds I bear we all bear
I am walking through my diary today. I shout I tear it
    up I moan in a fever I shake with fright. There is so
    much blood! If my shadow ever touched the ground,
    the whole earth would fill with blood!
my pain is your pain it is our pain
we come from the same pain. the wounds I bear we all
    bear. perhaps you don't know that. perhaps. you
    don't. no.

1979

Dari kaca jendela kamarku suata senja

Dua bayangan
Sergap menyergap
Dalam kaca.
        Kaca
                biru
        Kaca
                ungu
        Kaca
                hitam

Tersergap dalam bingkai
jalinan bunga tak tentu
(Sementara orang bilang:
Itulah seni gothik yang cemerlang).
Lalu kedua bayangan itu
merayap perlahan
dan tiba-tiba sergap menyergap
dalam pandanganku.
Dan aku pun menjerit:
        Magi Hitam!
        Magi Hitam!
        Kembalikanlah ketenteramanku!

(Bayangan bayangan itupun loncat meloncat
 dari satu bingkai
 ke bingkai lainnya)
        yuhuu!
(Dan kau pun akan terhenyak!)
Wah. Pada rambutmu yang tergerai
Nasib gatal merayap-rayap
Dan betapa tak pernah berhenti gelisah.
(Sejarah telah menganyam

Twilight on the window of my room

Two shadows
dogfight
on the window
 The blue
    window
 Purple
    window
 Black
    window

Snarling in the lead
of uncertain, woven flowers
(I have heard it called
excellent gothic)
they slowly prowl
then launch themselves at each other
as I watch
I scream:
 Black magi
 Black magi
 Give me back peace!

(The shadows jump
from one frame to another)
 A scream!
(You fall)
Fate crawls in your tangled hair
we worry all the time
(History binds our veins)

jalinan urat syaraf kita)
Aduh. Tidakkah kau peka
Akan sunyi titik air
menyanyi dari daun ke daun
menetes perlahan dari pelupuk mata kita
tersergap angin jahat
mengabur dalam seribu cahaya
biasan kaca
(Aturan peradaban
  yang dinamai 'Norma')
        Beribu orang mati tiap hari di Biafra
                (Kering bagai tulang disalut kulit / kering)
        Beribu orang mati tiap hari di Vietnam
                (Remuk bagai onggokan daging / remuk)
Setan pun menimang-nimang bayinya:
Wah puteraku, panglima generasi yang akan datang
        Plak ketibang, plak ketibang!
Pencipta sistim anti kemanusiaan yang cemerlang
        Plak ketibang, plak ketibang!
Buanglah anti kebudayaan yang sudah usang
        Plak ketibang, plak ketibang!
Yang
        Ketibang
Eh,
        Ketibang

Dua bayangan
Sergap-menyergap
Dalam kaca
Mereka adalah
Bukan kau
Bukan aku.

Don't you ever think
of the silent water drops
falling from our eyes
from leaf to leaf
dried by the cruel wind
fading in a thousand nights
adrift on the pane
(The rules of civilization
'norms')
        In Biafra thousands die every day
                (Dry bones wrapped in leather / dry)
        In Vietnam thousands die every day
                (Like broken heaps of flesh / broken)
Satan is a good father
One day you'll be generals, my boys
        Jack and Jill went up the hill
Brilliant innovators in inhumanity
        Jack fell down and broke his crown
Destroying past civilizations
        And Jill came tumbling after
Jack and Jill
        fixed their heads
with vinegar and brown paper

Two shadows
dogfighting
on the window
Two
and one is not you
the other is not I

                                *1974

Apa yang sesungguhnya harus kukatakan

Lewat jendela kamarku
Aku menjengukmu
'Adakah kau sehat-sehat saja
Seperti waktu aku dulu meninggalkanmu?'
    (Seperti Nuh membuka jendela kapalnya
    Berharap
    'Semoga ada daratan
    dengan bunga-bunga
    serta buah-buah'
    Kami pun sama-sama melepas burung dara)
Dulu
Kalau aku duduk di muka jendela ini
Kuberondongkan seribu tembakan
(Suara tanpa rupa)
Yang menghancurkan nestapa
yang menyergapku
apabila aku dihukum ibu.

Dan sekarang
Bahkan seribu tambah satu tembakan
Tak mampu melukai duka
yang menyerbuku.
    Sementara perhitungan teliti
    Memunculkan berbagai-bagai ancaman
    Lawan yang tersembunyi
    Serta medan yang tak terpetakan
    (Namun toh tiada malu-malunya kita berdoa:
    Semoga terjadilah
    Semoga)
    Sedang kepadamu kukatakan selalu
    'Wahai'
    'Hidupku adalah keajaiban
    Heran
    Kenapa belum padam-padam juga?!'

What can I say?

I can see you
through my window
"Have you changed
since I left?"
(Like Noah at the window of the ark
hoping
to find fruit
and flowers
we sent the dove away)

Once
I sat here
firing a thousand rounds
(silently)
at the threatening menace
of my mother's anger

Now
not even a thousand rounds
can wound
my sorrow

Various forms appear
—count them carefully—
strange enemies in a field of fog
(Yet we continue to pray
Pray for a miracle
Pray for
Pray)

I have always said
that life itself is a miracle
Yet you
still hope?!

Di bawah pohon-pohon kenari
Di sepanjang bukit-bukit
Kabut berjalan dengan diam-diam
Lalu berbisik:
Siapakah yang mati?
Aku pun pucat
Namun tak urung:
Manusia
Ya
Manusia terbaik abad ini.
    Bah!
    Apakah gunanya aku berbantah-bantah dengan
                          Tuhan
    Toh Ia selalu lebih benar?
Kabut menghampiri jendelaku
Sia-sia kuberondongkan tembakanku
Satu kali lagi
Sebelum sampai putus asa
Aku menyaksikan dosaku:
Cinta yang selalu bikin repot orang saja!
    Percuma usul kita :
    'Tuhan
    Harap yang begini-begini
    Kau beri hak hidup juga
    Betapa pun terbatasnya'
    Sebab Tuhan sendiri toh tak pernah kesepian
    Sekalipun Ia bujangan.

Under the candlenut trees
in the hills
the fog
advances slowly, whispering
of death
I am pale
but refuse to surrender:
Man, you know,
Yes, man, I say
has never been better off than he is now
Bah!
Why bother fighting with God
He always wins
The fog creeps to the window
I pull the trigger
again
then give up hope—
I have sinned:
never fall in love
it is always difficult

Wah.
lewat jendela kamarku
Kukirimkan surat kepadaNya
: Kristus
 Seandainya Kau kesasar dalam perjalananMu
Mampirlah ke rumahku
Aku sangat butuh bantuanMu
Aku pengin coba-coba menulis pesan
Cintaku
        Yang abadi
        Yang penuh pasi
        Yang manusiawi
Yang belum lagi jadi milikku kini.

Why complain
"God, I wanted this
and that, why didn't You make me
differently?"
He's too busy
even if he is a bachelor

I'll send Him a letter:
Christ,
if You get lost
come and stay with me
I need help
I have a list
        —eternal
passionate
human
love—
of all the things I've never had

*1974

Siapakah kau, aku?

I.

Siapakah kau
Matahari yang berguling-guling dalam tanur pabrik-
                             pabrik baja
Padahal dulu bulan yang tak henti diam dalam
                             ramahnya—
Ketika remaja meloncat-loncat di antara batu-batu kali
Dan sekarang merayap di lumpur-lumpur dengan bazooka

    Kenangan memadam
    Hidup detik ini dilontarkan
    Menembus nasib yang satu
    Menyusup nasib berikutnya
    tak tertangkap lagi logika.

Siapakah kau
Memburu burung menggelepar dalam jaring
'Tak mati hari ini ya besok pagi?'

Siapakah kau?
(Pada pohon-pohon kenari yang berbaris menderap
kuberondongkan tanyaku)
    : Aku adalah yang kau tanyai
    'Siapakah kau?!'
    dengan suara yang serak.

Siapakah kau?
(Pada air yang gemercik memukuli batu-batu kali
kuteriakkan tanyaku)
    : Ah. Ah. Ah.
    'Si a pa kah kau?!'
    Hmm?!

Who are you? Me?

I.

Who are you?
The sun rolls in the furnace
The moon is still friendly
Young men run among rocks in the river
crawl in the mud with bazookas
Memory fades
          Life is thrown like a dice
          fates and the future
          in the balance
          Logic? None
Who are you
hunting birds with a net
"If they don't die today, they will tomorrow"

Who are you
(I ask the running
candle-nut trees):
I am the one you asked about;
Who are you
my voice is thrown back like seed
Who are you
(I ask the shining water
beating against rocks):
Ah Ah Ah
Who are you?!
Who!Siapakah kau?

Siapakah kau?
(Pada kuda bendi yang berketipak sepanjang jalan
kulontarkan tanyaku)
 : plik
plak
(sunyi)
plik
plak

II.

Kupadamkan curigaku menemuimu
 Angin dingin yang menyanyi di antara
   pohon-pohon kopi
 (Karena aku percaya keampuhan jamu-jamuku)
Kupadamkan curigaku menemuimu
 Air yang bersijingkat di antara batu-batu kali
 (Karena aku percaya keampuhan jampi-jampiku)

Kuburu kau
Kutilang, Kutilang
Karena aku butuh sangat perasaan sehat
yang menggerakkan seluruh otot-ototku
Kuburu kau menyusup cahaya bulan
Karena aku butuh amat sangat kesegaran
yang membangun urat saraf baru bagi sukmaku
menghidupi hidupnya.
 Sudah tak kurasa lagi ada yang memburu-buruku
 Melewati umurku 27 tanpa mencucupnya.

Who are you?
(To the cart-horse clopping down the road):
clip
clop
(silence)
clip
clop

II.

My suspicion fades when we meet
        The cold wind sings in the coffee bushes
        (I believe in my spells)
Water crawls between the rocks in the river
(I believe in my spells)
I hunt you
thrush, thrush
for my health's sake
I hunt you in the moonlight
I want to be refreshed
in body and soul
and alive again
        Non-being chases after me
        Past 27, and nothing

Atas nama modernisasi
Momok-momok mekanisasi menjaringku
dengan 1000 diferensiasi
rumusan staus dan fungsi
dalam suatu sosiogram
di mana nasibku diputuskan
kemarin–hari ini–esok pagi.

Kudoakan nasib buruk bagimu
bandar-bandar lotere
supaya aku menang!

Kutabuhi kau dalam mabuk tari kuda kepang
Semoga nasib buruk jatuh padamu lawan politikku!

III.

Jam berdentang 12 kali
Aku ingat kau
Dan ingat 1000 wanita lain lagi

Wahai
Agaknya aku cinta mereka semua
Wahai
Berahiku yang menyala
Kubawa berlari masuk keluar bordil-bordil
        (Germo-germo menyebar air mata)
Kubawa berlari masuk keluar kasino
        (Bandar-bandar menyebar bunga-bunga)
Kubawa berlari masuk ke luar gereja
        (Pendeta-pendeta menyebar air mata)
Kubawa masuk keranjangku
Kupadamkan dalam bayanganmu
Tubuh padat ruh.

Jam berdentang 3 kali
Aku terkenang padamu
Dan hanya kepadamu belaka.

Mechanized ghosts ensnare me
in the name of modernization
with 1000 differentials
formulas of status and function
a sociogram
of my broken-backed fate
yesterday–today–tomorrow

I hope your luck is awful
I hope you buy lots of lottery tickets
and I win all the prizes

I beat the drum for your trance-dance
bad luck to all my enemies!

III.

    The clock strikes twelve
    I think of you
    and a thousand other women
I love them all
outrageous lust drags me from brothel to brothel
    (The prostitutes scatter rosewater)
from casino to casino
    (croupiers throw roses)
from church to church
    (priests sprinkle tears)
and back to bed
to extinguish lust in the shadow
of your body

    The clock strikes three
    I think of you
    and no one else

Aku mendengar suaramu
Sunyi
Di antara gelegar meriam di Vietnam
Demonstrasi para mahasiswa di kampus-kampus
Ataupun gemuruh mesin pabrik senjata

Suaramu
Sunyi
Melengking
Dalam Jazz & Soul

Siapakah kau
Remaja yang menanggalkan satu demi satu tawamu,
                          lirikanmu, gerak-gerikmu
Remaja yang menambahkan satu demi satu guratan
                dahi, putih rambut & kediamanmu

        (Bintang-bintang blingsatan dalam tabuhan Jazz)

Di matamu, dunia penuh dengan cahaya

        Kudendangkan namamu:
        Ai. Ai. Ai.

Jam berdentang 6 kali
Aku menghirup kopiku
Sangsi
Apakah kau pun mengingatku
(?!)

I can hear your silent voice
among the roar of cannon in Vietnam
the student demonstrations
and armament factories

A lonely voice
shouting
jazz and soul

Who are you
Young person shedding one by one laughter, grace,
                                    movement
assuming wrinkles, white hair and melancholy

     (the stars are dazed by the jazz drummer)

I see a world of light in your eyes

     I hear your name
     Ai Ai Ai

It is six
I sip my coffee
and wonder
if you remember me
?!

                                   *1974

Yudhistira Anm Massardi

Sajak sikat gigi

Seseorang lupa menggosok giginya sebelum tidur
Di dalam tidur ia bermimpi
Ada sikat gigi menggosok-gosok mulutnya supaya
                                                terbuka

Ketika ia bangun pagi hari
Sikat giginya tinggal sepotong
Sepotong yang hilang itu agaknya
Tersesat di dalam mimpinya dan tak bisa kembali

Dan ia berpendapat bahwa kejadian itu terlalu
                                berlebih-lebihan

A poem about a toothbrush

Someone forgot to brush his teeth
      before he went to bed.
All night long he dreamed
That a toothbrush
      scrubbed his teeth
      and kept his mouth wide open.

When he woke up the next morning
He had one toothbrush,
the other had gone—
lost in his dreams—
and never came back.

And he thought
      that the whole thing
was very strange.

1974

Biarin!

kamu bilang hidup itu brengsek. Aku bilang biarin
kamu bilang hidup itu nggak punya arti. Aku bilang
                                        biarin
kamu bilang aku nggak punya kepribadian. Aku
                                  bilang biarin
kamu bilang aku nggak punya pengertian. Aku bilang
                                        biarin

habisnya, terus terang saja, aku nggak percaya sama
                                        kamu
tak usah marah. Aku tahu kamu orangnya sederhana
cuman, karena kamu merasa asing saja makanya kamu
                          selalu bilang seperti itu

kamu bilang aku bajingan. Aku bilang biarin
kamu bilang aku perampok. Aku bilang biarin

soalnya, kalau aku nggak jadi bajingan mau jadi apa
                                  coba, lonte?
aku laki-laki. Kalau kamu nggak suka kepadaku sebab
                                        itu
aku rampok hati kamu. Tokh nggak ada yang nggak
                          perampok di dunia ini.
Iya nggak? Kalau nggak percaya tanya saja sama polisi

habisnya, kalau nggak kubilang begitu mau apa coba
bunuh diri? Itu lebih brengsek daripada membiarkan
                                  hidup ini berjalan
seperti kamu sadari sekarang ini

kamu bilang itu melelahkan. Aku bilang biarin
kamu bilang itu menyakitkan

I don't care

you say life is crazy. I say I don't care.
you say life is meaningless. I say I don't care.
you say I'm a nobody. I say I don't care.
you say I don't matter. I say I don't care.

all right, to be honest, I don't believe you.
Don't get angry. I know you're an ordinary
sort of a person. You feel uncomfortable, that's why you
                                        talk like that.

you say I'm a bastard. I say I don't care.
you say I'm a thief. I say I don't care.

the problem is, if I wasn't a bastard, what would I be, a
                                        slut?
I'm a man. If you don't like me as I am
I'll steal your heart. Everyone is a thief,
aren't they? If you don't believe me, ask the police.

all right, if you don't want me to talk like that, what
                                        should I do,
kill myself? that would be crazier than living like this.
as you well know.

you say I make you tired. I say I don't care.
you say I'm a pain in the butt.

                    1974

Sajak dolanan anak-anak

Sebuah boneka, namanya Poppy, punya Nency
Sebuah senapan, harganya mahal, punya Bobby
Sebuah mobil sedan, merk-nya Mercy, punya Tonny
Sebuah truk sampah, sopirnya mati, ditembak polisi

Tak mau

Banyak orang tak mau
Banyak orang tak mau banyak orang
Banyak orang tak mau sendiri di antara banyak orang

Dan orang tak mau
Sepi tak mau
Apa tak mau
Banyak yang tak mau

Dan akhirnya, banyak orang terpaksa
Mau tak mau . . .

A nursery rhyme

Nancy had a doll, called Poppy.
Bobby had a gun, a very big gun.
Tony had a car, a Mercedes Benz.
The man who drove the garbage truck died.
The police shot him.

1975

Don't want

Lots of people don't want
Lots of people don't want lots of people
Lots of people don't want to be alone
when there are lots of people around.

People don't want
Don't want to be lonely
What don't they want
They don't want lots of things

And, finally, lots of people have no choice
whether they want to or not . . .

1975

Chapter 4

DISENCHANTMENT WITH
THE NEW ORDER

1974: The End of Liberalism

THE NEW FREEDOMS associated with the rise of "the Generation of 1966" began to contract very markedly after 1974. The trigger for this shift was the two days of the *"Malari"* riots in January 1974. Ostensibly directed against the visiting Japanese prime minister Tanaka Kakuei, the riots began with anti-Chinese rioting and the burning of a Toyota showroom, but ended with a march on the presidential palace.[1] David Hill has argued that the true source of the riots was a "growing hostility towards government social and economic policy, and festering distrust for leading presidential confidants and associates."[2]

As a result of these public demonstrations, about 470 people were arrested, and twelve publications had their printing and publishing permits withdrawn, including *Nusantara, Harian KAMI, Indonesia Raya* (edited by Mochtar Lubis, who was himself detained for two and a half months), *The Jakarta Times,* and the weekly newsmagazine *Ekspres* (edited by Goenawan Mohamad).[3] These sweeping bans dramatically ended the government's fragile open relationship with the press, and the military's previously unambiguous "partnership" with the students.

The response marked a decisive new attitude toward individual and social participation in the policies of government. There would, henceforth, be little room for the expression of a diversity of opinions, and minimal opportunity to influence state policies or the distribution of power at the top.[4] As Richard Robison has written, "For the liberal intellectuals, 1974 was to be the beginning of the end. Since that time the New Order has successfully devoted its energies to controlling the bases of liberal influence: the universities, the press and the civil service. By the 1980s the apparatus of control and co-option has reached a level of efficiency and effectiveness far beyond that of the early 1970s."[5]

1975–1980: *The New Balance Consolidated*

This situation intensified throughout the rest of the decade as feelings of disillusionment with, and alienation from, the state were increasingly experienced by various segments of New Order society.[6] The role of Muslims as a potential force of opposition became clear in the 1977 general elections, following strong resistance to the proposal of new marriage laws and to efforts to make *kebatinan* (Javanese spirituality) into one of Indonesia's officially acceptable religions.[7] Indonesia's invasion of East Timor, 1975–76, was, in the words of Jamie Mackie and Andrew MacIntyre, "a military fiasco and a diplomatic embarrassment."[8]

With the hardening of government attitudes, students, who had vigorously supported the rise to power of the New Order, now felt betrayed by its perceived failures—corruption, repression, and lack of concern with social justice. In the lead-up to the 1977 elections, campus protests became frequent. The demonstrations had the support of parts of the army and were designed to force Suharto to step down—or at least consult with his peers.[9] Prior to the parliamentary election of the president in May of the following year, students in Surabaya, Yogyakarta, Medan, and Palembang continued to protest against government corruption.

In response to these exhibitions of dissent, the military leadership sent troops onto the campuses, rounding up some 223 student leaders.[10] The Campus Normalization Law of 1978 imposed tight controls on student political activity; student activities were confined to campus; and a ban was placed on all political action within the universities.[11] The campus press was muzzled and a further seven newspapers had their press licenses revoked.[12] As a result of the law, academic freedom was effectively extinguished.[13] In Vatikiotis's words: "The climate of intellectual freedom that once was taken for granted by Indonesian universities has become another casualty of the military's security approach."[14] The ban held until the late 1980s, when the army again began tacitly promoting student political action.

New Literary Constellations

During the 1970s, the clearly focused literary scene began to disintegrate rapidly. The arts center Taman Ismail Marzuki and the literary magazine *Horison* both lost their hold over the literary and artistic community.[15] The center became less adventurous, and more concerned to show a profit. Dissatisfied with the trend of the magazine, writers held a mock trial of *Horison* in Bandung during September 1974. Sapardi Djoko Damono met their conflicting demands by describing them as impossibly contradictory—publish more poetry, or more short stories, or more think pieces, include more new writers but also print only the best established writers![16] Instead, there was an increasing diversification and commercialization of literary production as the newsweekly *Tempo,* the intellectual monthly *Prisma,* and the daily newspapers, especially *Kompas* and *Sinar Harapan,* became more open to publishing short stories, poetry, and essays.[17] Regional newspapers, such as *Kedaulatan Rakyat* in Yogyakarta, also began to provide pages for writers. The magazine *Budaja Djaja* and its publishing house Pustaka Djaja, which had published works of literature extensively during the decade, closed down in 1979, and a range of new publishing houses with more obvious commercial interests began publishing fiction of a more popular type instead. Marga T's *Karmila,* for example, was released by Gramedia, an arm of the Kompas newspaper group, and immediately outsold all its more serious competition.[18] Cul-

tural centers were established in Bali (1976), Solo (1979), and Yog-
yakarta (1980), providing alternatives to the national capital.

Despite these greater and more diverse opportunities, many
writers, understandably, refused to comment on the changing cir-
cumstances of the wider society. Goenawan's poem, "Tentang se-
orang yang terbunuh di sekitar hari pemilihan umum" (A man
murdered near the day of the Indonesian general elections), written
in 1971, was one of the few poems that reflected on the perilous po-
sition of any citizen who might have had no social, political, or re-
ligious identification. But the poem was unclear as to who had
murdered the man, or why, just as Taufiq's poem had been unclear
about who should "give Indonesian back," or to whom.

Rendra

Rendra remained the one persistent literary critic of the New Or-
der government, and seemed to court trouble throughout the
1970s. He was first arrested in December 1970 for taking part in a
"Night of Meditation" in one of the main streets of Jakarta. The
vigil was, in part at least, directed against government extrava-
gance. In 1973, he was again held briefly by the police, in response
to his highly satirical play, *Mastadon dan Burung Condor* (The
mastodon and the condors).[19] The play claimed not to be set in In-
donesia but in some vague Latin American nation, where the dic-
tator, Colonel Max Carlos, ruled with an iron fist for the sake of his
developmental policies. When a revolution, led by university stu-
dents, appeared to be on the verge of taking over the whole country,
Carlos is forced to flee the country and seek foreign military aid. It
is clear in the play that the new government would be as repressive
as the old. Force would change nothing, without a corresponding
change of consciousness. As a consequence of performing this play,
Rendra was refused permission to present any further plays in Yog-
yakarta, his hometown, until 1977, "because of the special condi-
tions" which prevailed in the region. There were, however, no
objections to presentations in Bandung and Surabaya. The prohibi-
tion on Rendra's performing in Yogyakarta was lifted in 1977 for a

performance of a new play *Sekda* (The Provincial Secretary),[20] and again in 1978 for *Perjuangan Suku Naga,*[21] which pursued the same themes, with the same criticism of clearly recognizable political leaders and policies.

The poetry Rendra wrote throughout the seventies, like his plays, also heavily criticized the condition of Indonesian society and its elite. Rendra's "pamphlet poems,"[22] as he first called them, were not subtle. Their language was direct and held an obvious appeal to the emotions. The poems criticized the destructive effects of industrialization, and tourism, on the balance between humanity and nature. They attacked the grossly materialistic attitude of the elite, and the educational system they supported. Rendra read his works twice at TIM in 1977. By 1978, as the mood of confrontation heightened, Rendra was spending much of his time out of Yogyakarta, talking to student groups and reading his poetry at campus gatherings and even in student dormitories, at the University of Indonesia and the Bandung Institute of Technology. He was also featured reading his poems in the film *Yang Muda Yang Bercinta* (Young and in love). Huge crowds also attended his poetry readings and cheered the "savage portraits of greedy decadent leaders, confused corrupted youth and suffering poor."[23]

In this chapter of the anthology, the poems by Rendra derive from his pamphlet poems. The first, "Aku mendengar suara" (I hear voices), also used in the *Struggle of the Naga Tribe,* carried an urgent appeal "to bear witness" to the suffering he saw around him: the sound of "wounded, screaming animals," of "birds falling from their nest" and social destructiveness characterized by "men shooting at the moon." These are the themes of a longer poem, "Sajok burung-burung condor" (not included here),[24] in which the souls of the farm laborers turn at night into angry condors while *"di kota orang-orang bersiap menembaknya"* (in town, men prepare to shoot them).[25] The image of a divided society, in which the rich are licensed to exploit and oppress the poor in order to further their own interests, was extended in "Sajak Pulau Bali" (Song of Bali). Here the power of the elite was linked to the forces of international capitalism and, in particular, to the policies of the World Bank, which "helps backward nations / with huge projects / in which ninety percent of the goods are imported." "Orang-orang miskin" (Poor people) took the anger of the oppressed poor back into the homes of the elite, arguing, as Taufiq had earlier done, that the poverty of the poor not only was a consequence of the degeneration of the elite, but also carried its own potential vengeance. In this poem, the threat was carried right to the "curtains of the presidential palace."

After signing a statement in January 1978 with other intellectuals and artists protesting at the arrest and detention of student leaders and the banning of newspapers, Rendra was forbidden to make any public comments on the forthcoming election. On the first of May that year, after a bomb exploded at another of his poetry readings at TIM, Rendra was arrested and imprisoned on the grounds that his activities had been "politically provocative," and "for the cumulative effect of his activities and attitudes up to that time" might have on the masses' attitude toward development. He was charged in August for contravening sections of an early Dutch colonial law that provides a maximum jail sentence of seven years for "spreading hatred" against the government. Although released from detention almost immediately, he remained under "town arrest," until October 15, when all charges against him were dropped. Nevertheless, he was completely forbidden to give any further public performances and this ban remained in force until November 1985.[26]

Controls on arts sponsorship and censorship were further tightened during the late seventies. The sections of *Yang Muda Yang Bercinta* in which Rendra read his poetry were, of course, censored, because of "the possible negative effect they could have on society."[27] Overall, however, more Indonesial films were banned, cut, or revised for reasons other than explicit sex by different sections of the censorship machinery in 1977–78 than in any previous year.[28]

In the following decade, other poets such as Emha Ainun Nadjib and Linus Suryadi Ag were also refused permission to read their works on various occasions. Linus was not allowed to read his poem "Maria dari Magdala," for fear that the poem might offend Protestants and Catholics. Sapardi Djoko Damono commented that the ban made no sense, as the poem had already been published in the magazine *Hidup,* which was itself edited by a priest. N. Riantiarno and Emha Ainun Nadjib also had trouble receiving permission to stage their works. Generally the reasons for these restrictions were not clear and could only be guessed at by the public, because the works were usually already available in printed form. It seems probable, as Sapardi suggested, that the authorities were afraid of oral performances, but not of the written form, because of the limited readership of the latter and the powerful effect of the spoken word on a large crowds of people.[29]

The Corruption of Language

The 1945 Constitution states that *"Bahasa Negara adalah bahasa Indonesia,"* (The National Language [or: the language of the state] is Indonesian).[30] Because the language has always been an important part of Indonesian national culture, a number of cultural critics have spoken with concern of the "corruption" of the language as a tool for the accurate representation and analysis of social reality. Some of these critics have been foreign authors. Ben Anderson, for example, in his essay "The Languages of Indonesian Politics" (1966), has argued that the Indonesian spoken at the time of the Revolution represented "a project, an aspiration to unity and equality, a generous wager on the future—in the face of some increasingly intractable social facts." Contemporary Indonesian, however, "has something curiously impersonal and neuter about it, which sets up psychological distances between its speakers."[31] Michael van Langenberg identified forty "keywords" which he considered expressed the New Order's ideology in the areas of power, accumulation, legitimacy, and culture. These words, he concluded, articulated a state that was "authoritarian, theistic, corporate, institutionalised, and undergoing major structural change."[32]

Some critics, however, have also been Indonesian. The poets have often been implicit critics of the corruption of language. We have already seen the slavishness of the followers of the Great Leader in

Taufiq's poem "Kita adalah pemilik syah republik ini," with their obsequious phrase "As your majesty wishes." The absurdist poetry of the early seventies, I have argued, can be considered a way to affirm the dignity of an alternative discourse when public discourse has lost its meaning. Rendra's "newspaper language" strengthened the immediacy of his criticisms. More explicitly, Goenawan Mohamad had carefully argued as early as 1963 that political slogans shape a solidarity between the people and their leaders, whether or not the leaders have the people's interests at heart.[33] In late 1999, he regretted the poor quality of debate during the New Order, when words "lost their inspiration," bureaucrats tended to endlessly repeat cliches, and words were no longer spoken "from one heart to another." Suharto made a noise but he "did not speak."[34] Ajip Rosidi's poem "Kata-kata" (Words) was a clear statement of the potential violence caused by empty language during the New Order period: "mouths endlessly speaking words. ears endlessly deafened by words. hearts endlessly oppressed by words."

Tentang seorang yang terbunuh di sekitar
hari pemilihan umum

"Tuhan, berikanlah suaraMu, kepadaku"

Seperti jadi senyap salak anjing ketika ronda
menemukan mayatnya di tepi pematang. Telungkup.
Seperti mencari harum dan hangat padi. Tapi bau asing
itu dan dingin pipinya jadi aneh, di bawah bulan. Dan
kemudian mereka pun berdatangan—senter, suluh
dan kunang-kunang—tapi tak seorang pun
mengenalinya. Ia bukan orang sini, hansip itu berkata.

"Berikanlah suaraMu"

Di bawah petromaks kelurahan mereka menemukan
liang luka yang lebih. Bayang-bayang bergoyang sibuk
dan beranda meninggal bisik. Orang ini tak berkartu.
Ia tak bernama. Ia tak berpartai. Ia tak bertanda-
gambar. Ia tak ada yang menangisi, karena kita tak bisa
menangisi. Apa gerangan agamanya?

"Juru peta yang Agung, di mana tanahairku?"

Lusa kemudian mereka membacanya di koran kota, di
halaman pertama. Ada seorang yang menangis entah
mengapa. Ada seorang yang tak menangis entah
mengapa. Ada seorang anak yang letih dan membikin
topi dari koran pagi itu, yang diterbangkan angin
kemudian. Lihatlah. Di udara berpasang layang-layang,
semua bertopang pada cuaca. Lalu burung-burung sore
hinggap di kawat-kawat, sementara bangau-bangau
menuju ujung senja, melintasi lapangan yang gundul
dan warna yang panjang, seperti asap yang sirna.

"Tuhan, berikanlah suaraMu, kepadaku."

A man murdered near the day of the Indonesian general elections

"O God, may I be among the elect."

When the patrol discovered the body at the edge of the rice-field it was like the sudden silencing of a barking dog. Face down. As if searching for the fragrance and warmth of the rice. But in the moonlight the smell was strange and the cold on his cheeks unusual. The moon shone. Then they came—flashlights, torches, fireflies— but none of them knew who he was. He is not from here, said the civil-defense officer.

"May I be among the elect."

Beneath the hurricane lamps of the local office they found more wounds. The shadows shook and the verandah remained in whispers. The man had no identity card. He had no name. He had no party. He had no one to cry for him because we could not cry. We did not even know what religion he was.

"O great Mapmaker, where is my homeland?"

A few days later they read about him in the city papers. Some cried without knowing why. Others didn't, without knowing why. A pale child made a hat from a paper and the wind blew it away. See, there it goes. Into the air with the kites, masking the light. Then the afternoon birds perched on the wires, as the geese flew toward the twilight, past the bare plain and the lengthening colors, like ascending smoke.

"O God, may I be among the elect."

1971

W. S. Rendra

Aku mendengar suara

Aku mendengar suara
jerit hewan yang terluka

Ada orang memanah rembulan
Ada anak burung terjatuh dari sarangnya

Orang-orang harus dibangunkan
Kesaksian harus diberikan
Agar kehidupan bisa terjaga

W. S. RENDRA

I hear voices

I hear the sound
of wounded, screaming animals

There are men shooting at the moon
There are birds falling from their nests

It is time to rise
To bear witness
To protect life.

Yogyakarta

1974

Sajak Pulau Bali

Sebab percaya akan keampuhan industri,
dan yakin bisa memupuk modal nasional
dari kesenian dan keindahan alam,
maka Bali menjadi obyek pariwisata.

Betapa pun:
tanpa basa-basi keyakinan seperti itu,
Bali harus dibuka untuk pariwisata.
Sebab:
pesawat-pesawat terbang jet sudah dibikin,
dan maskapai penerbangan harus berjalan.
Harus ada orang-orang untuk diangkut.
Harus diciptakan tempat tujuan untuk dijual.
Dan waktu senggang manusia,
Serta masa berlibur untuk keluarga,
harus bisa direbut oleh maskapai
untuk diindustrikan.

Dan Bali,
dengan segenap kesenian,
kebudayaan, dan alamnya,
harus bisa diringkaskan,
untuk dibungkus dalam kertas kado,
dan disuguhkan pada pelancong.

Pesawat terbang jet di tepi rimba Brazilia,
Di muka perkemahan kaum Badui,
di sisi mana pun yang tak terduga,
lebih mendadak dari mimpi,
merupakan kejutan kebudayaan.

Inilah satu kekuasaan baru.
Begitu cepat sehingga kita terkesiap.
Begitu lihai sehingga kita terkesima.

Song of Bali

Because we believe in industry,
and are convinced we can make money
from our art and our scenery,
we have decided
to turn Bali into a tourist resort.

Well then,
let's not kid ourselves
about what we're doing when
we open Bali to tourists.
After all, jets exist,
airlines need passengers,
and passengers need places to go.
The airlines can compete
to process leisure
and family holidays.

We will shrink Bali,
its art, culture and beauty,
and sell it to the tourists,
wrapped in tinsel.

Jets fly over forests of Brazil,
past Badui mountain settlements,
appearing in the most unlikely places,
swifter than dreams,
bringing culture shock.

This is a different sort of colonialism.
It came so quickly we were taken by surprise.
It came so cunningly we were powerless.

Dan sementara kita bengong,
pesawat terbang jet yang muncul dari mimpi,
membawa bentuk kekuatan modalnya :
lapangan terbang, 'hotel-bistik-dan-coca-cola,'
jalan raya, dan para pelancong.

'Oh, look, honey-dear!
Lihat orang-orang pribumi itu!
Mereka memanjat kelapa seperti kera.
Fantastic! Kita harus memotretnya!'

*   *   *

'Awas! Jangan dijabat tangannya!
Senyum saja and say hello
You see, tangannya kotor.
Siapa tahu ada telor cacing di situ.'

*   *   *

'My God, alangkah murninya mereka.
Ia tidak menutupi teteknya!
Look, John, ini benar-benar tetek.
Lihat yang ini! Oh, sempurna!
Mereka bebas dan spontan.
Aku ingin seperti mereka . . .
Okay! Okay! . . . ini hanya pengandaian saja.
Aku tahu kamu melarang aku tanpa beha.
Look, now, John, jangan cemberut!
Berdirilah di sampingnya,
aku potret dari sini.
Ah! Fabulous!'

Dan Bank Dunia
Selalu tertarik membantu negara miskin
untuk membuat proyek raksasa.
Artinya: yang 90% dari bahannya harus diimport.

And while we were still dazed,
Jet planes came out of our dreams,
with new forms of financial domination:
hotels serving steak and Coca-Cola;
airports; highways; and sightseers.

'Oh, honey, look!
Look at the natives!
He's climbing that palm tree like a monkey!
Isn't he fantastic! Take a photograph!'

*　*　*

'Watch out! Don't touch his hand!
Just smile and say hello,
Look—his hand's filthy,
he might have lice.'

*　*　*

'My God, they're so innocent.
The women don't even cover their breasts.
Look, John, what magnificent breasts.
And look at this pair. Wonderful!
The people are so free and spontaneous.
I wish I could be like that . . .
OK! OK! . . . I was only joking.
I know you hate it when I don't wear my bra.
All right, John, stop complaining!
Stand next to her, honey
and I'll take your picture from over here.
Ah! Fabulous!'

The World Bank
helps backward nations
with huge projects,
in which ninety percent of the goods are imported.

Dan kemajuan kita
adalah kemajuan budak
atau kemajuan penyalur dan pemakai.

Maka di Bali
hotel-hotel pribumi bangkrut
digencet oleh packaged tour.
Kebudayaan rakyat ternoda
digencet standar dagang internasional.

Tari-tarian bukan lagi satu mantra,
tetapi hanya sekedar tontonan hiburan.
Pahatan dan ukiran bukan lagi ungkapan jiwa,
tetapi hanya sekedar kerajinan tangan.

Hidup dikuasai kehendak manusia,
tanpa menyimak jalannya alam.
Kekuasaan kemauan manusia,
yang dilembagakan dengan kuat,
tidak mengacuhkan naluri ginjal,
hati, empedu, sungai dan hutan.
Di Bali:
pantat, gunung, tempat tidur dan pura,
telah dicemarkan.

We progress like slaves,
middlemen and consumers.

In Bali,
Indonesian-owned hotels fail,
smashed by packaged tours.
Our folk-culture is destroyed
By the standards of international trade.

Our dances are no longer ceremonies;
they are simply entertainment.
Our carvings do not express our emotions;
they are mere handicrafts.

We live dominated by whim,
forgetful of nature.
We are subject to harsh,
strongly institutionalized rules,
which ignore our hearts,
our livers and kidneys,
the rivers and forests.

In Bali, they spit on us,
our beds, mountains and temples.

Pejambon, Jakarta
June 23, 1977

Orang-orang miskin

Orang-orang miskin di jalan,
yang tinggal di dalam selokan,
yang kalah di dalam pergelutan,
yang diledek oleh impian,
janganlah mereka ditinggalkan.

Angin membawa bau baju mereka.
Rambut mereka melekat di bulan purnama.
Wanita-wanita bunting berbaris di cakrawala,
mengandung buah jalan raya.

Orang-orang miskin. Orang-orang berdosa.
Bayi gelap dalam batin. Rumput dan lumut jalan raya.
Tak bisa kamu abaikan.

Bila kamu remehkan mereka,
di jalan kamu akan diburu bayangan.
Tidurmu akan penuh igauan,
dan bahasa anak-anakmu sukar kamu terka.

Jangan kamu bilang negara ini kaya
kerna orang-orang miskin berkembang di kota dan di desa.
Jangan kamu bilang dirimu kaya
bila tetanggamu memakan bangkai kucingnya.
Lambang negara ini mestinya trompah dan blacu.
Dan perlu diusulkan
agar ketemu presiden tak perlu berdasi seperti Blanda.
Dan tentara di jalan jangan bebas memukul mahasiswa.

Poor people

Poor people in the roads,
living in the gutters.
They have lost their battles.
They are tantalized by their dreams.
You must not forget them.

The wind carries the smell of their clothing.
Their damp hair clings to the full moon.
Legions of pregnant women in the sky
bear fruit conceived by the roadside.

Poor people. Sinful people.
Carrying dark babies in their souls.
Grass and moss beside the highway.
You must not neglect them.

If you push them away
your roads will be haunted by shadows.
Your sleep will be broken by evil dreams.
Your children will speak in ways you will not understand.

Do not say we are a rich country,
there are too many poor people in the cities and towns.
Do not say you are rich
if your neighbors eat cats.
Our national symbols should be wooden sandals and calico.
No one should have to dress like a Dutchman, wear a tie
to meet the president.
The army should not be allowed to beat up students.

Orang-orang miskin di jalan
masuk ke dalam tidur malammu.
Perempuan-perempuan bunga raya
menyuapi putra-putramu.
Tangan-tangan kotor dari jalanan
meraba-raba kaca jendelamu.
Mereka tak bisa kamu hindarkan.

Jumlah mereka tak bisa kamu mistik jadi nol.
Mereka akan menjadi pertanyaan
yang mencegat ideologimu.
Gigi mereka yang kuning
akan meringis di muka agamamu.
Kuman-kuman siplis dan t.B.C. dari gang-gang gelap
akan hinggap di gorden presidenan
dan buku programma gedung kesenian.

Orang-orang miskin berbaris sepanjang sejarah,
bagai udara panas yang selalu ada,
bagai gerimis yang selalu membayang.
Orang-orang miskin mengangkat pisau-pisau
tertuju ke dada kita, atau ke dada mereka sendiri.
O, kenangkanlah:
orang-orang miskin
juga berasal dari kemah Ibrahim.

The poor people in the roads
will enter your sleep.
The women of the streets
will bribe your sons.
Dirty hands
will grope at your windows.
You will not be able to stop them.

Do not pretend
that you can wish them away.
They will be a perpetual challenge
to your ideologies.
Their yellow teeth
will mock your religions.
TB and syphilis
from the squalid lanes
will hang on the curtains of the presidential palace
and the catalogues of the art galleries and concert halls.

The poor stretch endlessly back into history,
and are always present like the heat of the sun,
the shadow of the mist.
The poor take up their knives
and point them at us, and themselves.
Remember this:
the poor
are Abraham's children too.

Yogyakarta
February 4, 1978

Kata-kata

kata-kata memenuhi udara. kata-kata menempel pada dinding. kata-kata hinggap pada pintu. kata-kata bertumpuk di atas meja. kata-kata melekat pada jendela. lalu terbang memenuhi langit.

kata-kata menjadi awan. kata-kata menjadi hujan. kata-kata membawa banjir. kata-kata membawa bencana. kata-kata menjadi maut yang merenggut petani-petani terkapar tak berdaya.

kata-kata menjadi mesin. kata-kata merusak hutan-hutan. kata-kata menguras laut. kata-kata mengeringkan minyak bumi. kata-kata meringkus para penggalas. kata-kata memborgol para nelayan yang terdampar dengan perahunya yang rapuh.

kata-kata menjadi senjata. kata-kata menjadi peluru. kata-kata menjadi meriam. kata-kata menjadi bom. kata-kata memberondong para prajurit yang hendak memeluk anaknya sendiri yang terjerat dalam perangkap kata-kata.

kata-kata terus ditebarkan mulut. kata-kata terus memekakkan telinga. kata-kata terus menyesakkan dada.

AJIP ROSIDI

Words

words fill the air. words cling to the walls. words wait at
the door. words cover the tables. words stick to the
windows. words fly away and fill the sky.

words become clouds. words become rain. words cause
floods. words bring suffering. words bring death to the
farmer and leave him floundering without hope.

words become machines. words destroy the forest.
words empty oceans. words shut down oil wells. words
ruin petty traders. words imprison sailors shipwrecked
in their tiny boats.

words are weapons. words are bullets. words are cannons.
words are bombs. words shock soldiers who want to
embrace their children, themselves trapped in words.

mouths endlessly speaking words. ears endlessly
deafened by words. hearts endlessly oppressed by
words.

*1988

Chapter 5

EXPLORING RELATIONSHIPS

Into the Eighties: The Power of the State
DURING THE EIGHTIES, the state continued to become increasingly centralized and, also, further focused on the person of Suharto. As President, Suharto held enormous personal power in his own right; Jamie Mackie and Andrew MacIntyre have described him as being "in supreme control"[1] at that time. The 1945 Constitution provided the legitimate basis for his power in its provision that "All power and responsibility is in the hands of the President." There was no legitimate way in which that power could be challenged,[2] and in 1985 procedures were introduced into parliament which made it almost impossible to alter the constitution.[3]

Suharto had the prerogative of extending authority and material benefits to his supporters or denying them to his opponents.[4] As the decade progressed, he became increasingly free of his previous reliance on the Armed Forces within the cabinet and the bureaucracy. Instead, many members of the "1945 generation" of military officers retired and were replaced by the younger and less politically experienced officers trained in the military academy at Magelang, who were more dependent on his patronage.[5] While in 1980 eleven of the twenty-four cabinet members had been military personnel, by 1988, only four ministers were military officers on the active list. One was the commander of the armed forces; two of the others, however, had never seen active duty and were not supported by the officers of the armed forces.[6]

Because political and administrative power was confined to the upper echelons of the civilian and military bureaucracies, who were ultimately appointed by the president himself, the political parties had no influence over the decisions of the government. Even the area for maneuvering by the political parties prior to elections had been reduced in 1980 by a bill that prevented open campaigning, and this was progressively tightened in the lead-up to the 1982 general elections.[7] In the 1987 general elections, Golkar won 73 percent of the vote, an increase of almost 10 percent over the average figure achieved in the three previous elections, while the other parties were left with a mere 27 percent of the total vote between them.[8]

Mass organizations were tightly supervised. The 1985 Law on Social Organizations required that the executive board of each organization, and all its members, be registered with the government. The government also had the right to freeze any organization that disturbed public order or received aid from overseas sources without government approval.[9]

Legitimation through Ideology

The repressive hegemony of the state was underpinned by a substantial body of conspicuous ideological formulations,[10] backed up by a carefully cultivated concern with the possibility of the revival of communism.[11] (In 1986, it was still possible for two thousand oil workers to lose their jobs because of alleged involvement in the PKI during the sixties.)[12]

To ensure complete ideological conformity at all levels of society, the doctrine of *Pancasila* (the five principles enunciated in the Preamble to the 1945 Constitution) was accepted by the DPR in June 1985 as being the necessary and sole foundation *(asas tunggal)* of all social organizations and political parties. Any questioning of *Pancasila* itself, of state leaders, or of the role of the Armed Forces, all of whom were considered to be completely committed to *Pancasila,* was regarded as seditious.[13] The decision had serious consequences, as various groups struggled to implement the policy in ways which ranged from "reluctant, to pragmatic, to openly defiant."[14] (The conservative Muslim group, Nahdatul Islam, for example, resolved to accept *Pancasila* as its sole ideology in 1984 yet still declare itself a religious body. It then withdrew from politics completely, and returned to its original 1926 position as a social and organizational body. In the 1987 elections, many of its votes went to Golkar, thus earning it continued government favor.)[15]

There was also an emphasis on a theory of the integralist state, which was an attempt to link an explicitly totalitarian theory of politics with an Indonesian worldview.[16] The theory argued that "the Indonesian state must be an organic unity, a great collectivity, a harmonious and interdependent whole—and that Indonesia's political institutions should reflect and inculcate those values."[17] As a consequence, there was considered to be no place in Indonesian society for the presence of an opposition, for individualistic or liberalistic attitudes, or for potentially conflicting notions such as minorities and majorities, core and periphery, workers and bosses, military and civilians.[18]

Living in Fear

The stern pressures toward conformity of public thought, and the suppression of dissent, were reinforced by the provisions of the Anti-Subversion Law, which included the possible use of the death penalty. In particular, Articles 134, 154, 155, and 160 of the Indonesian Criminal Code banned insults directed at the president, "the public expression of feelings of hostility, hatred or contempt toward the government," or disobedience of a government law.[19] (These hate-sowing articles were, ironically, left over from colonial criminal law, which had criminalized the public expression of feelings of hostility, hatred, or contempt toward the Dutch colonial government.)[20] They were so often used in the eighties against supposed enemies or critics of the government, together with other forms of threat, that dissent was virtually silenced.[21]

Such protests as did occur, however, received a good detail of public attention, the more so as they were heavily punished. Two events especially stood out.

In 1980, a group of approximately fifty major public figures drew up a petition which they presented to parliament, accusing Suharto of using *Pancasila* in such a way as to encourage communal violence and to attack his opponents. The petition also criticized the political role of the Armed Forces and made allegations of preparations for subversion or even armed uprising ahead of the elections. As a consequence, members of the group were banned from travelling overseas, denied financial credit and access to state tenders, forbidden to air their opinions in the public press, and were often shunned socially.[22]

In September 1984, riots took place in Tanjung Priok, Jakarta's impoverished port district, protesting against inappropriate action by a group of policemen in a local mosque. At least sixty local people were shot dead (the actual number may have been as many as two hundred), and a further hundred wounded. Thirty persons were jailed for between one and three years. Lt. General H. R. Dharsono (ret.) wrote a paper, with some twenty other persons, in which he challenged the government's version of the riots. Dharsono was not a signatory of the "Petition of 50," but was close to some members of that group. He was arrested in September 1984, and sentenced in January 1986 to ten year's imprisonment, later reduced to seven years. The trial became, as Kingsbury has noted, "a public spectacle in which the regime and its justice apparatus was held up for ridicule and condemnation." But the same observer was also of the opinion that "If nothing else, the 'Dharsono affair' clarified once and for all the lengths to which the New Order government would go to repress even implied criticism."[23] (A similar massacre to that of Tanjung Priok again took place at Lampung, South Sumatra, in February 1989.)[24]

Again, an amendment to 1966 press law, made in 1982, stipulated that the press must conduct itself in a "free and responsible manner," and the press, on the whole, had little choice but to comply.[25] There were, perhaps, covert ways of resistance. Ariel Heryanto has claimed: "One common and effective pattern of resistance against imposed restrictions upon the press has been to evoke extended or added meanings, parallelism, or imagination."[26] Mangunwijaya has even suggested that these ways were "more subtle, more sophisticated and possibly more mature" than those used prior to 1965.[27] Nevertheless, magazines and newspapers were regularly closed: *Jurnal Ekuin* in 1983, *Expo, Topik* and *Fokus* in 1984, and *Sinar Harapan* in October 1986.[28] No wonder that the veteran journalist Rosihan Anwar was quoted as saying that there had been greater freedom of expression in the late 1940s and 50s than existed in 1990.[29]

During 1989–90 over one hundred political trials of students, intellectuals, Muslim teachers, and ethnic-nationalists took place.[30] These included the trials of three campus activists from Yogyakarta who were charged under the anti-subversion law for selling one of the novels of the greatest modern Indonesian prose-writer, Pramoedya Ananta Toer. For this, they received prison sentences of up to eight years.[31] Powers conferred on the attorney-general's office were widely used to ban books regarded as "disturbing to public order." During the eighties, an average of fourteen books were banned each year. (By 1996, some two thousand books had been banned during the New Order. This included a book listing banned books.)[32]

The consequence of these various physical and psychological pressures was that, as Adam Schwarz has written, "many Indonesians lead anxious and apprehensive lives. Their fears are rooted in their own vulnerability to the overwhelming power of the state."[33] Such feelings would surely be natural when arbitrary detention and subsequent release without a trial were by no means unusual and were often used on large scale, although often only the leaders were eventually tried.[34] Further, land could be appropriated, businesses closed, travel denied, arrests made, and jobs lost at the whim of a government official. The legal system was unresponsive, corrupt, politicized, and ineffective. There was little recourse for the individual seeking to right perceived wrongs.[35] It would have been difficult not to know of others, often quite close others, who had suffered for their political opinions, and to sense that the same things could happen to oneself.[36]

The New Middle Class

On the other hand, there were some pressures which served to limit this drive toward absolutism. The most obvious was the slow growth of a new middle-class sector of society after 1970. Jamie Mackie has extensively defined the Indonesian middle class in the following terms:

> It is a middle class characterized *not* by the ownership of property for the most part, for by far the largest part of it is made up of civil servants, professional people, the salariate generally, with relatively few businessmen ... but united—so far as it is—by a shared lifestyle ("the metropolitan superculture") and similar aspirations for the future of their children, by a gradually emerging sense of common interests in greater security of property rights, in less arbitrary government procedures, greater regularity and predictability of administration, even "the rule of law" in some still obscurely formulated sense.[37]

The collapse in oil prices after 1982 led to a severe revenue crisis for the government, which consequently increasingly moved to deregulate the economy and to build a far greater dependence on the private sector. As a consequence, the rate of growth remained high.[38] The middle class has also been seen as "a constituency for modernization and rationality";[39] the new situation produced striking changes in the values actually espoused by the middle class. They were now prepared to consider the possibility of more liberal economic ideas; to demand greater political liberalization, in one form or another; and to seek a redefinition of religious values in line with the growing Islamic revivalist movement.[40]

The two next phases in the development of Indonesian poetry during the New Order both grew from this middle-class search to elude the authoritarianism of the narrowing elite. The first, described in this chapter of this anthology as the process of "exploring relationships," involved an emphasis on the domestic sphere, as an area of personal self-expression which sought to be separate from the demands of public policy. The second was the turn toward various forms of Islam, which were the catalyst for the emergence of the "Post-Indonesian Generation" in succession to the Generation of 1966.

The Private Realm of Personal Relationships

The New Order not only sought to regulate public civil society, it also regularly prescribed patterns of behavior for men and (especially) women in their private lives. Sexually explicit material, whether its purposes were entertainment or even, sometimes, educational, was of course censored, where possible. The upper-class Javanese *priyayi* role-model of emotional self-restraint was widely deployed as an ideal pattern of masculine behavior.[41]

Most attention was given to forming attractive but docile and submissive female identities.[42] Laurie Sears has drawn attention to the idea of "femininity" in Indonesian society as "that which is marginalized by the patriarchal symbolic order."[43] From a masculine point of view:

> Women will then come to represent the necessary frontier between men and chaos; but because of their very marginality they will also always seem to recede into and merge with the chaos of the outside. Women seen as the limit of the symbolic order will in other words share in the disconcerting properties of *all* frontiers; they will be neither inside nor outside, neither known nor unknown.[44]

For Sears, "Women on the margins, or marginal women, are dangerous, are equated with chaos and seen as a threat to the state."[45]

Attempts were made to control this danger in various ways. Upperclass women married to men of the Armed Forces or the civil service were organized in terms of age, family ties, and social status, through women's organizations that promoted a philosophy of "State Ibuism."[46] The proto-nationalist figure Raden Ajeng Kartini (1879–1904), despite her resistance to marriage, her desire to educate girls, and her death in childbirth, was extensively promoted, to all strata of society and all ages of persons, as a true wife and mother, the proper *ibu*. The Family Welfare Guidance program, formed to promote "community well-being" to all levels of society, listed five precepts for proper female behavior. A wife's duties were (1) to support her husband's career and duties; (2) to bear children; (3) to care for and rear the children; (4) to be a good housekeeper; and (5) to be a guardian of the community.[47] Contrariwise, there was a fear of unrestrained female power and sexuality. Factory girls, sometimes away from parental control, were urged to be disciplined, chaste, obedient, and hard-working, because it was feared that this was exactly what they would not be.[48] The members of the communist women's movement, Gerwani, who were alleged to have participated in the murder of the six generals at Lubung Buaya in 1965 in ways which were obscene and shockingly violent, were represented throughout the New Order as unconstrained and destructive "maniacs."[49]

Despite the state's formal attempt to shape the gender roles of its citizens, recent postcolonial theory has argued that personal relationships may often be resistant to larger social identities. They express an oppositional desire for another "existence," away from public civil society. For a man, this existence could be undertaken "in the private sphere of his home, his personal interests and his leisure."[50] From this perspective, the inner space of the home was radically separate from other activities: it was an "inner" area where one could most fully express one's "true" or "real" individuality and desires, and least concern oneself with being an obedient subject, or following the will of one's superiors. Virginia Matheson Hooker, in her study of the Malay novel, has described literary writing on the personal and the domestic as not "boring and uninspired" but as likely to be "risky," because it is precisely at these points that authors were in a position to challenge conventional authoritative beliefs and practices.[51]

Representing Dreams

All of the poems presented here exploring domestic emotional relationships between men and women were written by men.[52] None of the men, it is fair to say, treated the enterprise with the cynicism born of disappointment that was to be found in Toeti Heraty's poetry, or considered themselves to be engaged in manipulative games that concealed their own feelings. Rather, the poems revealed an optimism, a delight in love, and, if anything, an easy sentimentality about the joys of mature adult companionship. In a society where even intimacy is organized hierarchically rather than between equals, the challenge was to develop a fully complementary and co-operative partnership, which accepted the woman as a full person, and as a participant in the deepest recesses of one's own life. In itself this implied a risk through the redefinition of conventional stereo-types of appropriate masculine and feminine behavior.

Arifin C. Noer's poems did this, it seems to me, extremely well. Their origin marked them as a gift of the self: they were presented to Yajang as a dowry *(maskawin)* on their wedding day, February 14, 1979. The first-person narrator of the poems, and the woman, Yay-ang, were represented in the poems very much as equals. They "be-lieve in love" and are "grateful to love," as "Selamat pagi, Yayang" (Good morning, Yayang) asserted. In the poem, the sensuality of the last night's lovemaking is still very present in the warmth of her body and the fragrance of her breath. Although they are soon to separate for the day—and it is clear she comes and goes on her own terms—the poem rejoices in "following the sun wherever it goes," the personal expression of freewill. The relationship, physical and as yet unmarried, is one in which she at least "knows no sin" ("Seekor kelinci ia," My love is a rabbit).[53] The quality of affection and playfulness shown in the male speaking voice is virtually unique in modern Indonesian poetry.

Sapardi Djoko Damono's poems were possibly the most "ro-mantic" of those in this chapter of the anthology. The first, "Benih" (Seed), admittedly presented an enigmatic picture, drawn from *wayang* shadow-theater and Indian mythology. The princess Sita, now restored to her husband, Prince Rama, after long years of cap-tivity by the giant Rawana, here described as her own father, is pregnant. It is extremely possible that the ogre is the father of the child she carries. Within the tradition, Sita has been characterized by her chastity during her time of captivity. In this poem, a more feminist suspicion appeared: Sita has determined for herself with whom she may or may not sleep. She, too, "knows no sin," and in-stead, seeks to interpret "the will of the gods."

The other poems were located in that shadowland of Sapardi's earlier neo-romanticism, where the world was beautiful and opposites dissolved into each other. "Aku ingin" (I want) (today often read at the weddings of Sapardi's own students) was a poem of complete self-surrender to the other, and the desire to merge completely, eradicating all individual personality. "Dalam doaku" (My prayer) hovered in a region between sacred and human love, seeking the beloved in every aspect of nature, throughout the sequence of the five hours of Muslim prayer and far into the night.

Fantasizing the Javanese Woman

Darmanto's two poems moved in an area that was strongly characteristic of Javanese folk religion: the celebration of fertility, both male and female. "Main cinta kwang wung" (Making love praying mantis style), written in Hawaii and filled more than ever with the mixture of languages that has continued to mark his writing, demanded the destruction of all differences and the rebirth of the world from that unity.

The second poem, "Isteri" (Wife), was spoken by a Javanese farmer named Towikromo, living in a small village outside Yogyakarta, and is filled with Javanese mythological references celebrating the relationship between male and female figures in the shadow-puppet world. The poem is Darmanto's most widely anthologized.[54] Seen within an overall climate of social conservatism and the celebration of regional cultural tradition,[55] the poem may be read as affirming a widely occurring pattern in Indonesian literature that links together conservative social values, Javanese cultural values, and the female identity.[56] The female figure was used to embody the archetypal Javanese cultural values of the acceptance of fate and submissiveness to higher authority, together with an acceptance of the role of a nurturing mother. Such an image also deliberately excluded the woman who turned away from Javanese values and the submissive supportive mother role in order to participate in the more egalitarian world of modern Indonesia.[57] The message of the poem was unusual in that it forcefully reminded men to respect their wives and never take them for granted. To some extent, this was still a conventional message, although not part of common national discourse patterns. The poem should not, therefore, be dismissed as merely patronizing.

Far more radical was Linus Suryadi's work *Pengakuan Pariyem*. This is without a doubt the longest poem in modern Indonesian. It also had the distinction of being the first-person narration of the life of a Javanese servant girl, who benefits from having had a child with the son of her employers. Pariyem determines her own life with great deliberateness, despite the apparent disadvantages of both humble origins and being a woman. She can certainly not be accused of reinforcing conventional proprieties, yet she is scarcely a "maniac" either. The extract presented here is sufficient to show the outrageousness of a poem which dared to mock contemporary elite constructions of traditional Javanese female peasant consciousness as properly submissive, dependent, and grateful for her position as the servant of an aristocratic household.[58] Whereas the message of Darmanto's poem "Isteri" was ambivalent, that of *Pengakuan Pariyem* was bold and clear. The wisdom of the shrewd peasant woman can rule the world.

Further, in its proud assertion of Javanese ethnicity, the poem took other risks as well. Within the tradition of modern Indonesian literature, it mocked those writers of an earlier generation, such as Chairil Anwar and Sitor Situmorang, who were uncomfortable with their own indigenous culture and background.[59] It also mocked the conventional themes of earlier women's poetry: love, nostalgia, waiting, disappointment, and hope.[60] Pariyem does not sit around feeling abused or unloved; she knows exactly what she wants and how to get it. She is self-expressive and purposeful.

Finally, the poem mocked the often-expressed New Order desire for the use of the Indonesian language in a way that was pure and correct.[61] Like Darmanto's writing, Pariyem's language was heavily loaded with Javanese words and phrases. In fact, the 230-page poem is followed by two appendices of almost 80 pages altogether, explaining the Javanese words and snatches of traditional verse included in the text. The Javanese language seemed warm and highly expressive to many of its readers, in a way that the more formal national language could never be.[62]

The Pain of Love

The remaining poems in this chapter of this anthology deal with a range of emotions and situations experienced in personal relationships, some of them extremely painful.

Subagio's poem "Malam pengantin" (Wedding night) tries to imagine the fears and ecstasy of a young girl on her wedding night, as her body takes on new meanings. "Hotel" is a longer poem, a one-sided conversation between a middle-aged couple who already have five children, as they rest close together in a strange hotel room, imagining themselves as lovers and not simply as husband and wife. The poem structures a number of points of reference around the couple. Besides the children, there were, firstly, their parents, "who never knew each other / and died still locked in their silence." It is clear that they do not know their parents either: "We are orphans / searching for the fathers we have lost," the poem states toward the end. And as the children of their own parents, the fear is surely that their children will judge them no more kindly they judge their elders. Beyond the room is the wider society, a place of "strangers," wearing "masks," who "prefer to have no faces at all." The wife has apparently been tempted by strangers before, and the husband is afraid of her being unfaithful while he is absent during the day again. "Travel," after all, "makes people unfaithful to each other." Ironically, at the end of the poem, they do indeed turn into hotel lovers: "We meet in this hotel, and at the corner of the road / to the old part of town, we turn away / and forget each other." Are they indeed married—to each other? Or is this the way things become in long-established marriages: familiarity and easy acceptance, moving into a mutual lack of interest in each other? The poem is an apparently simple but actually very complex exploration of a common relationship seldom treated in Indonesian literature at all. The source of Subagio's irony in his writing, as the next poem, "Mata Penyair" (The eyes of the poet), made clear, was his ability to recognize the difference between the imaginary beauty of common fantasies and the harsh reality of the everyday world.

Goenawan's poem "Suami" (Husband) also challenged the

conventional construction of the role of husband. The story behind
the poem, we may imagine, is a love story, between a woman living
in a village and a visiting soldier. The woman advises the soldier
that they will be unable to be together because her husband will be
returning home that night and she must adjust appearances to re-
ceive him as she should. Behind the story is an implied pathos, in
that traditional belief suggested that the woman's unfaithfulness
placed her husband's life in danger. (People are not always pun-
ished directly for their own sins in Indonesian and Malay litera-
ture.) But there is also the explicit pathos. As she turns away from
her lover, the woman speaks: *"Selamat malam . . . selamat malam,
suamiku,"* (Good night . . . good night, my husband). The words
may be a wish to her spouse but they more likely indicate that she
considers her lover to be more truly her husband than the other
man whom society and religion recognize as her legitimate partner.

The Pain of Memory

Sitor Situmorang's poetry at this time explored yet another dimen-
sion of the pain to be found in relationships: the pain of remember-
ing lost love.

Sitor was one of the most important members of the Generation
of 1945. He has had a long and prolific career as a poet, and is also
highly regarded for the short stories he wrote in the early fifties
when he was living and working in Europe. His earlier work ex-
plored two interrelated forms of inner conflict. The first relied on a
contrast between Indonesia and Europe: Indonesia was the home
where he no longer belonged, Europe was a place of rich experience
but also guilt and the loss of religious faith. Secondly, the experience
was particularly sexual; that contrasted with the fidelity he owed
his wife and family in Indonesia. Although imprisoned in Jakarta
between 1967 and 1975 for his enthusiastic literary support for
Sukarno during the period of Guided Democracy, Sitor has contin-
ued writing in the following decades. His collected volume of po-
etry from 1948 to 1988, *Bunga di atas Batu* (1989), is, in my opinion,
the most distinguished book of verse published during the eighties.

The first poems look back to the earlier stage in Sitor's life, to one or more old relationships in Paris. The word *"rindu,"* or the sense of loss which was a theme he often employed, is not used in these poems, yet all the facets of that culturally constructed emotion were present in his writing, mingled with the bitter sweetness of lost youth. The world in these poems is one of concrete objects centered around an absence, the absent and now no doubt also aging lover. Significantly, Sitor also drew across the first of those poems, "Jam 8 malam," the shadow of his prison experience, and it is that shadow which reappeared in "Belajar kembali alifbata" (Learning the alphabet again), dedicated to Alexander Solzhenitsyn. In the latter poem, Sitor rejected literary aesthetes but nevertheless also affirmed the worth of the writing of Rimbaud and Chairil Anwar, both surely extreme individualists, as he struggled to define a poetry in Indonesian for himself that would speak both of intimate human existence and dignified labor.

There is a hidden reference in "Learning the alphabet again." It occurs in the second stanza, in the words that poetry is "not a night carnival." The words *"Bukan Pasar Malam"* are the title of a short story[63] by another major left-wing author of the Generation of 1945, Pramoedya Ananta Toer, whose ongoing writing (done while he was on the prison island of Buru in Eastern Indonesia) stood with Sitor's as the most obviously impressive of the eighties. Whereas Sitor's works were circulated freely throughout Indonesia, Pramoedya's were systematically banned. In "Learning the alphabet again," Sitor sought to separate himself from his more radical peer in favor of a different literary commitment. Nevertheless, his presence in the literary community of the 1980s as an ex-political prisoner and a former admirer of Sukarno and the ideals of the Old Order was surely an extraordinary act of great courage. For Sitor to take the risk of publishing his personal poetry, his life's work, was, finally, to challenge conventional authoritative beliefs and practices about the fate of those whom the New Order had sought to silence.

Selamat pagi, Yayang

ketika cahaya matahari tumpah lewat kaca jendela
angin pun memainkan pucuk dedaunan, bunga-
                              bunga genit jadinya
kita sama-sama menggeliat tanpa saling menatap
diam-diam berterimakasih kepada udara
—kepada hidup
karena kita masih mau percaya pada cinta
di atas karpet berserakan sisa-sisa
percakapan-percakapan kita mimpi-mimpi kita
semalam
di antara sepatu-sepatu sandal-sandal
celana-celana baju-baju
asbak yang penuh putung, gelas-gelas kosong
botol-botol kosong

langit pagi ini langit kita
berwarna biru muda rata dan terbuka
biarkan bening biarkan hening
jangan putar kasset dulu jangan ada gerak dulu
aku hanya ingin mendengar menghirup
desah nafasmu
dan menatap matamu
pandanganmu yang selalu bagai malam

kita harus berterimakasih kepada hidup
karena kita masih mempercayai cinta
sekarang segeralah mandi berpakaian yang rapi
sisir rambut biarkan terjulai seperti biasanya
kalau mau pake sipat hati-hati, jangan kena bolamata
nah, segeralah

ARIFIN C. NOER

Good morning, Yayang

as sunlight pours through the window,
the wind plays with the tips of the leaves
        and the flowers tease,
we stretch, neither looking at the other,
silently thanking the air
—thanking life
that we can still believe in love.
scraps of last night's conversation
and our dreams
lie scattered across the carpet
among the shoes, sandals,
shirts and trousers,
the overflowing ashtray, empty glasses
and empty bottles.

the sky is ours,
crystal clear, silent,
blue from one end to the other.
don't turn the tape over. don't move.
i want to hear you breathing,
smell your breath,
look into your eyes
and see the night.

be grateful to life:
we still believe in love.
now, quickly, bathe, get dressed,
comb your hair, leave it long,
be careful with your mascara,
don't get any in your eyes,
hurry.

selamatpagi, yayang
kita akan mulai lagi

mengikuti matahari
entah ke mana

Tanpa mimpi tapi

Sudah larut benar, Sebaiknya
kau istirahat sebentar. Ini kamar
akan memberimu tidur
sebentar tanpa mimpi sama sekali tapi! Istirahat
sekali-sekali. Pengembaraanmu
yang sepi rupanya tidak akan ada
akhirnya. Semua kota
akan kau jelajahi. Satu demi satu kau
rebahi. Lalu berangkat lagi
Berangkat lagi
Sudah larut benar. Sebaiknya
kau istirahat sebentar. Di kamar ini
kau boleh tidur tapi tanpa mimpi
samasekali! Dan kalau besok kau akan pergi
tidak usah permisi. Pergilah diam-diam. Diam-diam
tutup saja kembali pintu pelan-pelan
Lalu berangkatlah. Bawa semua yang kau suka
(jangan lupa cuci muka)
O saya tahu saya hanya akan mendapatkan
beberapa helai rambutmu di bantal
dan bau keringatmu. Tak apa
(keki sih keki)
Nah, istirahatlah

good morning, Yayang.
we begin again.

let's follow the sun
wherever it goes.

October 4, 1977

No dreams but

It's late. Would you like
to rest a while? This
is a good room for sleeping.
No one ever dreams here. Stay
a while. Your long journey
has no end. You still
have many towns to visit. Many towns
to conquer. Leave . . .
leave later,
when the night is almost over.
Rest a while. You can sleep
in this room
and never dream. Don't wake me
in the morning. Just go. Go quietly.
Close the door softly
and go. Take whatever you want.
(Wash your face before you go.)
Leave me a few hairs
on your pillow
and the smell of your body. That's enough.
(My beloved.)
Now, rest.

October 21, 1977

Seekor kelinci ia

cintaku berlari-lari kecil
        berjingkat-jingkat
seekor kelinci ia
        dengan matanya yang jernih
        bercahaya

ketika pintu kamar itu terbuka
        sedikit:

                rupanya kau masih tidur
                selimut di sisi
                impian meniup sulingnya
                udara pun warna-warni

cintaku berlari-lari kecil
        berjingkat-jingkat
seekor kelinci ia
        dengan bulu-bulunya yang bersih
        bercahaya

ketika pintu kamar itu kembali tertutup
        mencuit:

                rupanya kau akan terus tidur

ia pun berlari-lari kecil
ke sudut-sudut gelap
        dalam lubang
        kelam
                sangat sempurna
                kesunyiannya
                secabik kubis
                sisa kemarin
                dikunyahnya

                sisa kemarin
                dikunyahnya

My love is a rabbit

my love scampers
       on tiny feet,
my love is a rabbit
       with bright shining
       eyes.
when I peep
through the door:

               i see you sleeping,
               the blankets by your side—
               flute dreams,
               colored skies . . .

my love scampers
       on tiny feet,
my love is a rabbit
       with bright shining
       fur.

when I close
       the door:

               she sleeps

she scampers
to obscure corners
       of a dark burrow:
               perfect
               in her solitude,

               nibbling
               on a scrap
               of yesterday's cabbage

               nibbling
               on yesterday.

dingin
—*apakah*
hangat
—*apakah*

seperti selalu dihindarinya
apa saja yang namanya keramaian
entah apa sebabnya
bekas bangsawan rupanya
namun seekor kelinci ia

sangat canggung tingkahnya
untuk dunia
dan alangkah sedih hatinya
setiapkali pintu kamar itu terbuka
kau masih saja tidur, dalam pose terbuka
sementara impian-impian memenjara

maka berjingkat-jingkat ia
ke sudut-sudut sunyi penuh rahasia
lantaran seekor kelinci ia
lantaran ia rasa tak ada dosa

are you cold?
"what?"
warm?
"what?"

she always avoids
what she calls "crowds,"
perhaps she was a noble,
though she is only a rabbit.

my love is too shy
for this world,
too sad:
you're beautiful when the door is open,
stretched out, asleep,
imprisoned in your dreams.

she scampers on tiny feet
to secret lonely corners:
my love is a rabbit.
my love knows no sin.

Jakarta 1969

Benih

"Cintaku padamu, Adinda," kata Rama, "adalah laut yang pernah bertahun memisahkan kita, adalah langit yang senantiasa memayungi kita, adalah kawanan kera yang di gua Kiskenda. Tetapi . . . ," Sita yang hamil itu tetap diam sejak semula, "kau telah tinggal dalam sangkar raja angkara itu bertahun lamanya, kau telah tidur di ranjangnya, kau bukan lagi rahasia baginya."

Sita yang hamil itu tetap diam: pesona. "Tetapi Raksasa itu ayahandamu sendiri, benih yang menjadikanmu, apakah ia juga yang membenihimu, apakah . . ." Sita yang hamil itu tetap diam, mencoba menafsirkan kehendak para dewa.

Seed

"My love for you," said Rama, "is as broad as the sea
which has divided us for years, as high as the sky which
sheltered us, as plentiful as the monkeys in Kiskanda
Cave. But. . . ." Pregnant, Sita listened in silence, " . . .
you have lived in that cruel king's palace year after year,
you have slept in his bed, he knows all your secrets."

Pregnant, Sita listened in silence: bewitched. "But the
Giant is your father, the seed that created you, the seed
which may have impregnated you, perhaps . . ."
Pregnant, Sita listened in silence, as she tried to
understand the will of the gods.

1981

Aku ingin

aku ingin mencintaimu dengan sederhana:
dengan kata yang tak sempat diucapkan
kayu kepada api yang menjadikannya abu

aku ingin mencintaimu dengan sederhana:
dengan isyarat yang tak sempat disampaikan
awan kepada hujan yang menjadikannya tiada

I want

I want
>> to love you
>>>> simply
in words
>>> unspoken
the way the wood
>>>> gives itself to the flame
>>>>>> to become ash

I want
>> to love you
>>>> simply
beyond
>>> all signs and symbols
the way the clouds
>>>> give themselves to the rain
>>>>>> to disappear
>>>>>>> forever

>>>> 1989

Dalam doaku

dalam doaku subuh ini kau menjelma langit yang
 semalaman tak memejamkan mata, yang meluas
 bening siap menerima cahaya pertama, yang
 melengkung hening karena akan menerima
 suara-suara

ketika matahari mengambang tenang di atas kepala,
 dalam doaku kau menjelma pucuk-pucuk cemara
 yang hijau senantiasa, yang tak henti-hentinya
 mengajukan pertanyaan muskil kepada angin
 yang mendesau entah dari mana

dalam doaku sore ini kau menjelma seekor burung
 gereja yang mengibas-ngibaskan bulunya dalam
 gerimis, yang hinggap di ranting dan menggugur-
 kan bulu-bulu bunga jambu, yang tiba-tiba gelisah
 dan terbang lalu hinggap di dahan mangga itu

dalam doak magribku kau menjelma angin yang
 turun sangat pelahan dari nun di sana,
 bersijingkat di jalan kecil itu, menyusup di
 celah-celah jendela dan pintu, dan menyentuh-
 nyentuhkan pipi dan bibirnya di rambut, dahi,
 dan bulu-bulu mataku

dalam doa malamku kau menjelma denyut jantungku,
 yang dengan sabar bersitahan terhadap rasa
 sakit yang entah batasnya, yang setia mengusut
 rahasia demi rahasia, yang tak putus-putusnya
 bernyanyi bagi kehidupanku

aku mencintaimu, itu sebabnya aku takkan pernah
 selesai mendoakan keselamatanmu

My prayer

at dawn I pray that you will take flesh in the sky of day
that your bright eyes will shine, ready
to receive the first light, that you will reach out silently
to receive the sounds of the morning

when the sun hovers gently over my head I pray
that you will take flesh in the dark green needles
of the pine trees, as they ask endless
impossible questions of wind, who comes whistling
from we know not where

in the afternoon I pray that you will take flesh
in a tiny sparrow flapping its feathers in the rain
perched on a branch and pecking at rose-apples,
before nervously flying away and settling
in a mango tree

at twilight I pray that you will take flesh
in the wind which slowly descends from far away,
crawls along a path, slips through a crack in the
    shutters,
and caresses my cheeks, my lips, my hair,
my forehead and my eyelids

at night I pray that you will take flesh
in the beating of my heart, patiently protecting me
from terrible dreams, faithfully weaving one secret
    after another,
singing the song of my life

I love you and I will never stop praying
that God's grace will protect you

1989

Main cinta model kwang wung

om swastiastu

kaleo o wahine: kahi. elua. ekolu!
        ayolah kamboja terbang
        ayolah burung berjalan
        ayolah gelombang tidur
        ayolah pasangan berpasangan - ayoo!
            ayo
                ayo   ayo
            — aloha!
        kaleo o kane: kahi. elua. ekolu!
        kamboja jangan berhenti jadi kamboja
        burung jangan berhenti jadi burung
        gelombang jangan berhenti jadi
                                gelombang —
            jangaan!   jangan   jangan
            jangan

        mahalo!

    siang-malam, musnahlah beda kalian
    laut-darat, musnahlah beda kalian
    laki-perempuan — musnahlah beda kalian
half korean, half chinese hawaiian american maiden —
satus persen wong lanang jawa yogya — indonesia

    m u s n a h l a h   b e d a   k a l i i a n !

hoong
iblis laknat setan bekasakan
kanioyo temen awakku:
    — kangen srengenge mongka awan-awan
    — rindu burung padahal ditengah ranjang
yearning for the waves yet on the ocean

Making love praying mantis style

—om swastiastu

kaleo o kane: kahi. elua. ekolu!
come frangipanni take wing
come bird walk
come wave sleep
come couples and join together—come!
come

come   come

—aloha

kaleo o wahine: kahi. elua. ekola!
Frangipanni don't stop being frangipanni
birds don't stop being birds
waves don't stop being waves
don't!   don't!   don't!
don't!

—mahalo

day and night, destroy all differences
sea and land, destroy all differences
man and woman, destroy all differences

half korean, half chinese hawaiian american maiden—one
hundred percent pure bred javanese from jogjakarta

merge all your differences!

Hoong
vile demon satanic slob
friend to my body
—floating in the clouds yearning for the sun
—floating in bed yearning for the birds
—floating in the ocean yearning for the waves

o dewa kamboja
o dewa burung
o dewa gelombang
kawinlah kalian kawinlah
hamillah kalian hamillah
lahirkanlah warna
lahirkanlah irama
lahirkanlah bentuk —
kekamian kami
untuk dibilang perkawinan
dalam jaman kumpeni kumpeni ini.

      om   shantih   shantih   shantih

kwang
     wung
         wung
             wung.

o cambodian god
o heavenly bird
o ocean god
marry, yes marry
be pregnant, pregnant
create color
create rhythm
create form —
our us
and call it a marriage
from the age of the Dutch East India Company
and the multinationals

    om shantih shantih shantih

praying
    mantis
        praying
            mantis

        *1980

Isteri

—isteri mesti digemateni
ia sumber berkah dan rejeki.
(Towikromo, Tambran, Pundong, Bantul)

Isteri sangat penting untuk ngurus kita
Menyapu pekarangan
Memasak di dapur
Mencuci di sumur
mengirim rantang ke sawah
dan ngeroki kita kalau kita masuk angin.
Ya. Isteri sangat penting untuk kita
        Ia sisihan kita,
                kalau kita pergi kondangan
        Ia tetimbangan kita,
                kalau kita mau jual palawija
        Ia teman belakang kita,
                kalau kita lapar dan mau makan
        Ia sigaraning nyawa kita,
                kalau kita
        Ia sakti kita!
                Ah. Lihatlah. Ia menjadi sama penting
dengan kerbau, luku, sawah dan pohon kelapa.
Ia kita cangkul malam hari dan tak pernah ngeluh
                                walau cape
Ia selalu rapih menyimpan benih yang kita tanamkan
                                dengan rasa
sukur; tahu terimakasih dan meninggikan harkat kita
                                sebagai lelaki.
Ia selalu memelihara anak anak kita dengan
                        bersungguh sungguh
seperti kita memelihara ayam, itik, kambing atau
                        jagung

Wife

> *"Respect your wife*
> *she offers you physical and spiritual well-being"*
> (My name is Towikromo, I live at Tambran in
> Pundong village, in the Regency of Bantul,
> outside Yogyakarta)

We need a wife to look after us
To sweep the yard
Cook in the kitchen
Wash at the well
send food to us when we are in the fields
and massage us when we have a chill.
Yes, a wife is very important

She is our partner
        when we attend celebrations
She is our helpmate
        when we sell vegetables
She works in the back of the house
        and feeds us when we are hungry
She knows our needs
        when . . .
She is our inner energy
        Ah, see. She is as important as our water-buffalo,
the plow, our fields and coconut trees.
We can plow her night and day and she will never
    complain, no matter how tired she is.
She will give thanks to God and store the seed we have
    planted;
her gratitude will make us glad to be men.
She will look after our children diligently, the way we care
for our hens, our ducks, the goat and our corn.

Ah. Ya. Isteri sangat penting bagi kita justru ketika kita
      mulai melupakannya:
            Seperti lidah ia dimulut kita
                  tak terasa
            Seperti jantung ia didada kita
                  tak teraba
Ya. Ya. Isteri sangat penting bagi kita justru ketika kita
      mulai
melupakannya.
            Jadi waspadalah!
            Tetep, madep, manteb
            Gemati, nastiti, ngati ati
            Supaya kita mandiri — perkasa dan pinter ngatur
                                          hidup
            Tak tergantung tengkulak, pak dukuh, bekel
                                          atau lurah
                  Seperti Subadra bagi Arjuna
                  makin jelita ia diantara maru marunya;
                  Seperti Arimbi bagi Bima
                  jadilah ia jelita ketika melahirkan jabang
                                          tetuka;
                  Seperti Sawitri bagi Setyawan
                  Ia memelihara nyawa kita dari malapetaka.
Ah. Ah. Ah
Alangkah pentingnya isteri ketika kita mulai
melupakannya.
            Hormatilah isterimu
            Seperti kau menghormati Dewi Sri
            Sumber hidupmu.
            Makanlah
            Karena memang demikianlah suratannya!
                  — Towikromo.

Ah yes. A wife is very important, especially when we begin
to forget her.
　　　She is as natural
　　　　　as the tongue in our mouth
　　　as integral to our being
　　　　　as the heart in our body
Yes, yes. A wife is very important, especially when
we begin to forget her.
So be careful!
Be strong, firm, resolute,
Loving, gentle, kind,
Feet fixed on the ground—courageous, know how to live
Do not rely on middle-men, politicians, merchants,
or the village headman

　　　　　She is Subadra to Arjuna
　　　　　the most beautiful of amazons
　　　　　She is Arimbi to Bima
　　　　　proud mother to his son
　　　　　She is Savitri to Satyawan
　　　　　she saves him from death

Ah. Ah. Ah.
A woman is never more important
than when we begin to forget her

　　　　　Honor your wife
　　　　　as you honor Dewi Sri,
　　　　　goddess of the rice,
　　　　　the source of your life.
　　　　　Eat her,
　　　　　for so it is written,
　　　　　and you will be changed
　　　　　forever.
　　　　　　　Towikromo

　　　　　　　　　1978

Pengakuan Pariyem

Saya ulur benang panjang
Saya ulur kenangan yang silam
Bagaikan air kolam: mengalir
mencapai titik perbatasan
Bersih, tenang dan lengang
mengapungkan daun-daunan

Waktu itu malam sudah larut
Kami pun pulang nonton wayang
Ki dalang Kimpul dari Seleman
Melakonkan Alap-alapan Sukesi
Dan simbok nyidhen sampai pagi
terang, pulangnya diantar seorang lelaki.
Sedang bapak ngethoprak di Tempel
pulangnya saban minggu sekali
Dan gamelan ditabuh seseg
keras, penuh dan bergegas
Dengan laras Slendro pathet sanga
pertanda Gara-gara pun sudah tiba
Dan rembulan condong ke kulon
tanda jam satu lewat dinihari
Kami pun menisik jalan berumput
—dingin, basah oleh embun
alam putih diliput oleh kabut
Sambil makan slondhok dan kacang
kami pun berjalan bergandengan

Pariyem's confession[†]

Let me spin a long thread
Let me spin an old memory
Memory is like a lake: the ripples
Flow to the farthest bank
The leaves float quietly on top
The waters are pure, deep and calm

It was very late at night
We were returning home from the wayang.
The dalang was Kimpul from Sleman
the story was *Alap-alap Sukesi,*
a story of brave prince Rama.
My mother would sing until morning
and then go home with a gentleman friend.
My father was an actor too, in Tempel,
and only came home once a week.
The gamelan was in full flight,
the notes were firm, full and quick.
I could tell from the *pathet sanga* scale
that it was almost time for the battle-scene.
The moon was low in the western sky
the first light of dawn had begun to shine.
The path was covered with grass,
the grass was cold, wet with dew.
The world was covered with mist,
the mist was cold and damp too.
Chewing on *slondhok*[‡] and peanuts
we walked home, hand in hand.

[†] An extract from *Pengakuan Pariyem* (Jakarta: Sinar Harapan, 1981), pp. 65–67.

[‡] A ring-shaped snack made from cassava.

Angin malam tembus ke tulang
dingin menggigilkan badan

Dusun Karang kami lewati
Dusun Wonosari ada di depan
Kami menempu bulak, gliyak-gliyak
dan selendang saya singsatkan leher
Dan tangan saya kuat dia pegang
Dan, oh, saya diseret ke gubug reyot
tempat menunggu padi di hari siang
O, saya belum tahu mau diajak apa
namun naluri sudah mengatakan
Rasa gagu menjebak saya—ingkar—
tapi gejolak darah membujuk gencar
Hati kemrungsung meraung-raung
saya pun tak bisa mengelakkan
Dia buka surjan, sarung dan kathok kolornya
dia pun buka kebaya, jarit, dan kutang saya
O, Allah, Gusti nyuwun ngapura
kami telanjang bulat!
Bibir saya diciumnya
ciuman pertama dari seorang pria
Penthil saya diremasnya
remasan pertama dari seorang pria
Dan kuping bawah saya dikulumnya
kuluman pertama dari seorang pria
O, Allah, gelinya luar biasa!
bulu kuduk saya mrinding lho
—berdiri sendiri

The wind pierced through to our bones,
the cold made our bodies shiver.

We left the village of Karang
and walked toward Wonosari,
strolling past the rice fields,
with my shawl wrapped tight
around my neck.
He held my hand tight
and I held his tight too.
Then, gracious, he dragged me
into a shabby old shed,
where the farmers rest during the day.
Although my mind didn't know
what he wanted,
my instincts certainly did.
I couldn't say a word—
I didn't dare, but my blood
was burning and showed me the way,
my heart was beating, urging me on,
I really couldn't stop.
He took off his woven jacket,
his sarong and underpants.
He took off my blouse, my skirt and my bra.
Allah, God forgive us,
We were stark naked!
He kissed my lips,
the first time a man kissed my lips.
He stroked my nipples,
the first time a man stroked my nipples.
He chewed my ears,
the first time a man
ever chewed my ears.
God, he tickled me.
All the hairs on my body
stood up straight.

Paha saya dirabanya
rabaan pertama dari seorang pria
Dan pusar saya dijilatinya
jilatan pertama dari seorang pria
O, Allah, jagad gelap gulita!
Napas saya berdebur keras
darah saya mengalir deras
Dan nalar, jangan tanya
Dia pun pasang kuda-kuda
menjatuhkan diri dan menggasak saya
Badan saya ditindihnya begitu rupa:

> Bumi gonjang
> langit ganjing
> Bumi dan langit
> gonjang-ganjing

Satu dalam kegemparan diri
memberikan restu pada kami
Dan mantera pun dia bisikkan
di kuping saya sebelah kiri:

> Ooh rasaku, ooh rasamu
> dudu mungsuh dudu satru
> Jagad wadonmu, jagad lanangku
> ngrasuk rasa ngrasuk kalbu

He caressed my thighs,
the first time a man caressed my thighs.
And licked my belly,
the first time a man licked me there.
God, the world went suddenly black.
My breath was pounding
my blood was racing,
And my mind, what can I say—
He hopped onto me
like he was riding a horse,
dropped into place
and went hard at me,
pinned me down and kept me at it.
> The earth bent this way
> the sky bent that way
> The earth and the sky
> this way and that

In the commotion
something blessed us,
as he whispered a prayer
in the lobe of my left ear:

> Ooh I can feel it
>   you can feel it too,
> we are not opposites,
>   we are not enemies,
> your woman's world,
>   my man's world,
> our feelings are one,
>   our hearts are one.

Berulang dia ucapkan
Berulang dia tikamkan
Ibarat keris ligan manjing warangka
demikian jagad pria dan wanodya
Dan tiba-tiba saya ingin pipis
dalam kegiuran tak tertahankan:
"Iyem"—dia panggil saya
"Kliwon"—saya panggil dia
"Ooohh"—serentak kami bercengkeraman . . .

Over and over he sang to me,
over and over he stabbed me.
He had a long sharp keris
and I was his sheath,
this was my world and his.
Suddenly I felt as though I wanted to pee,
I was excited, I couldn't help myself.
"Iyem," he called,
"Kliwon," I called,
"Ooohh," we shouted together . . .

1981

Malam penganten

Semalam ketika aku membaringkan diri di tempat tidur tiba-tiba aku berubah menjadi perempuan. Dadaku bersusu dan perutku bercelah.

Aku sudah mengharapkan hal itu, tetapi tidak mengira bahwa itulah saatnya akan terjadi. Aku lantas tahu, bahwa malam itu dia akan tiba.

Betullah, dia menghampiri aku dari balik kelambu, penuh napsu tetapi terkekang perasaannya seperti layaknya penganten baru.

Kami tidak berkata-kata, tetapi sekaligus kami saling mengerti. Kami berbicara lewat tubuh, lewat napas, lewat lambang. Dia ingin mengandungi aku dengan benih ilhamnya.

"Sudah lama kau menanti."

Dia diam saja dan memelukku sampai aku susah bernapas lagi. "Mati aku, mati aku!" keluhku.

Dia mengisyaratkan kepadaku supaya aku tidak usah takut. Tetapi aku tidak bisa menahan ngeriku waktu menyerah. Di puncak nikmat aku hampir tak sadarkan diri.

Waktu terbangun dari kesima terlepas dari mulutku tembang asmara.

Wedding night

As I lay in bed last night, I suddenly became a woman. I grew breasts and a slit formed in my stomach.

I knew this would happen but I hadn't expected it just then. At once I knew he would come to me soon.

I was right. That night he approached from behind the mosquito-net, full of desire but shy, as befits a new bridegroom.

We said nothing but understood each other at once. We communicated through our bodies, our breath, through our gestures. He wanted to fill me with the child of his imagination.

"You have waited a long time."

He did not answer but held me so tightly I could scarcely breathe. "Kill me, kill me," I moaned.

He indicated to me that I had nothing to fear. But I could hardly hold back my horror when I surrendered to him. At the peak of our ecstasy I almost lost consciousness.

When I woke from my coma, a love song flowed from my mouth.

*1982

Hotel

I

Kita bisa berhenti dan pesan satu kamar
Kita ingin lupa kita sudah tua dan punya anak lima
orang
Dinding di sini cukup tebal dan tetangga tidak akan tahu
kita berpeluk dan tertawa
Kau tutup mataku dengan tanganmu supaya aku hanya
merasa
tidak melihat
Kembang di jambangan di atas meja terbuat dari kertas
merah muda

II

Aku bermimpi : telah mendengar nyanyian kanak dari
kampung tak berhuni
Suara tak terujud tapi hadir, tak berkata tapi berbicara
Jamahan jari tak bermuka
Kata kerja tanpa benda
Waktu bangun aku terlupa semua nada dan tertawa
tak peduli
Bagaimana kau bermimpi?
Bianglala turun di pantai siang
Bukit karang menjorok ke pangku laut dan gugur batu
demi batu
Semua rebah tanpa suara dan air bercahaya
di bawah riang warna melengkung
Dingin pagi membuat tubuhku menggigil dan gila
mencium

III

Di kota ini semua orang jadi asing
Masing-masing memakai topeng

Hotel

I

We could stop and rent a room
Forget that we are old and have five children
The walls are thick enough, the neighbors will never

hear us

making love and laughing
You can cover my eyes with your hands
so that I can feel you
but not see you
The flowers on the table are made of pink paper

II

I dreamed I heard children singing
in a deserted village
I could not see them but they were there,
could not hear them but they spoke
I could not touch them
They were verbs, not nouns.
When I woke I forgot their singing and laughed instead
they no longer mattered
What did you dream about?
A rainbow over a beach in the middle of the day
Coral reefs hiding in the ocean
shedding their petals
one by one
Rocks falling silently into the sparkling water
beneath the vast colors of the sky
It is morning, I am cold, kiss me
I'm shivering

III

The city turns people into strangers
They wear masks

atau ingin tak bermuka sama sekali
Kita anak yang bersalah yang malu
akan kesalahan sendiri
Padamkan lampu. Kamar ini
lobang perlindungan di jaman perang
dan di waktu damai jadi persembunyian bagi maling
dan bagi orang tua yang ingin muda kembali
Isteriku, kau kini pacarku yang baru malam ini
berdamping

IV

Tunggu aku di kamar ini
kalau aku sedang pergi
Kalau merasa sepi bisa baca buku
atau duduk di jendela melihat
kehidupan lewat tak berhenti
Tapi jangan bicara dengan orang
tak dikenal dan meninggalkan
aku seperti dulu lagi
Jangan lekas percaya kepada orang baru datang
Petualangan menghilangkan perasaan setia. Engkau
janji

V

Kalau langit itu biru, semua
akan biru : bumi dan laut
mata dan rambut, juga
cinta dan kata yang terkulum
di mulut
Tapi matahari telah padam sejak semalam
Dan badan kita terbaring di ranjang
dalam kemelut kelam

but prefer to have no faces at all
We are guilty children
embarrassed by our own deeds.
Put out the light. This room
is our shelter from the war,
in peace it is a refuge for thieves
and for old people who like to be young again
Today you are my lover, not my wife,
we will be together again tonight

IV

When I go out
Wait for me here
Read a book if you're lonely
or sit at the window
and watch the world go past
But don't talk to strangers
or leave me
the way you did before
Don't trust people you don't know
Travel makes people unfaithful to each other.
        Promise me that.

V

When the sky is blue, everything
is blue: the sea, the earth,
your eyes, your hair,
your love, the words
you roll in your mouth
But the sun set yesterday
and our bodies rested in this bed
surrounded by storm

VI

Kita tidak akan berbicara tentang politik atau agama
Kita berbaring saja di dalam dekat lampu kelam
— Malam begitu dingin, kau pakai selimutmu yang
                                                          tebal
Dan omong-omong mengenai anak kita yang
                                              bersekolah
Tentang ketekunannya, tentang perjoangannya
                                      hendak mengerti
pengetahuan kita yang dewasa.
Apa yang kita tahu. Hanya setitik cahaya di atas lautan
                                              rahasia

Kita ingat orang tua, bapak dan ibu
Yang tak pernah tahu masing hati
Yang berpaling ke kubur tetap membisu

Dan kita sendiri, apa yang kita tahu
Tanganmu dingin di tanganku. Peganglah erat
Rasakanlah. Hanya itu yang kutahu. Bahwa kau ada.
      Hanya itu.

VII

Jangan kita cari tanah atau rumah
Kita tidak bisa tinggal lama
Malam kita menginap dan berangkat subuh hari
Kita anak piatu yang kehilangan bapak
dan mencari
Di hotel kita bertemu dan di pojok
jalan ke benteng tua berpaling muka
Kita akan saling lupa

VI

Let's not talk about religion or politics
Just lie here in the dark
—It was cold, we needed lots of blankets —
And talk about our children, their schools,
their studies and struggle to understand
what we adults know.
What do we know? A glimmer of light
        on an ocean of secrets.

We can talk about our parents,
they never knew each other
and died still locked in their silence

And us, what do we know?
Your hand is cold. Let me hold you
Feel you. This is all I know. You exist.
        Nothing else.

VII

We do not need to find land or buy a house
We cannot stay long
Rest a night, and leave in the morning
We are orphans
searching for the fathers we have lost
We meet in this hotel, and at the corner of the road
to the old part of town, we turn away
and forget each other

*1975

Mata penyair

Ketika terbuka jendela, terdengar hiruk-piruk kota. "Apa saja yang sudah kuberikan kepadamu," kata penyair, "kecuali nyawaku ini yang teraniaya."

Rakyat yang miskin merangsak ke muka. "Kami ingin matamu!" teriak mereka. "Kami ingin matamu, yang bisa merobah butir pasir yang tercecer dari karung menjadi emas di jalan. Beri matamu, matamu!"

Ada yang masih mau membela penyair itu. "Ingat, tanpa mata penyair menjadi buta!"

Tetapi rakyat yang putusasa tidak peduli. Mereka renggut mata penyair dari lubang matanya, dan lewat kedua bola matanya mereka melihat dunia sekelilingnya. Tetapi pasir yang tercecer tidak menjadi emas. Mereka menjadi kecewa dan merebus dan melahap kedua bola mata itu. Dan tidak terjadi apa-apa.

Penyair yang buta itu duduk di jendela dan tertawa menghadap ke kota. Tanpa mata dilihatnya semua begitu indahnya. Begitu indahnya!

The eyes of the poet

When he opened the window, he heard the bustle of the city. "I have given you everything," the poet said, "but my tortured soul."

A crowd of poor people pushed forward toward him. "We want your eyes!" they shouted. "Your eyes can turn sand scattered from a sack into gold on the road. Give us your eyes! Your eyes!"

Some of them wanted to help him. "Without his eyes a poet is blind," they said.

But the crowd didn't care. In their despair they tore the poet's eyes from his sockets and used them to see the world. The scattered sand did not turn to gold. Disappointed, the crowd boiled the eyes and ate them. It made no difference.

The blind poet sat at his window and laughed at the city. Without his eyes, everything was beautiful. Very beautiful.

*1995

Suami

Ia tahu wanita itu ingin cepat-cepat menutup pintu.
Ia tahu wanita itu ingin mengisyaratkan sesuatu.
Karena itu ia berhenti melangkah
pada setombak jarak, dan kebun yang basah.

Sesuatu telah berubah. Senja hanya berdiri.
Lampion kian lemah. Gerit tak ada lagi.
"Aku tak mengira kau akan datang.
Beberapa hari ini dusun hanya tenang."

Wajah itu pucat. Seperti huruf sunyi pada kawat
yang mendesakkan sesuatu—tapi tak termuat.
"Malam ini suamiku akan sampai
Malam ini malam kami yang damai."

Sudah berapa lamakah batu-batu itu tersusun
dalam kesedihan sebuah kebun?
Ada pernah ia lihat lukisan unggas
terbang, di atas teratai yang luas.

Lalu perempuan itu pun cepat-cepat menutup pintu.
"Aku harus menisik tanda pada kelambu," katanya.
"Karena itu selamat malam —
Karena itu selamat malam, suamiku."

Husband

He knew the woman wanted to close the door quickly.
He knew the woman wanted to tell him something.
So he stopped a spear's length away,
in the wet garden.

Something had changed. Twilight stood awkwardly.
The lamps were pale. The vines silent.
"I did not think you would come.
Nothing has happened in the village these past few days."

Her face was pale. Empty letters hung on the fence,
communicating something he could not understand.
"My husband will return tonight.
Tonight we will be together."

How long did the stones stand heaped
in the sadness of the garden?
He remembered a picture he had once seen
of cranes flying across a field of lotuses.

Then the woman quickly closed the door.
"I must mend the sheets," she said,
"So good night,
Good night, my husband."

1979

Jam 8 malam

Untuk Françoise

Kukhayalkan kau datang dari benua lain
setelah bertahun-tahun menanti kabar—
        percuma.

Kini kau datang seperti pencinta setia
dari dongeng pahlawan kuno.

Melintasi gunung dan laut,
terbang antar benua,
demi kasih dan persahabatan,
layak bagi Arjuna.

Kukhayalkan kau datang,
berhasil meyakinkan dunia,
perlunya dua makhluk manusia
dari dua benua dan dua dunia
diberi kesempatan saling tatap muka,
dari balik jeruji besi
untuk semenit-dua.

Kukhayalkan segalanya
dengan sepenuh jiwa,
yang meluluh jarak antar angkasa
dan masa menurut hitungan kalpa,
jadi kepekatan tatapan mata.

Tiba-tiba aku terjaga
Portir dengan kunci gemerincing
mencek pintu sel —
seperti tiap kali.

SITOR SITUMORANG

Eight o'clock at night

For Françoise

I have dreamed of you coming from a far country
and waited year after year for your letters. Nothing.

And now you're here, like some faithful lover
from an old legend.

Having crossed the seas and mountains,
flying from one continent to another,
come as a friend and lover,
fit for Prince Arjuna himself.

I have dreamed of you coming,
having convinced the whole world
that two human beings
from two different continents
and two different worlds
need to see each other
across iron bars
for a few minutes.

I have dreamed of it all,
with my whole heart,
breaking the distance between our skies
and the millions of years which divide us,
as our eyes meet.

Suddenly, the guard passes,
jangling his keys
as he routinely
checks the cell doors,
and I am awake again.

Tanda di belahan bumi sini
hari jam 8 malam.
Jam berapa di Eropa?
Kau di Paris sedang apa?

Hotel Emp(i)re-Paris

Berkunjung lagi setelah 30 tahun,
aku lewat di depan Hotelnya,
tapi tak masuk—
hanya mampir di Cafe, cafe di pojok itu
seperti esok paginya,
ketika kita sarapan Croissant

sekarang dengan meja kerusi berkilat,
nyaris mengingatkan malam-malam cinta,
malam-malam menerima dan memberi Nikmat
(Umur 23 terlalu indah, Manis)
di kamar-kamar hotel murah
bergorden beledru tebal
diterangi sebuah lilin

ketika kau copot pakaian, berkata
Padamkan saja!
Kupadamkan, lalu kamar bertambah terang
oleh cahaya tubuhmu

The sound tells me
that it is eight o'clock
at night, on this side of the world.
What time is it
        in Europe?
What are you doing
        in Paris?

*1976

Hotel Emp(i)re, Paris

A visitor after thirty years
I pass the hotel,
and do not go in—
I stop at the cafe on the corner,
as we used to do
for morning croissants.

The furniture shines now.
I can almost remember our nights of love,
nights of giving and receiving pleasure
(Twenty-three is a beautiful age)
in cheap hotel rooms
with thick velvet curtains
lit by a single candle.

As you undressed you said:
Blow out the candle!
I blew out the candle, and the room glowed
with the brightness of your body

di kamar remang
di kamar bergorden beledru tebal
diterangi cahaya, kini
ternyata masih menyala

di relung kenangan
di tengah keramaian Paris
yang sudah berubah

Apakah memang pasti
malam itu
Lilin kupadamkan?

Kamar kosong

Dari tumpukan pakaianmu tersisa
jamu-jamu kecantikan tertinggal
terserak kacau-balau
di kamar penuh namun kosong
sampai di sudut-sudut indera terdalam
menguap ruah bau ketidakhadiranmu
mengisi kesendirianku

terjerat jala ganggang
bekas-bekas pernah kausentuh
terdampar seperti ikan
di daratan

In a dark room
with thick velvet curtains
a light burned, and
still glows today

in a corner of my mind
in busy Paris
which has changed beyond all recognition

Did I really
blow out the candle
that night?

*1988

The empty room

The smell of your absence
drifts from a pile of old clothing
and the scattered bottles of make-up,
filling the empty room
and the deepest recesses of my mind
with loneliness

The things you touched
are caught in a cracked net,
like fish
on the sand

*1988

Belajar kembali alifbata

Satu hari dalam hidup
Solzhenitsyn

Sastra dunia? Bahasaku bahasa Indonesia,
semoga bicaraku mengandung diam,
diammu semakin jelas berkata.

Ternyata puisi memang
bukan sekadar gatra
tidak pula pasar malam
dan semudah menyerbang lapangan.

Yang mati pun belajar kembali
gagap melafal kata-kata : Arkipelag Gulag,
dan sajak-sajak Pasternak.

Sastra rahasia? Bahasa manusia,
paling sederhana. Sandi gelap
bagi kaum estetika.
(Yang bukan penyair tak ambil bagian
rahasia Rimbaud dan cintanya Chairil Anwar)

Tapi aku pun sedia belajar
alifbata sastra
bahasa sehari-hari
penghuni Nusantara,
bahasa lain aku tak bisa.

Learning the alphabet again[†]

A day in the life
of Solzhenitsyn

World literature? I speak Indonesian,
there should be a silence in my words,
so that your silence can be more clearly heard.

Poetry is not just grammar,
and not a night carnival,
its voice crosses vast distances.

Slowly the dead learn to read
again, spell out the syllables: Gulag Archipelago,
the poems of Pasternak.

A secret language? The simplest language
of mankind. Dim twilight
to the aesthetes.
(Those who are not poets will never understand
Rimbaud's mysteries, Chairil Anwar's love)

I want to learn
the alphabet of literature,
but all I know
are the everyday languages
of Indonesia.

[†] *Alexander Solzhenitsyn* (born 1918): great Russian author; his works include the documentary work *The Gulag Archipelago,* which was highly critical of the current implementation of Russian communism. *Boris Pasternak* (1890–1960): best known in the West for his novel *Dr. Zhivago* (1957), for which he received the Nobel Prize in 1958. Pasternak's major literary activity was as a poet. He particularly wrote on themes to do with nature. *Jean-Arthur Rimbaud* (1854–1891): French poet, author of *Illuminations* (1896) and *Une Saison en Enfer* (1891). *Chairil Anwar* (1922–1949): radical Indonesian poet of the "Generation of 1945," often considered the greatest of all Indonesian poets.

Aku harus bersedia
belajar alifbata, walau gagap:
Arkipelag Gulag, Arkipelag Gulag,
kepribumian Pasternak,

Sepanjang lorong-lorong penjara
ibukota-ibukota benua.
Sepanjang jalur-jalur angkasa
kejatuhan dan kebangkitan manusia

di hutan dan padang es
masa depan manusia.

I must learn
the alphabet, however slowly,
of the Gulag Archipelago, with its collective farms,
and the earthly integrity of Pasternak.

Along the corridors of one prison after another,
one city after another,
the fragments of sky seen between the bars,
humanity falls and rises again,

the forests and the glaciers
hold our future.

*1977

Part Two

The Post-Indonesian Generation

Chapter 6

THE RENEWAL OF ISLAM

Islam and the Rise of a New Generation

THE POETS PROMINENT in the late sixties and throughout the seventies, loosely referred to in the previous part of this anthology as "the Generation of 1966," gradually began to assume the positions for which their experience entitled them, as editors, administrators of the arts, literary scholars, and elder statesmen. They continued to write and publish during the eighties, although less often than before, and their work often developed the themes and styles for which they had already become known.

In their place came a second "generation" of writers, writers who were born into an independent state whose president had been Suharto throughout much of their life. The "Post-Indonesian generation" first began to separate from their elders within the area of Islamic verse, then asserted their complete independence during the period of relative "openness" which characterized the end of the 1980s. The next two chapters of the anthology deal with these further phases in the poetry of the New Order.

Islam in Indonesia

Eighty-seven percent of the population of Indonesia professes allegiance to the religion of Islam, making Indonesia the largest Muslim country in the world. Islam requires a belief in One God, Omnipotent Creator and Lord of the world; in angels; in the revealed scriptures, culminating in the Koran; in Prophets and Messengers as the emissaries of God; in the "last things," the Day of Judgement, heaven and hell; and in the divine determination of all that happens in human life. The practices it encourages are sincere recitation of the Profession of Faith, that there is One God, Allah, and that Muhammad (c.570–632 c.e.) was His Prophet; prayer five times a day; alms-giving; fasting during the lunar month of Ramadan; and, when possible, performance of the pilgrimage to the holy places in and around Mecca.

Across the Indonesian archipelago, the faith is lived out in many different ways. Drawing on Clifford Geertz' now classic work, *The Religion of Java,*[1] we may make a distinction between "conservative" (or "traditional") and "modernist" Islam. Conservative Islam tends to emphasize God's control over human behavior and to point to the hereafter as the ultimate reward for human actions. In a fairly indiscriminate way, it sees all aspects of daily social behavior as being "Islamic," whatever their source. Conservative Islam emphasizes emotional satisfaction as the immediate reward for ritual performance, and accepts a wide range of ritual experiences as being of spiritual benefit to those who practice them. Finally, conservatives tend to justify their beliefs and practices through reference to custom and by what Geertz describes as "scholastic learning in the traditional religious commentaries."[2]

"Modernist" Islam developed in Southeast Asia during the early twentieth century, under the influence of the reformist movement led by Muhammad Abduh at Cairo's Al-Azhar University. The reformist movement sought to "purify" Islam of non-Islamic mysticism, magic, and Indic beliefs and practices. It placed a strong emphasis on learning based on understanding, not mere rote study, in order to rediscover "the original, the pure, the true Islam," through a rational individual study of the Koran and Muslim traditions (the *hadith*)[3]. (Before he mastered Arabic, Mohd Radjab had written in a widely quoted but often misunderstood sentence in his autobiography, *Semasa Kecil di Kampung,* "God never said anything I was able to understand.")[4]

Again following Geertz, we may suggest that "modernists" in Indonesia tend to emphasize the importance of hard work and self-determination in daily behavior. They draw strong boundaries between what is Islamic and what is secular in life. There is no room in "modernist" Islam for the whole set of theories and practices of curing, sorcery, or magic, which Geertz sees as central to the animist or *abangan* variant of Javanese religion, and little place for the feast known as the *slametan.*[5] Rather, there is a strong concern with the careful and regular performance of the basic rituals of Islam: the five daily prayers, the annual fasting month, and with working toward the pilgrimage to Mecca. The major social unit is not the local unit of the family or the village but the Muslim community, the *ummat,* "a great society of equal believers constantly repeating the name of the Prophet, going through the prayers, chanting the Koran."[6] Finally, for "modernists," belief and practice are justified by their pragmatic value in contemporary life, their moral and social dimensions, and through "general reference to the Koran and Hadith interpreted loosely."[7]

Islam Religion, Yes! Islamic Ideology, No![8]

Despite its numerical significance, Islam has had little influence in Indonesian politics. Even before Independence was proclaimed, attempts to ensure the inclusion in the preamble to the 1945 Constitution of a statement that adherents of Islam would be "obliged" to implement Muslim law (the *syariah*) were firmly defeated.[9]

Muslim political parties have been pitted against each and have failed to win overwhelming support from the general public. Political scientists have often seen "conservative" Islam as best expressed by the Nahdatul Ulama, founded in 1926. NU comprises reasonably well off peasants and small landowners throughout East and Central Java and is led by traditionalist-minded *kyayi.* They have similarly focused "modernism" on the social and educational organization Muhammadiyah, founded in 1912. The Muhammadiyah has been strongest in the outer islands and west Java, and draws its following from lower-middle-class groups such as school teachers and government functionaries. In the first national elections, held in 1955, NU claimed only 18.4 percent of the vote and Masyumi (of which the Muhammadiyah was one component) 20.9 percent, while Sukarno's Indonesian Nationalist Party (PNI) pulled in 22.3 percent and the Communist Party 16.4 percent of the total.[10] The Masyumi Party was dissolved in 1960 on the grounds that it supported the regional rebellions then taking place in Sumatra and Sulawesi.

There has been even less respect for Muslim political parties from secular politicians and analysts. Ben Anderson has described their perception of the NU as being: "Thoroughly corrupt and thoroughly opportunist: a party for all seasons, a party which has made seedy accommodation with every national leadership since the birth of the Republic, a party interested only in the patronage of the Ministry of Religion, a party without policies, doctrines, or programs."[11] We have already seen how the Muslim parties were severely cramped in the seventies by their being required to work together in the single PPP, and even more so by the imposition of Panasila as the *asas tunggal* of all organizations, which led to NU leaving the political arena.

Secular politicians' distrust of Islamic values derived in very general terms from their own social background and education.[12] But it was even more grounded in experience. The struggle for the Islamic state, denied by the 1945 Constitution, took a new form in 1947, while the Revolution was in progress, at the hands of the Darul Islam militia, who were not finally defeated until 1962. The regional revolts of the late fifties were seen to be inspired, in part at least, by Islam. The rioting at Tanjung Priok and Lampung was initially attributed to Islamic agitators. An Islamic influence was also understood to be behind the ongoing disturbances in Aceh. Understandably then the most important targets for the attention of the intelligence and the security organizations in the 1980s were the Islamic community and labor, the parts of civil society "least amenable to subordination and incorporation" by the state.[13] As Keith Foulcher has argued, Islam offered "a coherent value system which is in opposition to the often perceived excesses in the culture of the state." With "its own conception of modernity," the term "Islam" also stood "in the shadow of 'Indonesia,' articulating resistance in the lives of individuals and in social organizations."[14]

Islamic Revival

We must now add a third form of Islam to the conservative and "modernist" forms already discussed. After the mid-seventies, Revivalist Islam began to make the same strong impact on Indonesian society that it was having elsewhere throughout the world.[15] The influence was felt particularly by young people. They began to give a greater place to Islam in their public behavior, language, and dress, to pray more regularly, and to form groups in order to study the Koran and the writings of contemporary theorists such as Sayyid Abul A'la Maududi and Sayyid Qutb, as well as the Indonesian theologians Nurcholish Madjid, Djohan Effendi, Abdurrahman Wahid, and the late Ahmad Wahib. Liddle has described the post-Indonesian generation as one that was "simultaneously modern, Indonesian and Muslim," wanting to be religious but not to be led either by the old-fashioned rural *ulama* or by the more extreme thinkers within modernist Islam.[16]

Islam and Islamic Poetry

Religious experience has played a minor role in modern Indonesian poetry. As Geertz so perceptively noticed in the late 1950s, the "national-art complex" has commonly reflected the intellectual values of "a group of restless, educated, urban young men and women possessed of a sharp dissatisfaction with traditional custom and deeply ambivalent towards the West."[17] The models of western literature dealt with the struggle to find faith, with doubt and uncertainty. The models of eastern religious literature were of obedience and praise. These attitudes merged in the few poems of Chairil Anwar where he expressed an antagonistic attitude toward the divine, yet, nevertheless, felt unable to escape from His power. They were also present in the pain and disappointment revealed in the personal work of the great prewar poet Amir Hamzah, which sublimated his desire for the woman he was not allowed by custom to marry into a search for a continually absent God.[18]

Under the effect of Revivalist Islam, popular songs of a religious and mystical nature began to appear within mainstream culture after the mid-seventies with increasingly frequency. By the eighties, religious belief and experience had also become, according to a number of contemporary observers, the most characteristic topic of poetic expression.[19]

The first Islamic poetry for this new audience was written by already established poets of the New Order, for whom a form of modernist Islam was an important part of their own lives: Abdul Hadi, Taufiq Ismail, and Sutardji Calzoum Bachri. Hadi's poem "Tuhan, kita begitu dekat" (Near God) arose from his interest in mystical Islamic writing—the works of Rumi, Hafiz, and other Persian poets, whom he translated into Indonesian—and the research into the writing of the sixteenth century Sumatran poet-theologian, Hamzah Fansuri, which was to culminate in Hadi's doctoral thesis. "Near God" uses a number of traditional nature images to indicate the closeness of God and His creature: heat in fire, cotton in cloth, the wind and its movement.

Sutardji's attraction to Islam undoubtedly came as a shock to many of his readers, after the flamboyance of his earlier life lived purely as "a poet." In his third volume, *Kapak* (Axe), published in 1979, there were signs of an initial willingness to submit himself to the "greatness of God," "Walau" (Even). The impact of his pilgrimage to Mecca in the late 1980s was unmistakable. His poems exulted in the physical details of the holy land and in the transformation which prayer, recited with faith, had made to his own life. These were poems of penance, of regret for a life so far wasted, but now determined to accept the call to submit to the "will of God despite (his own) suffering" ("Berdepan-depan dengan Ka'bah," In front of the Ka'abah).

Taufiq Ismail's "Membaca tanda-tanda" (Reading the signs) dealt, in his well-established manner, with social decay as evidenced through the pollution of the environment, but now read this as an indication of apocalyptic judgement. The description of the world as a series of "signs" follows a strategy that is used often throughout the Koran. In this way, Taufiq confirmed the centrality of Islam for this group of established poets. One could no longer dismiss the references to faith, as readers often did with Ajip Rosidi's poetry, as being merely "regional," interesting facets of a rural and traditional landscape.

"Sufism" and a New Generation of Poets

Following these older writers of faith, a new group of Muslim poets arose, the second generation of Indonesian writers to emerge under the New Order. Their background made them closer to the post-Indonesian audience than their seniors. All were born after 1950, most after 1960. They were, thus, some ten to twenty years younger: Emha Ainun Nadjib was born in 1953, Ahmadun Yosi Herfanda in 1956, and Acep Zamzam Noor in 1960. These writers had also received a significantly different education. All had close connections with residential Muslim school systems. Emha received his secondary education at the famous *pesantren* in Gontor; Acep at Cipasung, Tasikmalaya, West Java, and then at the *pesantren* As-Syafi'iyah in Jakarta. Ahmadun also spent six years in a *madrasah* at Kendal, East Java, and has taught art at the Muhammadiyah school in Kaliwungu. This education was followed by shorter periods in the state tertiary sector: Emha for four months in the Economics faculty of Gajah Mada University; Ahmadun in Education at the Yogyakarta Teachers' College; and Acep in Fine Arts at the Bandung Institute of Technology. The literature on which they had been raised, and to which they were to contribute, was literature written in Indonesian and that of Islam (the latter sometimes first read in Arabic or Persian, but also sometimes in English translation). None of them has chosen to spend any lengthy period in the secular commercial world of the national capital, Jakarta.

Emha Ainun Nadjib has been described by the publisher Joesoef Isak as *"seorang pesantren, pemikir muda islam, seorang dengan commitment social yang tinggi,"* a religious scholar, a young Muslim thinker, a man with a high degree of social commitment.[20] During the early eighties, he was closely involved with the Dinasti theater group in Yogyakarta, the heir to the legacy of Rendra's Bengkel Teater after he left for Jakarta. A number of other members of the group after 1980 were former students of Gajah Mada University, forced out by the Campus Normalization actions of 1978–9. The group presented various plays after 1982 that were sharply critical of the effects of the misuse of political power toward the common people. Emha was the co-author of some of these plays.[21] After the group's work was banned in Yogyakarta in 1983 and again in 1985, Emha left to spend over a year travelling in Europe. Upon returning, he joined with the group Sanggar Shalahuddin, and staged a theatrical version of his long poem *Syair Lautan Jilbab* (A Poem about a Sea of Head Scarves), defending the right of female students to wear the head scarf *(jilbab)*.[22] The play combined "theatre, poetry, religion and the resentment arising from historical change *(greget perubahan sejarah),"* and played to audiences of many thousands of devout Muslims.[23] Emha represented a new type of Muslim leadership, both intellectual and traditional, respected by mass constituencies "not by virtue of holding state office, or even . . . positions in Islamic organizations" but for their speaking and writing in an era of rapid mass communications.[24]

Emha's first volume of poetry, *"M" Frustrasi,* appeared in 1976 and already declared his interest in religion.[25] The volume *Cahaya Maha Cahaya* (Light, Great Light, 1991) derived, Sapardi Djoko Damono suggested in the introduction, from a restlessness that arose from the tension between Emha's desire to return to youthful ideals and the reality that he was an intelligent man who had already experienced too much and sacrificed himself too often to social conventions.[26] From another perspective, the poems explored the human fight to overcome sin and ordinary suffering, and surrender to the God who exists beyond all language, completely wrapped in light.[27] The two poems by Emha presented in this anthology both derive from *Cahaya Maha Cahaya* and explored the mystery of God who is incomprehensible to the human mind. "Aku mabuk Allah" (I am drunk with God) (intended perhaps to challenge the old Sutardji) affirmed the absolute supremacy of Allah as the purpose of human existence. "Sudah kubuang-buang" (I have rejected God) rejected, in fact, limited and false conceptions of the divine in order to find (in Meister Eckhart's words) "the God beyond God."[28]

It was the lyrical emphasis on interior religious experience which finally marked off these new "Sufis" (as they were often described) from the stricter externality of their seniors. The new Sufis were from the island of Java, their elders had come from the outer islands. Muhammad Slamat has suggested that the need of Javanese religiosity is for "a very personal, inward, transcendental experience."[29] In *Islam Observed,* Geertz, too, has described the characteristics of Javanese Islam as "inwardness, imperturbability, patience, poise, sensibility, aestheticism, elitism, and an almost obsessive self-effacement, the radical dissolution of personality."[30] The new Sufis wrote a type of verse that was youthful, light, playful, at ease with Koranic references as well the names of the prophets and the Persian mystics, set in the neo-romantic realm of the rural countryside, and deeply mystical. There was almost a radiance to their descriptions of a world filled with the God whose beauty attracted spontaneous worship, who was everywhere and yet "nearer to you than your jugular vein" (Ahmadun Yosi Herfanda: "Sajak Urat Leher," The veins of your neck, quoting *surah* 50, verse 15 of the Koran). Ahmadun Yosi Herfanda and Acep Zamzam Noor, whose work concludes this chapter of the anthology, were among the best exponents of this worldview, simultaneously modern (even post-modern) and yet also available to the most conservative of believers.

Tuhan, kita begitu dekat

Tuhan.
Kita begitu dekat.
Sebagai api dengan panas.
Aku panas dalam apimu.

Tuhan.
Kita begitu dekat.
Seperti kain dengan kapas.
Aku kapas dalam kainmu.

Tuhan,
Kita begitu dekat.
Seperti angin dan arahnya.

Kita begitu dekat.

Dalam gelap
kini aku nyala
pada lampu padammu

Abdul Hadi W. M.

Near God

God,
we are as close
as fire and flame.
I am flame
in your fire.

God,
we are as close
as cloth and cotton.
I am cotton
in your cloth.

God,
we are as close
as wind
and air.

In the dark
I burn
in your unlit
lamp.

1976

Walau

walau penyair besar
takkan sampai sebatas allah

dulu pernah kuminta tuhan
dalam diri
sekarang tak

kalau mati
mungkin matiku bagai batu tamat bagai pasir tamat
jiwa membumbung dalam baris sajak

tujuh puncak membilang bilang
nyeri hari mengucap ucap
di butir pasir kutulis rindu rindu

walau huruf habislah sudah
alifbataku belum sebatas allah

Even

even the greatest poet
will never be as great as God

once I looked for God within myself
now I do not

when I die
I will end like a rock, or end like sand
and my soul will live in my poetry

seven peaks cry out their cries
day's anguish screams its screams
I write my longing on the longing sand

were I to use every letter there is
my alphabet would never be as great as God

1979

Berdepan-depan dengan Ka'bah

Aku datang. Aku datang memenuhi penggilanMu.
Tapi ke mana engkau engkau datang. Engkau tak ke
mana-mana. Engkau datang ke dalam dirimu kosong,
bagaikan Ka'bah. Engkau terpesona, mungkin agak
terperangah. Dalam rumah dirimu, tak ada yang
menanti, tak ada yang mengucapkan salam. Sementara
tadi di airport Jeddah ada bienvenu, ada welcome, ada
selamat datang, dan entah apa lagi dalam kata-kata
Cina dan Jepang. Engkau di sini tamu sekaligus tuan
rumah. Baiklah ucapan seperti Umar mengucap:
*"Allahumma zid haadzal baita tasyriifa wa ta'zhiiman wa
takriiman wa mahaabatan wazid man syarrafahuu wa
karramahuu mimman hajjahuuawi tamarahuu tasyriifan
wa ta'zhiiman wa takriiman wa birra."* Jadi engkau
mengucapkan harapan pada dirimu. Memang
engkaulah tamu, engkaulah tuan rumah. Inilah rumah
dirimu. nah, mulai kini benahi lagi dirimu! O tamu
dirimu, O jiwa batinmu: roh yang lapar yang haus,
ingin mereguk berpuluh-puluh shalat, mengunyah
beratus doa! Jamulah dia. Ikuti maunya! Ingin
berkitar-kitar tawaf, ingin bergegas bolak-balik Safa
Marwa. O jiwa yang resah, kembalilah engkau kepada
Tuhanmu!

Berdepan-depan dengan Ka'bah, sampailah aku pada
perpanjangan sajak-sajakku. Setelah tanya dan resah,
setelah aorta diigau risau setelah kucing meraung
dalam darah, inilah jalan itu!

In front of the Ka'abah

"I come. I come in answer to your call." But where have you all come? You have come into your empty self. You are like the Ka'abah. This amazes you, even shocks you. In the house of the self, no one waits, no once welcomes you. Back at the airport, in Jeddah, you saw "bienvenu," "welcome," "selamat datang," and heaven knows what in Chinese and Japanese. Here you are host and guest, both. As Umar said: *"Allahumma zid haadzal baita tasyriifa wa ta'zhiiman wa takriiman wa mahaabatan wazid man syarrafahuu wa karramahuu mimman hajjahuuawi tamarahuu tasyriifan wa ta'zhiiman wa takriiman wa birra."* [†] You must encourage yourself. You are the guest. You are the host. This is your house, so make the preparations you know you will need. Guest of the self, inner spirit: your soul is hungry and thirsty, it wants blessings. Feed your soul with prayers and petitions. Let it have its fill! Let it have its own way. Let it encircle the Great Mosque and run between the hills of Safa and Marwa. Oh restless soul, return to your God!

In front of the Ka'abah, I come to the end of my poems. After my questions and my restlessness, after my heart has been driven wild by worry, after the cat has roared through my blood, this is the way forward.

[†] "Oh Lord give glory, greatness and love of the Ka'abah. And give glory, greatness, honor, and well-being to those who undertake the greater and the lesser pilgrimages, to all who honor and revere this house." Saidina 'Umar ibn al-Khattab was the second Caliph of Islam.

Kutanya urat, di mana darah? Darah mengalir dalam
doa, dalam tawaf, dalam tegukan zamzam, dalam
kecup Hajar Aswad. Bismillahi Allahu Akbar. Fana
fana fana. Tak ada Tardji. Tak ada kelompok orang
yang berkitar itu. Tak Afghan, tak Irak, tak Pakistan,
tak Iran. Kau panggil Ghulam, tak yang menjawab.
Kau panggil Gotbzadegh, yang jawab tak. Kau
teriakkan Burhan, tak ada sahutan. Kau panggil nama-
nama, hanya doa bergetar!

Kau menatap ke langit. Awan tipis tekun bertasbih.
Namun jangan kau cari Dia di sana. Tuhan tak ada di
langit. Cari Dia di hati mukmin! Kupandang dadaku,
denyutnya menggetarkan hari, tempat dunia
melengkapkan kepunahan. Sedang tawaf mengalir
mengisahkan jiwa muslim bertemu Jiwa. Di mana-
mana doa bergumam. O, jiwa mengalirlah engkau
mengitari Ka'bah, memulai lagi langkah! Dan dari
getar dadaku masih terdengar doa purba sajak lama
*papaliko arukabazuku kodega lagotokoco zukuzangga
zegezegeze zukuzangga zegezezegeze . . .*

Baitullah, tempat mulainya langkah tanpa batas,
perjalanan di luar daging dan kata-kata. Tempat doa
bukanlah sekedar alat menyampaikan harap. Tempat
doa adalah Dia! Dulu aku bawakan bunga padaMu
tapi Kau bilang masih. Aku bawakan resahku padaMu
tapi Kau bilang hanya. Aku bawakan darahmu
padaMu tapi Kau bilang cuma. Aku bawakan dukaku
padaMu tapi Kau bilang tapi. Aku bawakan mayatku
padaMu Kau bilang hampir. Tanpa apa aku datang
padaMu. Wah!

I look at my veins and search for my blood. My blood
flows in prayer, circumambulation, in kissing the Black
Rock, Bismillah, Allahu Akbar. Everything fades.
Fades. Fades. There is no Tardji. There is no crowd of
pilgrims circling the Mosque. There are no Afghanis,
no Iraqis, no Pakistanis, no Iranis. Call "Ghulam," no
one will answer you. Call "Gotbzadegh," no one will
answer you. Call "Burhan," no one will answer you.
Call any name, all you will hear is the roar of the prayer.

You gaze at the sky. Thin clouds play with their prayer-
beads. Do not look for God there. God does not live in
the sky. Look for him in the believer's heart! I gaze at
my chest, watch it daily throbbing, see the world
destroy me there. The circling crowds tell how the souls
of Muslims meet the great Soul. Prayers reverberate in
every corner of this great building. May my soul flow
around the Ka'abah, may I learn to walk again. Inside
my breast I hear the ancient prayer, the classical poem
*papliko arukabazuku kodega lagotokoco zukuzangga
zegezegeze zukuzangga zegezegeze* . . .

The journey without an end begins here, in the Great
Mosque, the journey beyond the body, beyond all
words. Here prayer is more than fantasy. God Himself
is the house of prayer. Once I brought You flowers and
You said wait. I brought You my blood and You said
not enough. I brought You my grief and You said it was
too small. I brought You my dead body and You said
that was better. I came with nothing. Ah!

Kau membawa aku ke Safa ke Marwa ke Safa ke
Marwa ke pasir ke gunung-gunung ke bintang-
bintang. Doa tumbuh menyapu-nyapu membenahi
diriku, untuk jalan Alina! Untuk tarekatku Alina, aku
buatkan sujudku di Makam Ibrahim, aku sampaikan
harap di Multazam, aku alirkan zamzam dalam urat
yang sering demam, untuk meluruskan jalan, Alina!

Alhamdulillah, Sakit, engkau telah mengakrabkan aku
padaNya. Terima-kasih Usia, engkau telah
mengantarkan. Dulu bisu batu sajakku. Kini engkau di
dekat Hajar Aswad ini telah mendedahkan rahasia.
Cahaya, Cahaya, Cahaya!

Apa yang gumam? Doa. Apa yang mengalir? Jiwa.
Apa yang tenggelam? Silam. Apa yang Dia? Cahaya.
Kupeluk Ka'bah, di pipi Hajar Aswad kekecupan
secupang doa. Kukecup lagi kali-berkali, lantas kucium
Ibrahim, Sarah, Ismail, Hajar, Maryam, dan Ahmad.
Dari hari Alastu mengalir air-mata.

You take me to Safa, to Marwa, to Safa, Marwa, to the
desert, to the mountains, to the stars. Oh Union, my
prayers replenish me, feast me, caress me! Oh Union, I
found my own religious order by bowing at Abraham's
Grave, taking vows at Multazam, pouring water from
the zamzam well into my fevered veins, and clinging to
the straight path. Oh Union!

Glory be, oh Illness you have brought me to God.
Thank you, Age, for leading me to Him. Once my
poems were as silent as rock. Now, near the Black Rock,
I see His secrets. The light! Light! Light!

What is that noise? Prayer. What flows? The soul.
What vanishes? The past. What is He? Light. I
embrace the Ka'abah and place prayerful kisses on the
Black Stone. As I kiss it again and again, I kiss
Abraham, Sarah, Ismail, Hagar, Mary the mother of
Jesus, and Muhammad. On this day of submission to
the will of God in the suffering of my life,[†] I weep.

1989

---

† The term Sutardji uses is *"hari Alastu."* The word *"alastu"* is found in
the Koranic verse 7:171, *"Alastu bi-rabbikum?"* (Am I not your Lord?)
The answer "yes" includes an acceptance of the affliction which has
been a part of earthly existence. The day of *alastu* is yesterday, by con-
trast with the Day of Resurrection.

Membaca tanda-tanda

Ada sesuatu yang rasanya mulai lepas
  dari tangan
  dan meluncur lewat sela-sela jari kita

Ada sesuatu yang mulanya
  tak begitu jelas
  tapi kini kita mulai merindukannya

Kita saksikan udara
  abu-abu warnanya
Kita saksikan air danau
  yang semakin surut jadinya
Burung-burung kecil
  tak lagi berkicau pagi hari

Hutan   kehilangan ranting
Ranting   kehilangan daun
Daun   kehilangan dahan
Dahan   kehilangan
               hutan

Reading the signs

There is something
    which has begun to fall from our hands
    and slip through the gaps in our fingers

Something which, in the beginning,
    was not very clear
but now we know
    we miss it

We see the sky
    turning gray
We see the lakes
    wasting away
Small birds
    no longer sing
       in the morning

The trees
in the forest   have no branches
the branches   have no leaves
the leaves   have no twigs
the twigs   have no
             forests

We see smoke
    filled with chemicals
    and carbon dioxide
    tears at our lungs

Kita saksikan
Gunung   memompa abu
Abu   membawa batu
Batu   membawa lindu
Lindu   membawa longsor
Longsor   membawa air
Air   membawa banjir
Banjir   membawa air

              air
              mata

Kita telah saksikan seribu tanda-tanda
Bisakah kita membaca tanda-tanda?

Allah
Ampuni dosa-dosa kami

Beri kami kearifan membaca
Seribu tanda-tanda

Karena ada sesuatu yang rasanya
        mulai lepas dari tangan
        dan meluncur lewat sela-sela jari

Karena ada sesuatu yang mulanya
        tak begitu jelas
        tapi kini kami
        mulai
        merindukannya.

We see
the mountains   pumping out ash
the ash   moving rocks
the rocks   starting earthquakes
the earthquakes   creating avalanches
the avalanches   diverting the rivers
the rivers   in flood
the floods   bear waters

the waters
of our tears

We have seen a thousand signs
Do we know what they mean?

God
We have read the earthquakes
We have endured the floods
Been hunted by fire and famine
Bombarded with ash and rock

God
Forgive us our sins

Give us the wisdom
To read these signs

Because
there is something
which has begun to fall from our hands
and slip through the gaps in our fingers

Because
there is something, which,
in the beginning,
was not very clear
but now we know
we miss it.

1982

Aku mabuk Allah

aku mabuk allah
semata-mata allah
segala-galanya allah
tak bisa lain lagi
aku mabuk allah
lainnya tak berhak dimabuki
lainnya palsu, lainnya tiada
nyamuk tak nyamuk
kalau tak mengabarkan allah
langit tak langit
kalau tak menandakan allah
debu tak debu
badai tak badai
kalau tak membuktikan allah
kembang tak mekar
api tak membakar
kalau tak allah
mabuklah aku mabuk allah
tak bisa lihat tak bisa dengar
cuma allah cuma allah
kalau matahari memancar
siapa sebenarnya yang menyinar
kalau malam legam
siapa hadir di kegelapan
kalau punggung ditikam
siapa merasa kesakitan
mabuklah aku mabuk allah
kalau jantung berdegup

I am drunk with God

I am drunk with God,
completely with God,
utterly with God,
there is no other way,
I am drunk with God,
everything else is unworthy,
everything else is false,
nothing else exists,
the flea would not be a flea
if it did not sing of God,
the sky would not be the sky
if it did not proclaim
the greatness of God,
the dust would not be dust
the storm would not be a storm
if they did not declare
the power of God,
the flowers would not blossom
the fire would not burn
if there were no God,
I am drunk, drunk with God,
I see nothing, hear nothing,
but God, only God,
when the sun shines
who is the brightness?
when night is dark
who is there in the gloom?
if you stab me in the back
who feels the pain?
I am drunk, drunk with God,
when my heart beats

siapa yang hidup
kalau menetes puisi
siapa yang abadi
allah semata
allah semata
lainnya dusta

who lives in me?
when I write poetry
who lives forever?
only God,
only God,
everything else
is false.

1986

Sudah kubuang-buang

Sudah kubuang-kuang tuhan
Agar sampai ke yang tak terucapkan
Namun tak sekali ia sedia tak hadir
Terus mengada mengada bagai darah mengalir

Sajakku beranak pinak
Dikungkung tuhan sendirian
Perih cintaku berteriak-teriak
Takut ditolak keabadian

Sudah kubuang-buang tuhan
Sudah kulupa-lupakan
Sampai ingat dan lupa
Lenyap jaraknya

Sampai tahu tak atau menjelma
Baginya tak beda
Sampai gugur mainan ada tiada
Yang menghimpitku di tengahnya

Sudah kubuang-buang
Sudah kubuang-buang
Ia makin saja tuhan
Makin saja Tuhan

I have rejected God

I have rejected God
So that I can reach
the one who has no name,
Even though He is never absent,
He is always present,
flowing in my blood.

My poems are my children,
Shaped by God.
My love cries out,
Afraid it may lose eternity.

I have rejected God,
I have forgotten all about him.
Now remembering and forgetting
are one and the same.

I know
that whether He is present or not,
He is always here.
Presence and absence
make no difference.
They are only a game,
with me in the middle.

I have rejected God.
Rejected God.
That makes Him more God,
Makes Him more God.

1986

Doa pembuka

hanya milikmu cahaya pagi hingga senja
dan rahasia kegelapan ketika malam tiba
pada muhammad kauanugerahkan kemuliaan
pada sulaiman kaulimpahkan keberadaan
kautunjukkan keindahanmu melalui yusuf
dan cinta kasihmu melalui isa
dan hati kekasih sejati pun kautanam
rahasia kemakrifatan

kaujadikan perut burung-burung
kenyang ketika petang
dan lapar kembali di pagi hari
hingga terdengar selalu kicaunya
menghiasi kelopak hari yang terjaga

kaujadikan bintang-bintang
selalu bertasbih padamu
kauciptakan pohon-pohonan
selalu berzikir padamu
o, allah, anugerahi aku kesetiaan
tanganku menjadi tanganmu
kakiku menjadi kakimu
lidahku menjadi lidahmu
mataku menjadi matamu
telingaku menjadi telingamu
hatiku menjadi istanamu

: bumi dan langit tak mengandungku
tapi hamba berimanku mengandungku

Opening prayer

the light of the day is yours, from morning to dusk,
and the secrets of the darkness, when night falls,
you gave honor to muhammad,
wealth to solomon
you showed your beauty through joseph
and your love through jesus,
the secret of union
rests in the hearts of those you bless

you fill the birds
in the afternoon,
and make them hungry
in the morning,
their chirping flows softly
over the petals of the day

you have made the stars
to praise your name,
you have made the trees
to sing your glory,
lord, make me faithful,
may my hands be your hands,
my feet your feet,
my tongue your tongue,
my eyes your eyes,
my ears your ears,
may my heart be your palace:

"heaven and earth cannot contain me
but I live in the hearts of those
who worship me"[†]   1989

[†] From a tradition relating to a non-Koranic revelation made to the
Prophet Muhammad.

Sajak urat leher

karena cinta tuhan meletakkan
dua malaikat di pundakmu
—inilah pengasuh-pengasuhmu
kata tuhan. sayap-sayapnya
bisa membawamu terbang ke langit
sekaligus berpijak di bumi lagi

engkau tak perlu takut
malaikat bukan polisi atau satpam
bersih dari amplop dan uang sogok
tak suka dijilat maupun menjilat
malaikat bersih dari nafsu-nafsu burukmu

karena cinta tuhan meletakkan
dua malaikat di pundakmu
karena cinta tuhan lebih dekat
dari urat lehermu

The veins of your neck

in his love God has set
an angel on each of your shoulders
—they will guide you, said the Lord,
one will bear you on his wings
to heaven, the other
will hold you here on the earth

you need not be afraid
the angels are not policemen
they cannot be bribed,
they cannot be flattered
and they will not flatter you,
the angels know nothing
of the desires which torment you

in his love God has set
an angel on each of your shoulders
in his love God is nearer to you
than your jugular vein.†

1990

---

† *Koran,* 50:15.

Sungai iman

sungai itu panjang sekali
mengalir ke dalam tubuhmu
dengan penuh cinta aku pun belayar
bersanandung dalam konser ikan-ikan

sungai itu dalam sekali
berpusar dalam palung jiwamu
dengan penuh gairah aku pun menyelam
menangkap makna hidup pada mata kerang

sungai itu panjang sekali
di arusnya aku memburumu
tak sampai-sampai

The river of faith

a long river
flows through your body
full of love I sail
singing with the fishes

the river is deep
it whirls through the sluice of your soul
I dive, eagerly seeking
the meaning of life among the shells

the river is long
I hunt you throughout eternity
in each of its currents

1990

Angin dan batu

1

Kenapa harus batu yang diam
Dan bukan angin? Ia padat dan dingin
Tapi bergolak bagai api
Di perutnya sungai mengalir dan keheningan
Sembahyang. Ia diam dan bisu
Sekaligus menderu

2

Kenapa bukan angin.
Dan harus batu? Ia tersepuh waktu
Matang oleh rindu

Requiem

Apa yang kaucari
Dari kediaman? Belajar pada batu
Berguru pada air
Membaca cuaca
Bicara dengan angin

Kautinggalkan rumah
Kautinggalkan buku-buku
Kaulepas seluruh pakaian

Wind and rocks

I

Why should the rocks be silent
But not the wind? The wind is hard and cold
It rolls like fire
In the belly of the river and the stillness
Of prayer. The wind has no tongue
Yet it roars all around us.

2

Why the rocks
And not the wind? The wind is covered
With golden flakes, ripened
By desire

1984

Requiem

What are you seeking
In silence? Learning from the rocks
Studying with the water
Reading in the weather
Hearing from the wind

You have left your home
Left your books
Taken off all your clothing

Kaubanting cincin
Kaumasuki malam yang dingin

Apa yang kaucari
Dari kebisuan? Bersekutu dengan malam
Tapi menolak bintang-bintang
Suaramu bagaikan sunyi
Tapi hatimu besi

Kautempuh topan
Kaujelajah waktu
Kaubakar rambutmu yang indah
Kauabukan hidupmu
Dalam perapian cinta

Tapi apa yang kaucari
Dari ketiadaan?

Para kekasih

Attar telah bernyanyi tentang burung
Yang terbang dari dahan-dahan jiwa
Sana'i telah menanam dan memetik mawar abadi
Telah banyak nyanyian dan juga kesedihan
Dibisikkan angin yang memuja keramahan Sulaiman

Thrown away your rings
And entered the cold night

What are you seeking
Among those with no tongue?
You are one with the night
But you do not see the stars
Your voice is filled with loneliness
But your heart is made of steel

You fought your way through the storms
Crossed vast expanses of time
You burned your beautiful hair
And turned your life to ash
In the furnace of love

But what are you seeking
In the nothingness
Of death?

1988

The lovers of God[†]

Attar sang of birds
Flying from the branches of the soul
Sana'i planted the roses of eternity and picked them
After many songs and much sadness
The whispering wind praised Solomon's hospitality

[†] The "lovers of God" mentioned in this poem include major prophets,
most common to the Judaic, Christian, and Muslim traditions, as well
as a number of Sufi Muslim mystical poets who wrote in Persian:
Farid al-Din Attar (1119–1220), Sanai (d. 1131), Jalal al-Din Rumi
(1207–1273), Muhammad Shamsuddin Hafiz (1320–1389), and
Maulana 'Abdur-Rahman Jami (1414–1492).

Batu-batu digosok para kekasih menjadi nilam sejati
Dan udara dipenuhi aroma hati yang terbakar

Begitu mendengar senandung Daud yang merdu
Pohon-pohon terhenti dari kejatuhannya ke tanah
Dan airmata langit mengkristal di udara
Jalaluddin telah mengundang matahari turun ke
                                            hatinya
Rumput-rumput terkejut dari keterikatannya pada
                                            akar
Sedang jiwa bumi bergerak dalam tarian yang riang
Hingga batu-batu berterbangan bagaikan kapas

Di sepanjang Laut Tengah yang tawar
Langit bagaikan logam yang disepuh keemasan
Di sana Yunus memahat sajak-sajaknya dalam
                                            kaligrafi
Yang sulit dibaca. Tapi ikan-ikan dapat membacanya
Kadal-kadal telah membacanya dengan mata terpejam
Karang-karang menyusut menjadi butiran pasir
Dan lautan membukakan lembaran-lembaran buku

Hafiz menyuling anggur dari kebun hatinya
Lalu mengundang burung-burung untuk mabuk
                                            bersama
Jami bergoyang-goyang di antara dua cawan besar
Yang disajikan langit dan bumi pada kehidupan
Tak terhitung berapa lagu dan juga airmata
Disalurkan sungai-sungai rahasia ke Safa dan Marwah
Menjadi gelombang para kekasih yang mengalir

God's lovers caressed rocks and turned them into
                                    sapphires
And the air was filled with the incense of hearts on fire

When they heard David's sweet singing
Leaves refused to fall
Rain turned to crystal tear-drops
When Jalaluddin invited the sun into his heart,
The grass leaped high,
The earth's spirit moved in happy dance
Sending stones flying like tufts of cotton

The leaden skies over the salty Mediterranean
were streaked with the golden calligraphy
of Jonah's poems, which no one could read.
Except for the fish, and the large-lidded lizards,
The long reefs shrinking into grains of sand,
And the opening pages of the sea.

Hafiz' flute drew wine from the garden of his heart
And invited the birds to share in his drunkenness
Jami staggered between two large cups
Offered to life by heaven and earth
No one can tell how many songs, how many tears,
Have rolled like rivers, as God's lovers,
Crowds of holy pilgrims, have flowed
Between the sacred mountains of Safa and Marwah.

1992

Chapter 7

A NEW OPENNESS

Promises of Spring

BY THE END OF THE eighties, much had changed in Indonesia. The Indonesian economy had been transformed from one based on the interests of "a regime constituted by the interests of a rent seeking ruling group of military officers" to one dominated by several vast industrial and trading conglomerates. The regime may have largely consisted of the same individuals, but with the retirement of various key figures from military service, they no longer held the same access to power as before.[1] This reconfiguration provided greater scope for elite rivalry, most especially between Suharto and the Armed Forces.[2] Because it was widely recognized that the president was in his late sixties and not in good health, the question of who might succeed him also began to be of considerable interest.

Previously, only alienated members of the political elite or desperate working-class groups had dared to launch sporadic attacks on the regime. After the long winter of the repression of the eighties, the year 1989 saw a sudden public outpouring of opinion, discussion, and debate about important political and economic issues facing the country. Controversial issues such as the role of the presidency, the emasculation of political parties, the militarization of society, the business interests of the president's family, the degradation

of the environment, and the widening gap between rich and poor
were all increasingly discussed in public forums.[3] This was widely
described as *"keterbukaan"* ("openness," even sometimes translated
ironically by outside observers as *"glasnost"*)[4] and it seemed to prom-
ise many new freedoms.[5]

The debate came from various directions. One was from the middle
class, eager to see less ideological conformity and greater tolerance to-
ward dissent.[6] A second came from Islam, now more publicly accept-
able than ever before. As the relationship between President Suharto
and the Armed Forces deteriorated in the late eighties, he began to
court Islamic groups as a possible new source of support.[7] In Suharto's
sixth term, Islamic courts were strengthened; the wearing of *jilbab*
(head coverings) by female students in state schools was allowed; the
editor of the news magazine *Monitor* was arrested and sentenced for
apparent disrespect to the Prophet Muhammad; the establishment of
an association for Muslim intellectuals, ICMI, was approved in 1990;
and approval was given for the creation of an Islamic bank.[8]

Thirdly, in late 1988 and early 1989 there was a growth in student
protests, the first since early seventies, as the call for an end to Su-
harto's rule spread across Java.[9] The protests were especially con-
cerned with land disputes between the government and agricultural
communities, and with public welfare. Almost always peaceful, these
demonstrations were surprisingly well reported in the mass media.[10]
The association of students with rural peoples and industrial workers
was surely significant as a sign of widespread dissatisfaction with the
government.[11]

The political parties joined in this desire for more open debate
and participation as well. After the re-election of the president in
1988, and the appointment of a contentious vice president, there
were calls for greater opportunities for freer political expression.[12]
The leaders of Golkar, originally founded by the army, talked
about greater civilian involvement in politics, and greater "democ-
ratization." Much was made of the decision to allow for individual
membership of Golkar rather than corporate membership. The
constraints placed on political parties were widely regretted.[13]

However, without military support, especially in parliament, for "openness," it seems unlikely that this change of attitude could have developed at all. The distant beginnings of military expression of a desire for greater freedom of speech may be placed as early as May 1987 when the chief of the Armed Forces, General Bennie Murdani, warned that too much control over the younger generation would produce "a generation of robots."[14] (Moerdani was given the less powerful position of defense minister early in the following year and replaced by General Try Sutrisno. With the support of the Armed Forces, Sutrisno became vice president in 1993, against Suharto's wishes.)[15]

The more immediate source stemmed from the complaint made in 1989 by Police Brigadier General Dra. Rukmini Koesoemo Astoeti Soejono, a member of the military fraction in the parliament, that the contemporary press had been reduced to "a government bulletin."[16] Although far from agreeing with Rukmini, Sutrisno subsequently told a parliamentary commisssion on the Armed Forces' Doctrine of Leadership and Social Communication that "healthy" communication between the Armed Forces and society depended on a real, although carefully circumscribed, openness, which was an integral part of *Pancasila*.[17] Following in his steps, General Edi Sudrajat, commander of the armed forces, called on a meeting of active commanding officers held at the Magelang Military Academy in December 1989 to create an atmosphere in which differences among Indonesians could be discussed in a more open manner, rather than the old "foot-stomping, father knows best style of leadership." He repeated these comments several times during 1990. Each time his comments were followed by extensive discussion among civilian intellectuals about changes needed in the established political culture over the next twenty-five years.[18]

What may have begun as a series of complex moves by some members of the ABRI leadership to place the armed forces in guarded opposition to Suharto was countered by the president's moves to contain these initiatives. He appeared to give at best some qualified support to "openness" when, in response to Sutrisno's comments in mid-1989, he suggested that there should be four major limitations to political openness. These were: opinions should be expressed in a "rational manner"; they should not conflict with the important interests of the people; they must not damage national unity; and they must not conflict with *Pancasila* as the basis of the nation. In his August "state of the nation" address to the DPR, Suharto again referred to *Pancasila,* as he had indeed done as far back as 1984,[19] as "an open ideology" *(ideologi terbuka)* whose principles were unchanging.[20]

He continued to repeat this opinion over the next two years. In June 1990, he was obliged to acknowledge that political leaders need not be concerned about open debate and even redefined differences of opinion as necessary for economic development.[21] He expanded on these remarks in his subsequent national day address, and these comments led to a special edition of the magazine *Editor* on "openness." Perhaps as a consequence, Suharto was more guarded in 1991 when he reminded his listeners that although Indonesia was moving toward a period of greater openness, including a freeing of the media, any openness also required responsibility.[22] Few listeners believed that Suharto's commitment to social and political change was genuine,[23] the more so as there were never any guidelines issued as to how the policy might be administered or what its limits were.[24]

Openness in Public Culture

Culture too seemed to come alive again at the end of the eighties, sometimes in obvious ways, sometimes only if one knew where to look.

The newly refurbished and more commercially oriented Jakarta Arts Center provided opportunities for greater expression of opinion.[25] Rendra was once again able to read his work and to stage plays, including *Panembahan Reso* (Lord Reso), which was, as Barbara Hatley has written, "a grand drama of power struggles among ambitious officials and soldiers when the ruler of a mythological Javanese kingdom becomes too old and weak to exert proper control."[26]

The group Teater Koma even presented musicals which also satirized political corruption and injustice. In the trilogy, *Bom Waktu* (Time Bomb), the first two plays dealt with the close relationships between the president and business and the growing disparities in wealth in Indonesia.[27] They were enthusiastically received by large audiences of "middle-class but relatively unintellectual young men and women, willing to pay thousands of rupiahs to be entertained by a heady mixture of Broadway musical and low Surabaya and Jakarta folk comedy."[28] Of course, they were also criticized by Jakartan intellectuals for "their purported commercialism, low aesthetic quality, and lack of social message."[29]

Teater Koma undoubtedly went further than was prudent in October 1990 when it presented the third play, *Suksesi,* satirizing the major political topic of the end of the decade. Eleven days into the fifteen-day season, the play was banned. Although the audience quietly left the theater,[30] there then followed a public outcry over the banning, which stressed the ability of Indonesian audiences to deal sensibly with "a little outrage, commercialism, suggestive humour, experimentation and conflicting ideas."[31] A delegation of artists protested to parliament and the security forces, and were sympathetically heard. Artists were promised clearer guidelines for censorship and more equitable treatment in future.[32]

The ban served to remind citizens that freedoms given under duress could be quickly withdrawn, very much to the disadvantage of those who had spoken out rashly. Over the next few months, a number of public readings by Rendra were banned, *Monitor* was closed, and Riantiarno's next play, *Opera Kecoa* (Cockroach Opera), first staged in 1982, was banned before it had even opened.[33]

The second round of openness, which began in 1993, ended even more decisively with the arrest of some two dozen students at the end of the year for "insulting the head of state."[34] In June 1994, three leading newsweeklies, *Tempo, Detik,* and *Editor,* were banned for their critical reports on conflict within the government and Armed Forces over certain financial decisions.[35] Prior to this, the magazines had also published detailed analyses of presidential family businesses, human rights abuses, misuse of authority, maladministration of government funds, and factional splits within the government and the military.[36] These were the first mass closures since 1978. They again led to great public debate. David Hill has argued that "The bans were arguably a sign of political ineptitude, a rear-guard action by a President, poorly advised, engaged in a futile attempt to slow the march to democratisation."[37]

Openness and Poetry

Between 1975 and 1980 no fewer than two hundred volumes of poetry had been published in Indonesia.[38] This situation changed during the eighties when creative writing was most regularly published only in magazines and newspapers. In 1990 only a few volumes of poetry appeared.[39] *Horison* remained the only literary periodical, a "little magazine" with a circulation of no more than 3,000 copies.[40] Goenawan Mohamad gloomily noted in 1991 that "the literary market has become less and less recognizable, having been progressively decimated by economic and political chaos in the young republic, with readerships dramatically reduced by decades of faulty schooling. Indonesian prose writing now consists mainly of short works published in undistinguished and disposable magazine forms."[41] There was some loss in this. In reaching out to a different audience, literature seemed to have moved closer to the pop-culture characteristic of much of the rest of the world,[42] being neither "particularly self-conscious or introspective."[43] But there was also a gain in vigor, and the growth of a new audience in a different climate seemed to allow the possibility of saying things that had not been said for a long time.[44]

In chapter 6 of this anthology, "The Renewal of Islam," we observed the emergence of a new group of Muslim poets, who, I argued, marked the beginning of a second generation of Indonesian writers within the New Order. As Islam was no longer outside the mainstream of contemporary social awareness, Emha Ainun Nadjib, Ahmadun Yosi Herfanda, and Acep Zamzam Noor were soon part of a much wider cohort which emerged under the subsequent conditions of openness and have continued to develop throughout the nineties. That larger group included the writers presented here in chapter 7, the major poets of the nineties. Members of the wider group were of the same age as their Muslim peers but more secular in their orientation and more widely read in European literatures. Some lived in Jakarta, others continued the trend of living outside of the capital.

The brief period of openness allowed for the greater public recognition of this Post-Indonesian generation of poets; it did not necessarily lead to an outpouring of writing critical of the New Order and its shortcomings. The time was too short for that; the writers, perhaps, too young and too well-trained.[45] From one perspective, that "fabulous creature, the new generation"[46] seemed still to follow the aesthetic norms that had been established by the poets of the seventies and early eighties.[47] Their works were lyrical, concerned with nature, and introspective. They enjoyed irony and humor. They sought transcendental meaning in a changing universe, and pondered on, sometimes even laughed at, their own personal insignificance. From another perspective, these writers, raised on *Horison* and *Budaya Jaya,* as well as the literary pages of popular magazines and papers, had also absorbed the various and sometimes conflicting influences of their immediate predecessors, and they now set about to blend and develop them in a way which would become distinctively their own. They advanced and changed the paradigm, rather than overturning or challenging it.

As the earlier writers had done, the poets of the nineties also used an emphasis on the private and the personal as a wall against the intrusive power of the state. In a decade which would increasingly debate the significance of "postmodernism,"[48] the ongoing interest in the irrationality of the subconscious and the primacy of emotional spontaneity, pioneered in the seventies, continued to provide a welcome alternative to ideas of linear progress; absolute scientific truth; the efficacy of social, political, and economic engineering; and the control of formal systems of knowledge, all of which marked official discourse.[49]

The link between the first and the second generation can best be found in the work of Kriapur (Kristanto Agus Purnomo), which was, unfortunately, cut short by his death in a motor accident in 1987. (The car in which he and his father were travelling ran off the road into a river, and was crushed by a truck loaded with cement that followed them into the water.) A first volume of his poetry entitled *Mengenang Kriapur (1959–1987)* (Remembering Kriapur [1959–1987]),[50] was assembled one year later in commemoration of his passing. It consolidated the powerful impact which his previously scattered writing made on the minds and emotions of many of his readers.[51] A second, more radical volume, *Tiang Hitam Belukar Malam* (Black posts in the forest of night),[52] edited by Afrizal Malna, followed in 1996 and confirmed the importance of Kriapur's work to those who came after him.

Kriapur's "Para pembakar" (Men on fire) is the only poem included in this chapter that deals with politics openly; it was written as far back as 1980. Significantly, it was not included in the first posthumous selection of his work. The theme of the poem was the resentment of rural society toward the larger cities, and the poem contained a real threat of violence from those the state most feared, the "floating masses." This was not the only poem Kriapur wrote on politics. Other poems which were included in the commemorative anthology included "Kota kota kota" (City city city) (1981) and "Sajak buat Negaraku" (A poem for my nation) (1983). The earlier poem described thousands of hungry clay corpses shipwrecked in large cities, together with children without dreams and street women caught up in "a black heaven." In two pointed lines, it dared to ask *"kemerdekaan tanah / untuk siapa?"* (for whom was the land made free?). The latter poem pointed to a repressed rural rage that would sooner or later break out in murderous rage in the larger cities. It promised *"rakyatku siap dengan tombaknya / siap dengan kapaknya"* (my people are ready with their spears / ready with their axes).[53] It is possible that the publication of these two works out of sequence in the rest of Kriapur's poetry was an act of bravery which could pass during the early thaw, but that *"Para pembakar"* was still seen as too provocative until the mid-nineties when real rage against Suharto was beginning to reach its peak.

More typical of Kriapur's work in the early eighties was "Pencarian" (Search). In order to better understand what he was attempting in this and subsequent poems, it is useful to reflect on the similarities and differences between Kriapur's views of poetic language of poetry and those of Sutardji Calzoum Bachri. "The meanings of words," Kriapur wrote in 1986, "exist in a world before meaning. Their logic exists before logic (pre-logical). Because of that they are prior to meaning—which is most definitely not to say that they have no meaning, or are meaningless—they can mean anything at all. Poems written within the 'obscure' or 'imagist' tradition can, at one and the same time, mean what they mean and the opposite of what they mean. Which is precisely why they can have more meanings. Be more compact."[54]

The bulk of Sutardji's early poetry emphasized sound. Kriapur's focus was far more on images. Kriapur wanted his poems to have meaning, many meanings, and did not feel that this was oppressive. It is surely significant that the second poem presented here began with two lines from the French symbolist Mallarmé. In 1986 Kriapur further explained: "The poet is a person who wanders in the middle of a forest of symbols which is inhabited by words. He describes this as a supernatural world, where language has already formed grand and enchanting transcendental structures. Its logic is an acrobatic and broken logic that seems to be transparent but in fact offers new possibilities which no one had ever suspected before."[55] Poetry for him was a way of creating an alternative, private world, through new and unusual images, in which the invisible became visible, and presented an alternative to the routine and clichéd reality of the everyday world.[56] With the advantage of romantic hindsight, many readers discovered the major theme in Kriapur's poetry to be not simply an exploration of unconsciousness but the actual apprehension of his own death. The theme of lovely death recurs in all of the other poems presented here. Each of these poems played with a dreamlike landscape, woven around silence, uncertainty, loneliness, and the comfort of freedom from earthly suffering.

Kriapur was in many ways a poet's poet, often hiding individual identity behind an elegant use of language. Cecep Syamsul Bahri's beautifully crafted poems of fairy-tale love and confusion followed Kriapur in the surrealist practice of joining strange images in a web of beautiful words which were to be read with the subconscious and not with the mind. Afrizal Malna, to whom Cecep refers in one of his poems, went even further. Afrizal remained a symbolist but he used the material images of the city, instead of rural landscapes of night, rivers, and trees. As was noted in an Indonesian review of Afrizal's work published in 1996, "Afrizal's themes tend to revolve around depictions of the modern world and urban life and on pre-sentation of material objects from this environment . . . [It] is this correspondence between objects that creates his poetic sense and style."[57] The review also noted that Afrizal's poems sometimes con-fused their readers, especially those looking for clear meanings or moral messages!

Readers looking for clear meaning and unmediated individuality found greater comfort in the work of Sitok Srengenge. Sitok's first collection appeared in 1992 and bore the startling title of *Persetubu-han Liar* (Wild sex).[58] Lacking Kriapur's intensity and dark imagery, Sitok's poetry appealed to a far wider audience, because of its youth-ful playfulness and comfortable awareness of the complexities of liv-ing in the capital, Jakarta. In his various poems, Sitok was able to mock the fading older generation of writers (or this at least is how I read "Rangkasbitung"), and the concessions to sheer survival made by a middle-aged, middle-brow, middle class. He was able to an-guish over the uncertainties of young adult love. He lamented the problems of an inadequate education system, both for his own gen-eration and the next. Within a few years, his poems had expanded from tight concise verses to long-lined, highly rhythmical works, which were more and more interested in the exploration of non-logical symbols. In keeping with the new literary respect for Islam, the tone of his writing affirmed a positive attitude to the world and the presence in it of God, encapsulated in the mystery of His "Name." In 1995, Sitok was involved in the International Poetry

Festival held at the major Istiqlal Mosque in Jakarta. The news weekly *Asiaweek* listed him in 1999 as one of twenty "Leaders for the Millennium in Society and Culture." It described him as "Indonesia's best young poet," part of "a post-repression renaissance," and compared his role and personality in the nineties to that of Rendra in the eighties.[59]

The work of Dorothea Rosa Herliany was more confrontational than that of any of the male poets of the newer generation. A natural feminist, Dorothea increasingly wrote from the shadow-side of Indonesian gender relations, the image of woman as nature: the "ancient female archetype . . . of fertility, autonomous, sexually potent, magically dangerous."[60] Her work revealed the anger and aggression that was a part of female experience in a strongly patriarchal society. There was none of the games and lightness that one finds, for example, in Sitok's poems about relationships. Her poems affirmed the desire to be counted as an equal in sexual relationships. They spun dreams, hopes, despair, and violence around the marriage bed. Her writing was less intellectual, perhaps, than Toeti Heraty's, but it was also less resigned to the acceptance of female misery as a result of the failure of love. Dorothea's work has developed quickly over the past decade and the personal dimension of her writing can be expected to continue to grow in intensity and force.

This chapter of this anthology is itself open-ended. Although the collection closes with the resignation of Suharto in 1998, the writers represented here will, hopefully, continue to write in different and more complex ways during the new millennium.

Para pembakar

pembakar-pembakar berjalan dari kampung
menuju kota yang bersimbah luka
lalu membakar harta, membakar rumah-rumah
membakar angin dan jam

daun-daun putih
mencatat pohon-pohon, hujan mencatat
kota-kota
pengembara dalam kabut bangsa-bangsa
dari kampung pembakar-pembakar melempar batu
melempar api

pembakar-pembakar berjalan
menuju kota
berterompah sangsai
menuju arena lapar
membakar darah
membakar lukanya sendiri

Men on fire

Leaving their villages, men on fire
head for cities spattered with blood,
to destroy property, houses,
the wind and time

white leaves
written on the trees, rain
written across the cities,
men wandering in a haze of ideas,
hurling rocks from their villages,
hurling fire

men on fire walking
toward the cities
on battered clogs,
heading for the arena
where hungry men fight,
their blood burning
their wounds alight

Solo, 1980

Pencarian

> *. . . La chair est triste, hélas!*
> *et j'ai lu tous les livres.*
> —Stéphane Mallarmé—

Perjalanan begitu jauh matahari larut dalam mimpi
dan ganti suram
dalam hujan lautan dengan ombak panjang-panjang
menghibur angin yang mabok kepayang
kumakan langit dan bintang-bintang
kota tanpa lampu dan lolong serigala
dari gelap hutan
menyeringai cahaya malam
tetapi tak kutemukan di sana hanya ada pohonan
berwarna asing tempat berteduh segala ruh
kapal hitam kulayarkan dalam darah
tenggelamkan saja aku ke dasar duka resah
biar kutemu arti paling dalam
kuburan senyap tidur dan tak ada lagi cinta
tak ada lagi penghianatan
sebab tanah telah bilang pada tulang-belulang
tak ada lagi dunia dengan pemandangan lama
hanya di sana kanak-kanak buta
meraba-raba udara
pemburu! di mana pun burung tak ada

Search

<blockquote>

La chair est triste, hélas!
et j'ai lu tous les livres.[†]
—Mallarmé

</blockquote>

The journey was so long
    that the sun vanished into dreams
and became black
in the distant waves of ocean rain
which caressed the ecstatic wind.
I devoured the sky and the stars,
cities without lamps, wolves
howling in the forest
as they snarled at the moon,
and found nothing there
    but strangely colored trees
filled with spirits.
I sailed gray ships in my blood
and nervously scuttled them
    on the sea-beds of my own doubt,
searching for the true meaning
    of silently sleeping graves,
where there is no more love
and no more betrayal,
because the earth has told its bones
    there is no new world
    and nothing new to see,
only blind children
    grasping at the sky.
the hunter comes
    but the birds have flown away.

Solo, 1980

[†] "The flesh is sad, alas! and I have read all the books." From "Brise
Marine" (Sea Breeze). This text is available in *Stéphane Mallarmé*, ed.
Mary Ann Caws (New York: New Directions, 1982): 16–17.

Memasuki sunyi

memasuki sunyi, kulihat kota
terayun di udara
dan di pagi sedingin itu, kau menangis lagi
kabut belum luruh
air matamu jatuh

sebenarnya semua mudah saja terlempar jauh
atau hujan bisa saja turun
tanpa diawali dengan mendung tergantung
tapi kematian harus dibebankan
dan kata-kata harus berjalan
seperti sedia kala

matahari yang biru bergulat dengan dingin
dan sisa malam yang menyusut jadi batu
kau tetap, seperti menata nasibmu sendiri
yang berdiri sebagai pohon rapuh
di tepi kali

memasuki sunyi, semua jadi menggigil
pagi akan jadi lain
dan Tuhan begitu baik
tapi aku tak pernah tahu
segalanya memang berlaku

Entering the silence

entering the silence, I saw the city
suspended in the sky,
the fog clung to the earth,
it was cold
as you wept

it would have been easy to ignore you,
to forget the fog
and let the rain fall,
but death was present
and words were needed

the blue sun wrestled with the cold
as the last scraps of night turned to stone,
unmoving, you shaped your future,
like a broken tree
beside the river

entering the silence, the world shivered,
day would be different,
God would be good,
but I never understood
what really happened.

Solo, 1981

Aku ingin menjadi batu di dasar kali

Aku ingin menjadi batu di dasar kali
Bebas dari pukulan angin dan keruntuhan
Sementara biar orang-orang berhibuk diri
dalam desau rumput atau pohonan

Jangan aku memandang keluasan langit tiada tara
Seperti padang-padang tengadah
Atau gunung-gunung menjulang
Tapi aku ingin menjadi sekedar bagian
                                        dari kediaman

Aku sudah tak tahan lagi melihat burung-burung
                                        pindahan
Yang kaubunuh dengan keangkuhanmu–yang mati
                                        terkapar
Di sangkar-sangkar putih waktu
O, aku ingin jadi batu di dasar kali
Menanti datang saat abadi

Berpikir tentang maut

Hanya sebuah jendela, sewaktu selalu dipermainkan
                                        angin
Dan aku tak bisa lagi memberi warna gerimis
Srigala bersarang dalam darahku, di kepala ada sebuah
                                        kota
Yang hancur oleh tatapan mata bulan
Perempuan dan kanak-kanak berteriak di sepanjang
                                        jalan
Minta kesunyian dan air dari mimpiku yang mawar

I want to be a rock in the river

I want to be a rock in the river,
free from the beating of the wind, unchanging,
Let others do as they want
in the rustle of the wind, the blowing of the leaves

I do not want to stare at the sky,
like the endless open fields
and the soaring mountains,
I want to be a small part
of the silence

I hate to see birds shifting from tree to tree,
dying because of your cruelty, lying rigid
in the white cages of time,
I want to be a rock in the river
Waiting for eternity

Solo, 1981

Thinking about death

Only a window where the wind always plays,
and the mist has no meaning,
Wolves nestle in my blood, in my head
a city falls under the gaze of the moon,
women and children shout in the streets,
begging for water and silence from my rose-colored
dreams

Ini rumah penjara, kata matahari
Yang mulai membusuk di tengah-tengah onggokan
sampah
Lalu burung membuat hujan di sudut malam
Bulan tak lagi bergantung di langit pengembaraannya

Dan hanya sebuah jendela, waktu mencuat, nafas
memberat
dari penjuru tidur, tanah terpampang gambar-gambar
Antara ada dan tiada

Kupu-kupu kaca

Sehabis meninggalkan jejak kemarau lama
lalu kupu-kupu menjadi kaca
Aku makin mengerti keluh bumi ini
Malam menjadi jalan dan mencari pemilik diri

Juga terasa jiwa, memuat pedih lalu lenyap
Udara telah menutup semua peristiwa
dan suara ombak melimbur
Menggelepar di pinggir pagar yang merah terbakar

Setiap menyusup dalam bumi kelam
Tangan-tangan mayat menjulur ke bulan
Kota yang bangkit karena hujan
Menguber luas jaman.

The house is a prison, says the sun,
surrounded by rubbish, it stinks,
the birds brought rain to the corner of the night,
the moon no longer wanders across the sky

Only a window where time shivers, and breath hangs
                                                heavily
in a corner of sleep, where the earth stretches out in
                                            paintings,
life on one side, death on the other

                                    Solo, 1983

Glass butterflies

Having left heavy footprints
        in the long dry-season,
the butterflies become glass.
I begin to understand the earth's sigh,
Night turning into a path
        and searching for its owner.

Once the sky hid the past,
the soul filled with bitterness
        and vanished,
covering the world with the sound of waves
shattered by burning red fences.

Everything slides into the dark earth.
Bony hands reach out to the moon.
In the rain cities rise
determined to live
        for centuries.

                                    Solo, 1987

Rangkasbitung

O betapa ia gamang
kalimat batinnya sendiri
matahari tak garang lagi
Betapa ia tak sadari
musim berganti

Pagi melempit malam
embun di pelepah
daun luruh demi buah
kembang kelampis bertebaran

O baunya
angin mengirim wangi
jepit gading rambutnya

Siang dipacukan
malam ia sanding matahari
menyusur jalan berlubang
Percakapan halte bis kota
pisang panggang kaki lima

O banowati
bukan tak garang lagi
tapi matahari
padamu berbagi mati

Rangkasbitung[†]

See how my lord stands
nervously reciting his lines
in the late afternoon sun.
How little he realizes
that the seasons have changed.

Morning edges into night,
dew rests on the palms.
The leaves fall as the fruit
blooms, shrivels, then drops.

The wind bears the fragrance
of his long ivory curls.

He is busy all day.
At night he joins the sun
as it slowly moves along the pot-holed roads,
chatting with strangers
and eating fried bananas.

Oh Banowati,[‡]
it is not that you are feeble,
but simply that the fading sun
can no longer give you life.

Jakarta
November 1986

[†] The village of Rangkasbitung provided the setting for the famous nineteenth century Dutch novel *Max Havelaar* by Multatuli. Rendra's volume *Orang-orang Rangkasbitung* (1993) identified himself and his contemporary society with this suffering but idealized rural Javanese community.

[‡] In wayang shadow theater, Banowati is the daughter of Prabu Salya, the king of Mandraka, and marries the oldest Kaurawa brother, Duryodana. She is an ambiguous figure, in that she helps the Pandawa side at the cost of betraying her lawful husband. See B. R. O'G. Anderson, *Mythology and the Tolerance of the Javanese,* Modern Indonesia Project, Monograph Series (Ithaca, N.Y.: Cornell University, 1965): 36, 51.

Ruang, satu

Kita telah bertukar kunci
dan sama-sama menghilangkannya
Aku tersekap di kamarmu
kamu tersekap di kamarku

Kapan ketemu?

Ruang, dua

Ir, kepadamu aku pernah bicara
dan kepadaku kamu berkata pula
Kenapa kita baru saling dengar
justru setelah masing-masing di luar pagar?

Akankah kita tetap berkeras hati berlari
cuma karena sebelumnya saling tak mengerti,
atau mungkinkah berbincang lagi
menepiskan keakuan
menuruti gerak nurani,
dengan mendobrak pintu gapura
yang sesungguhnya tak pernah ada?

Rooms, one

We gave each other our keys
and then lost them
I am locked in your room
you are locked in mine

How can we ever meet again?

Depok,
July 1987

Rooms, two

Ira, I talked all the time
and so did you,
why is it only now
    we hear each other's voices
from beyond our different fences?

Shall we harden our hearts
    and continue to run from each other,
because once we did not understand each other,
or can we speak again,
forget our pride and
follow our true feelings,
can we break down the doors
which were never there?

Depok,
June 1987

Engkau angin

Semula aku sangka kau gelombang
tapi setiap kali aku renangi
engkau menggasing bagai angin
Peluh membuncah dan ruh dan tubuh gelisah
adalah ibadah bagi Cinta tak berjamah
Di situ, kunikmatkan teduhmu
sesekali sebelum kau berhembus pergi

Aku buru suara seruling di jauhan
yang kutemu dedahan bergesekan
Aku termangu tertipu gerakmu
sehening batu di kedalaman rinduku

Kini aku tahu, tak perlu memburumu
Engkau hidup di dalam dan di luar diriku
— tak berjarak namun teramat jauh
teramat dekat namun tak tersentuh

Jika benar engkaulah angin itu
semauku akan kuhirup kamu
Dalam jantung yang berdegup
engkau gairah baru bagi hidup
Mengalirlah darah, mengalir
dalam urat nadi Cintaku
karenamu, Kekasihku!

You are the wind

At first I thought you were the waves
but each time I swam in you
you whirled me about like the wind.
My body sweated, my soul shook,
in my chaste devotion to Love.
There, I enjoyed your calm
before you spun away again.

I sought the distant sound of the flute
and found the rustling of leaves
I was restless, deceived by your movements,
as silent as a rock, as deep as desire.

Now I know, I need seek you no more.
You live in me, and around me,
close to me and far away,
so near I cannot touch you.

If you are the wind
I want to breathe you, always.
You are the passion
which makes my heart beat.
Love flows in my blood, in my veins,
because of you, my Beloved.

Jakarta,
July 1991

Osmosa asal mula

> Aku bertanya kepada angin,
dari mana asalnya angan
> > angin menggoyangkan pucuk-pucuk daun
dan kusaksikan pohon-pohon melukis lingkaran tahun

> Aku bertanya kepada pohon,
dari mana datangnya waktu,
> > pohon merekahkan kelopak bunga
dan kusaksikan lebah hinggap menghisap madu

> Aku bertanya kepada lebah,
dari apa sel yang tumbuh jadi tubuhku,
> > lebah menggumam terbang ke dalam gua
dan kusaksikan kelelawar menangkup kuping di
> > > dinding batu

> Aku bertanya kepada kelelawar,
dari mana awalnya suara,
> > kelelawar mengepak sayap ke langit malam
dan kusaksikan embun bergulir serupa sungai

> Aku bertanya kepada sungai,
dari mana sumber air susu,
> > sungai menjulangkan gunung
dan kusaksikan lembah bergaun kabut

> Aku bertanya kepada lembah,
dari mana mulanya tabu,
> > lembah menyingkap gaun
dan kusaksikan bumi bugil menggeliat anggun

In the beginning was osmosis

I asked the wind
where dreams come from,
the wind shook the leaves
and I saw the trees paint the passing of the years.

I asked the trees
where time came from,
buds opened on the trees
and I saw the bees sipping honey.

I asked the bees
which cell created my body,
the bees hummed as they flew into a cave
and I saw bats hanging up-side-down,
their wings around their ears.

I asked the bats
where sound came from,
the bats flapped their wings against the night sky
and I saw dew flowing down like a river.

I asked the river
where milk came from,
the river rose like a mountain
and I saw a valley wrapped in mist.

I asked the valley
where prohibitions came from,
the valley lifted its skirt
and I saw the naked earth proudly stretching its body.

Aku bertanya kepada bumi,
siapa yang melahirkan Ibu,
    bumi tersipu, tapi kudengar laut menyahut,
"Ia bersaksi atas fakta, namun tak berdaya untuk
                                        bicara!"

    Aku bertanya kepada laut,
siapa yang menampungnya,
    laut menggelora, tapi kerontang
sebelum usai membilang Nama

Obituari bulan

    Anakku tidur menduga-duga bulan,
dan di kelas matanya masih menyimpan malam
    ketika ibu guru mengajari matahari
Anakku lalu menggambar cakrawala, lautan,
    perahu layar tanpa nakoda, dan
rok ibu guru dipermainkan ombak pasang,
    ibu gurunya dimakan ikan

    Di tempat tidur anakku menangis
airmatanya tetes ke buku tulis
    yang penuh coretan merah, jingga, kuning,
hijau, biru, nila, ungu

                    I asked the earth
who gave birth to my Mother,
                        the earth turned away
but I heard the ocean say:
        "Although she sees everything,
                she cannot speak."

                    I asked the ocean
who set her boundaries,
                the ocean howled,
                            seethed
and finally said
            The Name.

                    Solo, March 10, 1995

An obituary for the moon

    My child fell asleep, dreaming of the moon,
and at school the next day her eyes were filled with the night,
    as her teacher talked about the sun.
So she drew a picture of the sky, the ocean,
    a boat with no captain, and
waves playing with the teacher's dress,
    while a fish ate her.

    That night, my child cried in her bed,
and her tears smudged the scribbles in her exercise book:
    red, orange, yellow, green,

Ia bilang itu kolam,
ia ingin menolong ibu guru
        Lantas ia gambar seorang bocah memancing
sambil memandang bulan di atas kolam itu
        Dan sesudahnya, ikan di bait pertama
menjadi santapan anjing ibu guru

        Anakku kembali tidur
sembari menduga-duga bulan berpendar
        di dalam matanya yang menyimpan malam
tetapi anjing itu melolong panjang minta ikan
        Anakku segera menggambar ikan
di dalam matanya yang menyimpan lautan
tetapi ikan itu tersedu minta ibu guru
Anakku lekas menggambar ibu guru
        di dalam matanya yang menyimpan sekolah
tetapi ibu guru kembali mengajari matahari
        Anakku mengulang gambar cakrawala, lautan,
perahu layar tanpa nakoda . . .
        di dalam matanya yang menyimpan dunia
tetapi ibu guru tidak suka
        dan memberinya angka lima

        Hari-hari berikutnya,
anakku tak berani menggambar lagi
        kecuali mengenang bocah di bait kedua
yang kesepian kehilangan bulan di atas kolam

blue, indigo and purple.
She said it was a lake
          and she wanted to help her teacher.
So she drew a picture of a child fishing,
          staring at the moon,
                    and she fed the fish in the first stanza
                              to the teacher's dog.

          My child fell asleep again,
dreaming of the phosphorescent moon,
          her eyes filled with the night,
but the dog barked out loud, wanting more fish.
          My child drew a picture of a fish,
her eyes were filled with the sea,
          but the fish cried out, wanting the teacher.
My child drew a picture of the teacher,
          whose eyes were filled with the school,
as she talked about the sun.
          So my child drew another picture
of the sky, the ocean,
                    a boat with no captain . . .
          her eyes were filled with the world,
but the teacher didn't like her picture
          and gave her five out of ten.

          After that
my child was too frightened to draw
          anything, except for the child in the second stanza,
who felt very lonely, because the moon no longer shone
                    on her lake.
                              Cipayung Jaya, 1991

Lagu yang diulangulang

akupungut setangkaibunga yang engkaulemparkan
di kotaksampah itu. masih tercium wanginya
: menyegarkan mimpi dan terjagaku.

lalu akukemas dalam vas hitam, seluruh lukamu.

biarlah ia sendirian di sudut kamar. akan
senantiasa setia dengan warnamerah dan putihnya.
—bernama mawar dan melati. bernama cinta dan
                                    sangsi.

tapi wanginya takkan lepas dari bingkai hati.

akupungut setangkaibunga yang engkaulemparkan
di kotaksampah itu. masih tercium wanginya.
masih tertinggal tunasnya. kelak dalam hatiku
: bakal kusihir jadi taman.

Aku mengandung puisi yang tak jadi

aku menciptakan surga kecil pada rahimku.
penghuninya: sebuah puisi tanpa judul tanpa
rima dan irama. tapi ia mengalun disiulkan
anakanak bermain yang menunggu dengan rindu
malaikat kecilnya.

Endless songs

Ipickedup theflower youthrew
onto the rubbish, its fragrance
sweetened my dreams and waking hours

then Iput it into a black vase
shaped like your wound

and left it alone in a corner of the bedroom
to remind me of the colors redandwhite,
roses and jasmines, love
and betrayal

their fragrance never left me

Ipickedup theflower youthrew
onto the rubbish, its fragrance
scattered seeds in my heart.
I will bewitch the buds
and grow me a garden

1987

I am pregnant with an unborn poem

I created a small heaven in my womb.
its inhabitant was an untitled poem,
with no rhythm or rhyme. it rocked back and forth
as the children sang to it, waiting
for their tiny angel.

anakanak menyenandungkannya, sebab
hurufhuruf hanya lambanglambang yang tak
tereja. telah bertahuntahun kita menciptakannya.
hayatilah perjalanan panjang itu. tanpa menunggu
ia bersenandung sendiri, ketika anakanak letih
mengenangkannya.

Nikah pisau

aku sampai entah di mana. berputarputar
dalam labirin. perjalanan terpanjang
tanpapeta. dan inilah warna gelap paling
sempurna. kuraba gang di antara sungai
dan jurang.

ada jerit, serupa nyanyi. mungkin dari
mulutku sendiri. kudengar erangan, serupa
senandung. mungkin dari mulutku sendiri.

tapi inilah daratan dengan keasingan paling
sempurna: tubuhmu yang bertaburan ulatulat,
kuabaikan. sampai kurampungkan kenikmatan
sanggama. sebelum merampungkanmu juga: menikam
jantung dan merobek zakarmu, dalam segala
ngilu.

they hummed, the letters
were only symbols for words
no one could spell. we wove it for years,
gave life to its long journey. soon
it hummed to itself, when the others
were too tired to remember it
anymore.

1991

Married to a knife

I have arrived somewhere, spinning
in a labyrinth, it was a long journey,
without a map. and the darkness
is perfect. I followed a lane
between a river and a chasm.

there was a scream. it sounded like a song.
perhaps it come from my mouth. there was a moan,
like a lullaby. perhaps it came from my mouth.

but I have landed in a place
of perfect alienation: your body is covered with maggots
which I ignore. until I find complete
sexual satisfaction. then I finish you too,
I stab you in the heart and
tear off your prick
in my pain.

1992

Nikah ilalang

engkau nikahi ilalang. berumah di negeri
semaksemak. diamlah dalam kemerisik angin
yang mengecoh cakrawala.

tapi orangorang lalu melayat padamu. terasa
kelam perkawinan dan pesta syahwat. engkau
butuhkan bungabunga ditaburkan. doadoa
penghabisan, dan ziarah bertubitubi.

engkau nikahi ilalang. luas kebun luas bumi
luas langit luas jagat batinmu. engkau
nikahi kesunyian yang ditinggalkan abadabad
nanti. berkumur cabikan tanah kering dan
pestisida. berkumur jagat hewankecil yang
mencari rumahrumah dalam tangis dan sekarat.

Nikah sungai

engkaubawakan aku bungabunga. di sini pasir,
semak dan lumut melulu. kadang bauan busuk
dan bahkan bangkaibangkai. kepiting tak
menyisih menyambutku.

di mana ruang yang kausediakan buatku?
buat percintaan mahadahsyat. buat pertempuran
takusaiusai. nafsu yang senantiasa membuahkan
kebencian dan bencana.

aku rebah di tanah basah. mengandung
racun dan beranak peradaban kering nurani.

Married to the grass

you were wed to the grass. your home
was a land of weeds. you lived in the rustling wind
and told lies to the heavens.

people sympathized with you. they knew
it was a dark wedding and a celebration
based on sex. you needed them to scatter flowers for you,
to pray, and sit by your grave.

you were wed to the grass. the garden was vast,
so was the earth, the sky, and the world
of your soul. you were married to the loneliness
left by future generations. you ate the earth,
toxic sprays, a world of small animals
seeking shelter among tears and death.

1992

Married to a river

you brought me flowers. here,
where there is only sand, weeds and mud. sometimes,
a foul smell. sometimes, rotting corpses. the crabs
take no notice of my coming.

where is the room you promised me?
our bridal chamber, ready
for unending battle, for desire
which flowers in hatred and confusion.

I fall onto the wet earth, pregnant
with poison, and give birth
to a sterile civilization with no morality.

1992

Nol

tanpa tepitepi, ranjangkita dirangkul
malaikatentahapa. tanpa cahaya, ruangtidurkita
bagai petimati. tanpa langitlangit, rumahkita
bagaikubur.

apakah yang ingin kaucipta dengan tanahliat itu?
atap yang tak tembus langit. atau dindingdinding
tak berjendela.

kaupilih lantai. diam, dan kautolok keterancaman.
inilah hidup yang takkuharapkan.

Skenario drama percintaan

anakkumuntah ketika televisi memainkan
lagu-lagucinta.

dan inilah adegan yang harus dimainkan
: bunga, perempuan, pisau, darah, dan lakilaki. birahi
hanyalah serentet narasi yang tak rampungrampung
dibacakan. kalimatkalimat bagai rumput liar yang terus
berbiak. mereka melukiskan fatamorgana.

dan inilah adegan yang harus dimainkan: cacingcacing-
tanah yang berbiak. kuman-kuman bergerombol dalam
hatimu. dan tanganmu yang mengayunkan pisau.
sebuah jeritan, diteriakkan tanpa penghayatan.

anakku. . . .

Nothing

unending, ourbed is surrounded
bysomesortofangels. unlit, our bed
is like a coffin. uncovered, our house
is like a grave.

what do you hope to create from this clay?
there is no sky. there are no windows
in the walls.

you prefer the floor. it is quiet, safe.
I never thought
      I could live this way.

1992

Video script for a love song

my children vomit
when they hear love songs on TV

the story is always the same:
flowers, a woman, a knife, blood, and a man. desire
forms endless unfinished stories
for them to read. the sentences flourish
like weeds. they paint an illusion.

the story is always the same: a mass
of worms, disease
spreading through your heart, a knife
in your hand, a scream which means
nothing to anyone at all.

my children . . .

1992

Metamorfose kekosongan

seperti inilah, aku letakkan ranjang dalam dadamu.
kujadikan ronggarongga sempit itu kamarcintaku.
suatu hari nanti, akan berjejal lagulagu dan tangisan.
rintihan kecil dan jeritan tibatiba. dan kaukirim aku
ke tanahasing: dengan dentum dan suaraangin dari
nafasmu.

seperti inilah, aku letakkan tempatsampah dalam
otakmu. kujadikan gumpalan zat itu suduttakberguna.
suatu hari nanti, akan berjejal entahapa. telah sesak
ruang sempit itu oleh rencanarencana dan bencana.

tadi, kita telah berkhianat dengan cinta. kauledakkan
aku dengan zakarmu. kuletakkan ulatulat di sana.
sampai saatnya nanti, siap memangkas daunhatimu.

seperti inilah kita: merenda kemungkinankemungkinan.
suatu hari nanti—dalam otakmu, dalam dadamu, dalam
perutmu—kutanami bangkaibangkaiulat. suatu hari nanti,
akan kupanen kupukupu.

Transforming emptiness

this is how it was: I made my bed
in your chest, and turned that tiny space
into a bridal chamber. in time it filled
with songs and tears, small sighs
and sudden screams. you sent me away
to an unknown land, with your explosions
and the breeze of your breath.

this is how it is: I fill your brain
with rubbish. I render your atoms
useless. one day, I will fill your mind
with something, if I can find a space
among your plans and wicked schemes.

a moment ago, we used our love
to betray each other. you blew me up
with your prick, I placed caterpillars
there, and waited for them
to chew on your heart.

this is how it will be: I shall weave
various possibilities—in your brain,
your chest, your belly—and plant my cocoons,
one day I shall harvest butterflies.

1993

Pengantin yang terbaring

kaubaringkan diriku di atas tanah. betapa
fana gairah yang meletupkan kebencian. dan
aku mabuk bercumbu dengan pikiran sendiri.

seperti inikah kenikmatan sanggama?
kita tebar ribuan benih yang menjamurkan
kebencian dan kecewa. gemeretak bunyi tulang
yang membajak tanah kering dan batu bebukitan.
kecipakair dalam sungai tanpa arus. tak
ke manamana.

seperti inikah? kaubaringkan diriku di atas
tanah. dan nafasku menyebarkan aroma yang
dihirup para serangga. dan mengembunkan uap
yang menyejuki cacingcacingtanah dan ulatulat.

The reclining bride

you lay me on the ground. brief passion
exploded into hatred. I was drunk,
intoxicated by my own thoughts.

is this the pleasure of sex?
we scatter a thousand seeds
and they mushroom into anger
and disappointment, the grinding bones
fertilize dry ground and stony mountains,
a splash in a blind river, going
nowhere.

is this how it was? you lay me
on the ground. insects sucked
on my fragrant breath, while
maggots and worms
bathed in the moist air.

1993

Post scriptum

Ingin aku tulis
sajak porno sehingga
kata mentah tidak diubah
jadi indah, pokoknya
tidak perlu kiasan lagi
misalnya payudara jadi bukit,
tubuh wanita = alam hangat
senggama = pelukan yang paling akrab

yang sudah jelas
tulis sajak itu
antara menyingkap dan sembunyi
antara munafik dan jatidiri

Postscript

I want to write
pornographic poems
in which the words are raw
not made beautiful, without
those metaphors in which
breasts become hills
a woman's body = a warm world
fucking = an intimate embrace

obviously
to do so
I would have to reveal myself
    and hide
tell lies
    and the truth

*1995

Di negeri ajaib

"Ini malam ke empat puluh empat," kabarmu pada vas
bunga, tempat lilin dan asbak porselin. Miniatur kapal
selam melaju cepat dalam dadamu: Kau bertemu Verne
di situ. "Di mana Alice?" tanyamu. "Ia raib dari
Wonderland," jawab sebuah suara. Barangkali Peter Pan
atau Paman Sam. Tergesa-gesa kau keluar dari dalam
lubang kelinci ajaib dan menemukan landscape asing
yang lain

dalam dadamu. "Ini malam keempat puluh empat,"
gumammu, pada tiang listrik, kedai jamu, bulan mati
dan papan papan reklame. "Tetapi apa peduli kalian. Aku
mencari Alice. Alice!" Terburu-buru kau tutup semua
pintu, jendela dan seluruh tirai kamarmu. "She's escape
from Wonderland," bisik sebuah suara. Barangkali
Tinker Bell, atau Peter, atau Sam. . . .

In Wonderland

"This is the forty-fourth night," you told the vase, the candlestick holder and the porcelain ashtray. A miniature submarine sails into your chest, under the command of Jules Verne. "Where is Alice?" you ask. "She has vanished from Wonderland," a voice replies. It might be Peter Pan or Uncle Sam. Quickly you scurry from the magic rabbit hole and discover another strange landscape

in your own heart. "This is the forty-fourth night," you mumble to the electric light posts, the herbal medicine shops, the dead moon, and the billboards. "But you don't care. I must find Alice! Alice!" You rush to shut the doors and windows in your room. As you draw the curtains a voice whispers, "She has escaped from Wonderland." It might be Tinker Bell, or Peter Pan, Uncle Sam . . .

1993

The wedding song

Apa yang tersisa dari sepi selain separuh
kenangan? Malam, tak seperti biasanya, gaduh
dan kasmaran. Inikah malam pengantin itu,
id? Ketika separuh yang lain dari sepi diam-diam
disembunyikan tuter mobil di kejauhan, suara lembut
tirai yang melambai-lambai dan isak tangismu
yang kau simpan jauh

dalam batinmu. Pagi, kau seduh teh kental
manis dengan senyummu yang lembut. Secarik
pesan yang biasa bagi sebuah kehidupan
yang lain: Dunia bukan Antah Berantah. Tanpa peri,
cangkir-cangkir aneh yang pandai menari,

segala yang ajaib dan mimpi.

Empat mil dari kenangan

Sepasang angsa di sudut taman pom bensin: Kusaksikan
keajaiban dongeng dan biografi bersatu di situ. Seperti
Wilde yang murung di depan sajak Ginsberg dan
Rendra. Kota-kota tanpa patung "Happy Prince"
menyimpan dendam dan keinginan diam-diam pada
kematian. Bagai puisi Malna dalam saku celana

kekuasaan. O, ke mana orang-orang pergi begitu
bergegas pada dini hari yang riuh ini? Di luar jendela

The wedding song

What remains of loneliness but a few slices
of memory? It was different last night, you
fought and made love. Was it your wedding night,
Ida? When half of your loneliness
was hidden by distant car-horns, the soft
flapping of the curtain, and the tears
held deep within yourself?

In the morning, you drank sweet black
tea and smiled. A simple lesson
for a different life: This is not Never-Never Land.
There are no fairies, teacups cannot dance,

the world is strange, like a dream.

1993

Four miles from memory

Two geese in a garden near a diesel engine: I see strange
myths and biography unite as Oscar Wilde sits sadly
reading the poems of Rendra and Ginsberg. Cities have
no statues The Happy Prince is angry and wants to be left
to die alone, with Malna's[†] poetry in his pocket

to give him courage. It is dawn, why is everyone in such
a hurry? Outside a window,

---

† Oscar Wilde (1854–1900): Irish playwright, novelist, essayist, poet and
wit. Sutardji Calzoum Bachri, the author of the poem "Kucing/ Cat,"
and Afrizal Malna are both Indonesian poets (see elsewhere in this
volume). Sa'di (1184–1292): the greatest didactic poet of Persia.

para penyair, borgol dan selongsong peluru mengubah
dirinya menjadi bahasa. Sayangku, di sebuah tempat
dalam kenangan, Sa'di kehilangan lentera, Tardji
kehilangan ngiau, aku kehilangan

engkau.

Pada wajah daun-daun

- ziata

Pada wajah daun-daun senja yang lembab itu, kulihat
engkau sendiri menari. Lambaian demi lambaian
telapak tanganmu menciptakan pusaran angin,
menjelma badai dalam batinku. Di negeri tak lagi
bernama itu, malam menggigil dalam pelukanmu. "Ah,
seperti liebestraum," gumammu pada angin sambil
menyebut sebuah nama. Barangkali Liszt, Anne Frank,
Alice, atau sekeping bunyi muntahan mortir

pecah pada dini hari berkabut negeri porak-poranda itu.
"Di sini cinta," katamu di masa lalu, "kekal pada
kesunyian kayu salib dan bulan sabit." Namun pada
senja yang lembab itu, kulihat engkau pada wajah daun-
daun. Sendiri menari. Riang dan kekanak-kanakan;
seperti sejarah negeriku. Kerlingan demi kerlingan bola
matamu menciptakan pusaran

sepi, menjelma duka dalam batinku.

poets, wearing handcuffs and bullet-belts,
turn themselves into words. My darling, somewhere
in my memory, Sa'di loses his lamp, Tardji
loses his meow, I lose

you.

1994

The face of the leaves

For Ziata

One damp twilight, I saw you dancing alone
across the face of the leaves. You waved your hands
creating a whirlwind, a storm
in my soul. In an unnamed country
night shivered in your arms. "Ah, liebestraum,"
you whispered to the wind, calling
someone's name. Liszt, maybe, Anne Frank,
Alice, or perhaps it was a distant fragment of cannonfire

exploding at dawn in some far chaotic
land. "Here," you once said, "love lives
between the silence of the cross and
the sickle moon." But one damp twilight I saw you
on the face of the leaves. Dancing alone. Happy,
like a child, like my new nation. The movement
of your eyes created whirlpools

filled with silence, created sorrow
in my soul.

1994–95

Chanel oo

Permisi,
saya sedang bunuh diri sebentar.
Bunga dan bensin di halaman.

Teruslah mengaji,
dalam televisi berwarna itu,
dada.

Pohon pisang di pinggir kali

Sekali engkau datang di luar keramaian benda-benda,
dan menulismu, seperti mengubah setiap yang bergerak
jadi kematian. Waktu menyimpan engkau di situ, tak
berpikir lagi tentang hari-hari datang dan pergi.

Seseorang terus menulis di situ, seperti pohon pisang di
pinggir kali, menyaksikan air mengalir tak sama dari
hari ke hari. Setiap melangkah, dunia di belakangnya
berubah jadi jurang yang memelukmu. Ia datang
padamu seperti gagasan, bahwa semua akan mati.

Sekali engkau datang di luar keramaian benda-benda,
kakimu kisah-kisah semata, yang menulis setiap sisi
gelap, dari yang terdiam tak terucapkan. Lalu jurang
menganga lagi di belakangnya, menulismu, seperti
tahu, semua yang harus pergi menyudahi kata.

Channel oo

Excuse me I'm busy
killing myself
The flowers are in the yard,
    so is the petrol

Let the holy man
keep praying
on coloured television,
Ta-ta.

1983

A banana tree beside a river

Once you came outside the noise of material objects,
and wrote yourself, saying that every living thing was
dying. Time held you there, never thinking of the way
the days came and went.

Alone someone kept writing there, like a banana tree
beside a river, watching the water flow differently every
day. With each step, the world behind him became a
ravine reaching out to embrace you. It came to you as
the realization that death is inevitable.

Once you came outside the noise of material objects,
your feet trailing dishonest stories, written on all sides
of the darkness, in words which were never spoken.
Then the ravine opened behind him, you wrote, as
though you knew, that everything must go and that
there would be nothing more to say.

1988

Telah aku kirim kamar mandi untuk membangunkannya. Seperti membangunkan tubuhmu, 10 menit dari kedengkian yang lalu. Aku pernah bersamamu di situ, dan berpisah lalu, lewat jatuhnya segumpal tanah: Aku telah terhina jadi dirimu, tumbuh di setiap jemari tangan . . . Semua telah jatuh dari tubuhmu. "Aku tunggu, Adam, warna-warna kesedihanmu pada setiap ilmu."

Di jalan, malam hari, ketika setiap orang menyimpan tangannya dalam saku celana, diam-diam aku keluar. Jangan lagi bicara malam bersama mantel, lampu senter, dan pisau lipat dalam saku. Aku telah terhina jadi dirimu. Seluruh ketakutan telah mencium kakiku, malam itu, seperti pada gagasan kelahiran Adam pertama kali.

Tetapi jemari kakiku seketika gemetaran, aku temukan diriku bercucuran di setiap pengeras suara. Ada yang ingin mendapatkan wahyu lain di situ, dari kamar mandi yang lain lagi, bahwa kematian telah menghina pikiranku.

Semua telah jatuh dari tubuhmu.

Tetapi suatu hari, di mimbar yang mengantarmu pergi, jalan-jalan penuh mobil terbakar, asap hitam mengepul di setiap gedung, pecahan-pecahan kaca etalase beterbangan mengubah kota, Adam merebut mikropon dalam sebuah khotbah. Beribu tangan meraihnya. Ia dilarikan, dengan masa silam berjatuhan dari tubuhnya.

**For 100 years Adam, searching for Eve,
tried to convince himself that he was human**

I sent a bathroom to complete the house. Just as I shaped
your body ten minutes ago from rage and frustration. I
was with you there, and separated from you, in a falling
clod of earth. I was insulted to be you, to grow in your
hands . . . Everything dropped from your body. "I will
wait, Adam, the colors of sorrow in all that I learn."

On the road, at night, while everyone stood around with
their hands in their pockets, I quietly left. No more night
conversations with coats, torchlights, a penknife in your
pocket. I was insulted to be you. Fear kissed my feet that
night as I realized that the first Adam had been born.

But my feet quivered and I perspired each time I passed
a loud-speaker. Some sought other forms of inspiration,
from other bathrooms, telling me that death was an
insult to my mind.

Everything dropped from your body.

But one day, at the pulpit which went with you, the
roads were full of burning cars, black smoke rose from
each building, broken shop windows exploded
creating new cities, Adam grabbed the microphone
before the preacher could finish. A thousand hands
reached out. They ran away with him, the past
dropping from his body.

Aih, Adam, di malam-malam tanpa mikropon, orang-
orang mencari sesuatu, sebuah pikiran di antara pisau
lipat, tempat orang-orang akhirnya berkata: keabadian,
keabadian telah menghina kematianku.

Cucian kotor suatu pagi

Hidup mungkin bisa berubah—kata orang. Rupanya
ada asbak jatuh dari meja, abu dan puntung rokok
terserak: Aku jatuh cinta pada seorang lelaki.
Hidungnya berair, suaranya melengking seperti asbak
pecah, 5 minit yang lalu. Tetapi ia sering mengejekku
dalam bahasa Inggeris. Tahu, aku tak bisa bertengkar
dalam bahasa itu, setelah penjajahan yang lalu: Negeri-
negeri dunia ketiga yang tak bisa menjual jagung. Hari
berlalu, asbak yang lain jatuh, juga tak mudah
membuat persahabatan. Kedengkian jadi tak terduga,
menyuruh orang berhenti di sebuah tikungan,
menjelang jam 7 malam. Ada tetangga di situ,
menunggu nasib di depan pintu, seperti seorang nyonya
menyimpan diri, dalam 130 kilo berat badannya.

Suatu pagi—hidup mungkin bisa berubah, seperti
seseorang yang menyentuh tubuhnya dalam genangan
sabun: "Tak ada lagi *kata* yang bisa dihayati, di sebuah
tempat, tanpa melihat jam dinding." Kota memang
telah meninggalkannya, jam 6 pagi yang lalu. Cucian
kotor menumpuk di situ. Lalu setiap benda yang
disentuh terasa bersabun, seperti hidung lelaki itu.

Suatu pagi, cucian kotor menghias koran-koran, berita-
berita nasional, surat pembaca, busa sabun yang
berjatuhan dari tangan. Dan sebuah puisi, yang dibaca
orang lewat kecemasan.

Alas, oh Adam, night after night without a microphone,
people search for something, a thought caught between
the blades of a pocketknife, somewhere they finally say:
eternity, eternity is an insult to my death.

1989

One day's dirty washing

Things can always change, they say. Just as an ashtray
can fall from a table, scattering ash and cigarette butts.
I fell in love with a man. He had a runny nose and a
high-pitched voice that sounded like a breaking ashtray,
5 minutes ago. But he used to ridicule me in English. Do
you know, I've never been able to argue in that
language, it's because of the empire: Third world
nations can't sell corn. The days passed, other ashtrays
fell, it isn't easy to make new friends. Intense hatred
made one pause at the corner, about 7 o'clock at night.
A neighbour was there, waiting outside his front door
to see what might come along, like a married woman
weighing 130 kilos keeping to herself.

One day, things can always change, as someone said
washing his body with soap: "You can't say *anything*
anymore, no matter where you are, without looking at
the clock." It was true, the city had abandoned him at 6
o'clock in the morning. There were dirty clothes
everywhere. Everything one touched felt as though it
had soap bubbles on it, just like the man's nose

One day, the newspapers, magazines and letters to the
editor were covered with dirty clothes, and soap bubbles
falling from his hand. And a poem, which people could
read nervously as they hurried past.

1995

Chapter 8

THE END OF THE NEW ORDER

The Achievements of a Quarter-Century

THERE CAN BE NO doubt that Indonesia changed enormously over the first quarter-century of the New Order, amply fulfilling, so it seemed, the goals of economic development and political stability which it set for itself. The Indonesia of the mid-1990s was "virtually unrecognizable" from that of the mid-sixties.[1]

At the beginning of the New Order, the nation had been deeply divided. The outer islands had frequently rebelled against the control of Java. The sharp social and ideological divisions within Java had led to the horrendous massacres that followed the abortive Coup of 1965. The bureaucracy was so inefficient and corrupt that the central government was often unable to maintain even the most minimal standard of administrative services. The poor maintenance of the transport and communication systems further contributed to the danger of national disintegration.

The economy was in chaos, with inflation headed toward 1,000 percent per annum. Foreign exchange reserves were exhausted, and per capita income was about US $40.[2] The extensive droughts common in the early sixties led to widespread hunger. Educational standards were low. There had been little private investment since the 1930s and the process of industrialization had barely begun.

Hal Hill and Jamie Mackie frankly describe Indonesia's condition in 1965 as an economic "basket case."[3]

Indonesia's relations with its neighbors were tense and often violent. Indonesia had taken West New Guinea into its territory by force and still waged a war of *"konfrontasi"* with Malaysia. It had expressed strong antagonism toward the United States, moved to align itself with the People's Republic of China and the communist bloc, and angrily withdrawn from the United Nations. Sukarno's views of Indonesia and its place in the world were defined by complex ideological symbols, not by the rigorous analysis of the problems of daily existence.

Suharto provided Indonesia with a strong and integrated form of government, which was low key and pragmatic. It focused not on his charisma but on the twin goals of political stability and economic development. During the New Order, Indonesia became unambiguously more capitalist and more integrated into the international economy. Markets were allowed to operate comparatively freely, and generated the accumulation of private wealth on an ever-increasing scale. There was a steady economic growth of an average 6.8 percent per year for almost the entire period. Per capita income reached about $100 in 1970 and rose to about $1,000 in 1994.[4] Individual living standards improved dramatically. According to figures accepted by the World Bank, the proportion of the population living in poverty fell from sixty percent to about thirteen percent.[5] People were better fed, the average per capita calorie intake having risen by fifty percent,[6] and better clothed. The emerging middle class generated new patterns of mass consumption and thinking, and had created their own commercial culture based on extensive consumption of the mass media, especially television and popular magazines. Infant mortality was almost halved through the extensive introduction of a successful program of family planning.

Rice yields almost doubled on Java. Indonesia not only became self-sufficient in rice after 1985 but actually had a surplus which it exported. In 1991 for the first time the value of manufacturing output exceeded that of agriculture, indicating that the nation had crossed a key threshold on the path to industrialization and might soon graduate into the ranks of the newly industrializing countries. The labor force had diversified, becoming less Java-centric, less concentrated in primary industries, less rural, less masculine and, through the implementation of universal primary education, better educated. Improvements in transport and communications served to unify previously disparate and isolated regions. In November 1994, Australia's Minister for Foreign Affairs, Senator Gareth Evans, estimated that Indonesia could well be "the world's fifth-largest economy by the year 2020."[7]

Finally, Indonesia was again "deeply enmeshed" in global politics. It had mended its quarrel with Malaysia and contributed to regional stability through its major role in ASEAN. It had also rejoined the United Nations and, apart from some differences with that body over the status of East Timor after 1975, seemed to be acting as an exemplary world citizen.

The Price of Development

There were costs involved in these changes, many of which were due to the fact that the president had managed to position himself as the nexus of both state and economic power. He was allowed to operate the state as a self-perpetuating patronage system, rewarding those who supported him with major contracts, concessions, "extra-budgetary funds" and other economic resources.[8] In a system where the Armed Forces carried a "dual function," the president intervened heavily in military promotions and transfers, and this interference continued to have serious civil consequences. More and more, cabinet and senior government positions were filled by "sycophants and loyalists" who lacked significant personal support bases and had little credibility in the ruling elite. The avaricious financial interests of his family and some close business cronies were increasingly given free reign. Those who opposed the president's interests were heavily penalized. The regime was repressive and authoritarian. It had a poor record on civil rights as demonstrated by the restrictions it imposed on the freedom of association, the press, and free speech in general. To some observers, too, Indonesia was a more deferential, less egalitarian society than the Revolution and the early years of independence had promised.

The form of economic growth that had been encouraged rested on dangerous foundations. Protectionist measures were widespread. There were too many banks, badly monitored. Corruption was widespread. Much of foreign investment went into non-productive areas or projects that depended on continued import protection.[9] Legal support for business activities was highly defective.[10] Importantly, the benefits of growth were unevenly distributed. The apparent reduction in poverty was only possible because the official poverty line was set very low (and the situation was so bad in 1965 that any return to a normal condition would have marked a significant improvement). Although infant mortality had been reduced, the corresponding improvement in the quality of health and longer life expectancies meant that the population had still increased by about 75 percent, placing enormous pressure on resources and the employment market. The introduction of universal primary education had not improved the actual quality of education.[11] Unemployment and underemployment were rife, particularly among Indonesians aged between fifteen and twenty-four.[12]

As a consequence, there was, as Edward Aspinall, Herb Feith, and Gerry van Klinken have noted, a strong and increasing undercurrent of political and social unrest.[13] The terror which military violence could unleash upon unarmed civilians was made clear by the Dili massacre in East Timor during late 1991. After the second round of "openness" abruptly ended in 1994, political turbulence and uncertainty spread more widely throughout the country. In 1996, the PDI headquarters were subject to violent attack in order to replace Megawati Sukarnoputri with a leader more to Suharto's liking. Megawati had been properly elected as the chair of the opposition party PDI in 1993; the attack on the PDI headquarters on July 27, 1996, resulted in the most widespread street rioting seen in Jakarta under the New Order. In order to divert attention from this challenge, the rioting was blamed on an unofficial party, the Partai Rakyat Demokrasi (PRD, People's Democratic Party), that was then linked to the PKI. A number of young opponents of the regime received long jail sentences.[14]

Religious and ethnic conflict surfaced as anti-Chinese and anti-Christian riots erupted in Situbondo, East Java, and Tasikmalaya, West Java in late 1996.[15] In West Kalimantan, there were violent clashes between the indigenous Dayak people and Madurese transmigrants. The May 1997 general election campaign and later the presidential election were accompanied by further, unprecedented public violence against the blatantly engineered campaign in favor of Golkar and Suharto respectively. On May 14, 1997, over one million people were estimated to have protested in the streets of Jakarta.[16]

Economic Downturn

It may have been true that "[s]trong economic growth rates provided their own political legitimation" for the regime.[17] Despite a brief period of illness in December 1997, and his refusal to name a successor, Suharto was unanimously elected president by the MPR for a seventh term on March 10, 1998, together with his protégé, the unpopular and financially highly inept Professor B. J. Habibie, Minister for Research and Technology, as vice president.

So far, none of the violence had affected the economy. None had touched the position of the president, who again appeared to be in supreme control within two months after the parliamentary elections.[18] Suharto's position was safe until the trade-off on which the New Order rested—material well-being in exchange for political submission—was no longer possible.[19]

The first step in this destabilization occurred when the "economic miracle" turned into an "economic disaster."[20] The Asian financial crisis that began in Thailand in July 1997 spread to Korea, the Philippines, and Malaysia before hitting Indonesia particularly heavily during the second half of that year. There were a number of reasons for this. The impressive record of growth had been propped up by low-wage export manufacturing and the massive investment of foreign capital. Because the value of the rupiah had been closely tied to the American dollar, the exchange rate plummeted from about Rp 2,500 to the dollar to Rp 17,000 in January 1998 as capital began flowing out of Indonesia. Further, Indonesia's extensive foreign debt was based largely on short-term loans; this too rendered the situation extremely volatile. Finally, the domestic financial system was poorly managed and supervised, and there was little confidence in the banking system, especially once the Central Bank (BI) closed sixteen banks in November.[21]

Following the collapse of the rupiah, inflation rose by about 20 percent per month in early 1998.[22] Unemployment or under-employment spread to more than 40 percent of the population, as 5.4 million workers lost their jobs when their employers became technically bankrupt or were only able to function at a reduced ca-pacity.[23] Even companies working wholly within a domestic frame-work could not escape the soaring interest rates. Due to drought, there was no agricultural buffer that could support those hoping to return to the countryside from the cities; indeed, it forced many farmers into the city instead.[24] By the end of the year, almost eighty million Indonesians lived in poverty.[25]

The Indonesian government responded to the crisis by floating the currency, eventually calling on the IMF for assistance, closing some banks, and postponing some major projects. International markets, and the Indonesian political public, saw the crisis as insep-arable from the government's accumulating political problems. Despite agreements entered into half-heartedly with the IMF by the president, there were no signs that either political or economic reform was ever seriously contemplated.[26]

Political Collapse

The second step in the president's downfall depended on the fur-ther withdrawal of political support for him by the public and then, crucially, by the military and parliamentary elite on whom he most relied.

The beginning of this loss of confidence stemmed from Su-harto's announcement of his new cabinet. The cabinet's primary responsibility ought, surely, to have been dealing with the financial crisis. Instead, the cabinet contained no economic experts and no moderate reformers. Rather, it drew heavily on "a narrow palace coterie," especially business cronies and associates of the president's daughter Tutut, who, it seemed, was being groomed to follow her father into national leadership.[27] For many, the cabinet was the erratic decision of an old and sick man, blind to the moral corruption of his family, disdainful of his critics, and indifferent to the welfare of the nation.[28]

During the lead-up to the presidential election, a number of prominent mainstream figures had spoken out for the first time against Suharto, and against his choice of Habibie as vice president. The critics included Dr. Amien Rais,[29] the chairman of Muhammadiyah, and Professor Emil Salim, who had held economic posts in four previous cabinets. In the absence of legitimate formal institutions to express different opinions, including (but not necessarily) outright opposition, the largest and more consistent group calling for change, other than the crowds in the street, was once again university students. With the enormous spread of state, private, and Muslim tertiary education during the New Order, students had potential influence across the whole nation. Owing their origins to a broad social spectrum that now reached down into the lower working class and rural society, students were also in a position to be able to gather wide support for their cause.[30] With wide divisions developing within the army, particularly between General Wiranto, the Commander of the Armed Forces, and Suharto's son-in-law, Major General Prabowo Subianto, commander of the Army Strategic Reserve, they had the possibility of support by significant factions within the Armed Forces.[31]

Although locked inside their campuses, students protested first about the high prices of basic commodities, then about Suharto's forthcoming re-election, and finally, the need for extensive political and economic reforms.[32] The protests began between December 1997 and January 1998 in small regional universities in Lampung and Solo, then spread to other provincial cities.[33] In late February 1998, they were taken up at the University of Indonesia, before again spreading to other campuses in major cities such as Yogyakarta, Bandung, Ujung Pandang, Semarang, Solo, Medan, and Surabaya.[34] After the presidential election, students on dozens of campuses mourned the result, "mocking the pomp and ceremony with streams of toilet paper, and money stuck across their mouths."[35] The campus-based protests thereafter continued on an almost daily basis. In early May they began to approach their climax, after the removal of subsidies on petrol, kerosene, and electricity, in over-hasty compliance with IMF demands, had led to public rioting in Medan, North Sumatra.

The response of the Armed Forces toward the student movement was divided. Some leaders, including Wiranto, appeared to be tolerating, or even at times encouraging, dissent. Others, particularly Prabowo, were harsh. A number of radical student leaders simply "disappeared." The point of no return was passed on Tuesday, May 12, 1998, when four students from Trisakti University in West Jakarta were shot by soldiers while returning to their campus after an attempt to walk the five kilometers to the parliamentary building had been blocked. Their funerals the next day were followed by two days of extensive rioting, starting near the campus then spreading throughout the capital. The riots caused more than 250 million dollars damage to commercial centers, businesses, homes, and motor vehicles.[36] Some 1,188 persons died in the rioting, mainly looters trapped in burning supermarkets.[37] There was also extensive sexual violence against Chinese women.[38] The Jakarta riots were followed by further rioting in Palembang on May 13, and in Solo and surrounding areas on May 14–15.

Suharto attempted to contain the rioting by the announcement on May 18 of a different cabinet. He promised some reforms and even offered to hold new general elections. On the same day, students were allowed to enter the parliament building, and then to occupy it in increasingly large numbers.[39] Suharto's promises fell on deaf ears. No one was willing to stand with the discredited president. His closest allies had turned against him. Over the next few days, high-level military officers, academics, and members of parliament, including the speaker, former cabinet members, senior members of Golkar, and the military faction, all called on Suharto to resign. The choices appeared to be either that the president be encouraged to resign through constitutional means, or that the nation undergo further massive social unrest, with possible military reprisals and the emergence of a military dictatorship.

The final step took place when Amien Rais threatened to bring Jakarta to a standstill on May 20 by calling large numbers of people onto the streets in honor of National Awakening Day. Although he was dissuaded from doing so by a threatened re-enactment of the Tienanmin Square situation in Jakarta,[40] the city was totally paralyzed on that day.[41] In Yogyakarta, an estimated one million people did take to the streets.[42] In other cities too, such as Bandung, Semarang, Solo, Ujung Pandang, Samarinda, Lampung, Medan, and Padang, demonstrations against Suharto also occurred.[43] His various advisers continued to press Suharto to resign until late into the night, when it became clear that he had finally exhausted all his options.[44]

At 9:05 on the morning of Thursday, May 21, 1998, President Suharto quietly read out his resignation to a press conference held at the Merdeka Palace. He stated that his inability to form the reform committee and the development cabinet he had proposed would make it difficult for him to fulfill his further duties as president. He also expressed his thanks to those who had supported his leadership and asked forgiveness "if there were any mistakes and shortcomings."[45] Then Habibie was sworn in as president, as the constitution required, "for the remainder of the current presidential term." The New Order was over. Although students continued to occupy parliament for an extra two days, demanding that Habibie step down, an era of what was hopefully called "Reformation" had begun.[46]

Sastra Reformasi

Despite the dispersal of writing across the nation and into ephemeral forms of publication, *Horison* again asserted its literary dominance when it dedicated its June 1998 issue to *"Reformasi."* The issue carried two leading articles. The first, by Agus R. Sarjono, was entitled (in English), "No More Bloodshed Reformation." Sarjono began by recounting the message of the classic Chinese work, *The Three Kingdoms:* yesterday's heroes often become today's tyrants. He argued that the most important task for the reformation agenda was not a change of rulers but "the development of a just system, a just legal system, in which the king and the masses could stand as equals. A system which would give a high worth to every individual. A system which believed that one human being was worth more than a hundred skyscrapers and shopping complexes. A system which freed people from fear, which enabled them to be courageous, and gave them the right to hold different opinions." Sarjono called for openness in society, and for literature to be more open to the depiction of the whole of Indonesian society.[47]

The second was "Agenda Reformasi Seorang Penyair" (The Reformation Agenda of a Poet) by Rendra. Rendra called for a change of culture, away from a feudal-peasant-agrarian culture, toward a modern culture in which all citizens participated as equal creators of a new society, freed from competing power groups and the theft of human legal rights and possessions.[48]

Then followed forty poems on the current situation of Indonesian society. The poems were a mixture of old and new works. Some were by first-generation writers: Taufiq Ismail, Rendra, Hamid Jabbar, Ikranegara, Slamet Sukirnanto, the short story writer Danarto, Sutardji Cazoum Bachri, and even the novelist Mochtar Lubis. Others were by second-generation writers such as Ahmadun Yosi Herfanda, Agus Sarjono, Sitok Srengenge, Sono Farid Maulana, Iyut Fitra, and Sutan Iwan Soekri Munaf. The journalist Seno Gumira Ajidarma, author of a striking previous volume of short stories on the Dili massacre, also contributed a graphic account of the pillaging and violence which formed part of the riots in Jakarta after the Trisakti killings.[49]

I have selected three poems from *Horison* for this anthology. Two are by Taufiq Ismail. The first, "12 Mei, 1998" (May 12, 1998), was dedicated to the "four martyrs" of Trisakti University. Elang Mulya, aged 19, who had been shot through the chest by a sniper's bullet, died on the campus. Hery Hertanto, 21, shot in the back while washing tear gas from his face and hands with water from a plastic bottle, also died on the campus. Hendriawan (Sie) Lesmana, 20, was shot twice while running, once in the back and once in the right side of his neck; he bled to death while being driven to hospital. Hafidhin Royan, 21, was shot by a bullet through the head, just above his ear; he died in hospital.[50] The second poem dealt with one of the common themes of the *"reformasi"* cause: *"korupsi, kolusi dan nepotisme"* (known in short as "kkn," corruption, collusion, and nepotism).[51] Here, Taufiq was able to use humor to criticize modestly paid officials, who neverthless managed to live in luxury in the elite suburbs of Jakarta, travel overseas regularly, and educate their children in overseas universities.

The third poem is by Ikranegara. It is the only poem by him included in this volume and it consisted of only two words. The first word formed the title and was *"merdeka,"* the goal of the Indonesian Revolution, "freedom," "liberty," "independence." The second word contained the whole poem: *"belum."* The word is a negator; it indicates "no" in the sense of "no, not yet; one day, perhaps, anything is possible, but no, not yet." In reading the poem during the demonstrations, Ikranegara and the crowd would play with the title and single line, repeating them both at some length. In conventional political "dialogue," the crowd normally returned the cry *"Merdeka!"* when the politician delivered it to them during a speech. The use of the negator was, thus, extremely subversive. In as far as the poem was dated the evening before Suharto's resignation, anything was still possible.[52]

12 Mei, 1998

mengenang Elang Mulya, Hery Hertanto
Hendriawan Lesmana dan Hafidhin Royan

Empat syuhuda berangkat pada suatu malam, gerimis air
    mata tertahan di hari keesokan, telinga kami
    lekapkan ke tanah kuburan dan simaklah itu
    sedu-sedan,
Mereka anak muda pengembara tiada sendiri,
    mengukir reformasi karena jemu deformasi,
    dengarkan saban hari langkah sahabat-
    sahabatmu beribu menderu-deru

Kartu mahasiswa telah disimpan dan tas kuliah turun
    dari bahu. Mestinya kalian jadi insinyur dan
    ekonom abad dua puluh satu,

Tapi malaikat telah mencatat indeks prestasi kalian
    tertinggi di Trisakti bahkan di seluruh negeri,
    karena kalian berani mengukir alfabet pertama
    dari kata reformasi-damai dengan darah arteri
    sendiri,

Merah Putih yang setengah tiang ini, merunduk di
    bawah garang matahari, tak mampu
    mengibarkan diri karena angin bersembunyi,

Tapi peluru logam telah kami patahkan dalam doa
    bersama, dan kalian pahlawan bersih dari
    dendam, karena jalan jauh dan kita perlukan
    peta dari Tuhan.

Taufiq Ismail

May 12, 1998

In memory of Elang Mulya, Hery Hertanto,
Hendriawan Lesmana and Hafidhin Royan

Four martyrs departed one night, a light mist of tears
    fell the next day, in the cemetery
    we heard the muffled sound of weeping

Young people, wandering with many others, committed to
    reformation because they were tired of deformation,
    who every day heard thousands of their friends
    calling for change

They put away their student cards, took their bags from their
    shoulders. They should have been engineers, and
    economists, shaping the twenty-first century

The angels honor their achievements above all at others at
    Trisakti University, indeed throughout the whole
    nation, because they dared carve out the first letters
    of peaceful reformation with the blood from their
    own arteries

The nation's flag hangs at half mast, bowed beneath the fierce
    heat of the sun, unwilling to flutter as long as the
    wind hides itself

Our common prayers have smashed their metal bullets, and
    you are heroes, freed from hatred.
    The road is still long,
    and we need a map from God

1998

Yang selalu terapung di atas gelombang

Seseorang dianggap tak bersalah, sampai dia
dibuktikan hukum bersalah. Di negeri kami,
ungkapan ini terdengar begitu indah. Kini simaklah
sebuah kisah. Seorang pegawai tinggi, gajinya sebulan
satu setengah juta rupiah,

Di garasinya ada Volvo hitam, BMW abu-abu, Honda
metalik dan Mercedes merah. Anaknya sekolah di
Leiden, Montpelier dan Savannah. Rumahnya
bertebaran di Menteng, Kebayoran dan Macam Macam
Indah,

Setiap semester ganjil, isteri terangnya belanja ke
Hongkong dan Singapura. Setiap semester genap, isteri
gelap liburan di Eropa dan Afrika,

Anak-anaknya pegang dua pabrik, tiga apotik dan
empat biro jasa. Saudara sepupu dan kemanakannya
punya lima toko onderdil, enam biro iklan dan tujuh
pusat belanja,

Ketika rupiah anjlok, terperosok, kepleset macet dan
hancur jadi bubur, dia ketawa terbahak-bahak karena
depositonya dalam dolar Amerika semua. Sesudah
matahari dua kali tenggelam di langit barat, jumlah
rupiahnya melesat sepuluh kali lipat,

Krisis makin menjadi-jadi, di mana-mana orang antri,
maka seratus kantong plastik hitam dia bagi-bagi.
Isinya masing-masing lima genggam beras, empat
cangkir minyak goreng dan tiga bungku mi cepat-jadi.
Peristiwa murah hati ini diliput dua menit di kotak
televisi, dan masuk berita koran Jakarta halaman lima
pagi-pagi sekali,

The man who always rises above the flood

A man is considered innocent until the law proves him guilty. This is a beautiful saying we have in this country. Now listen to my story. There was a senior civil servant, who earned one and a half million rupiah a month,

In his garage he had a black Volvo, a gray BMW, a silver Honda, and a red Mercedes. His children went to school in Leiden, Montpellier and Savannah. His houses were scattered over Menteng, Kebayoran and all the Happy Valleys,

In the first semester, he used to take his wife shopping to Hong Kong and Singapore. In the second semester, he holidayed with his mistress in Europe or Africa,

His children owned two factories, three pharmacies, and four insurance offices. His cousins and his nephews owned five automotive repair shops, six advertising agencies and seven shopping centers,

When the rupiah slipped, slid, fell and turned to mush, he laughed out loud because all his bank accounts were in dollars. After sun set twice in the western sky, their worth in rupiah had skyrocketed ten times,

The crisis grew much worse, everywhere people started to queue for basic necessities, so he gave away a hundred plastic bags. Each bag contained five handfuls of rice, four cups of cooking oil and three packets of instant noodles. This act of great generosity took two minutes on television, and was featured on page five of the early morning papers of Jakarta the next day,

Gelombang mau datang, datanglah gelombang, setiap
air bah pasang dia senantiasa terapung di atas banjir
bandang. Banyak orang tenggelam tak mampu timbul
lagi, lalu dia berkata begini, "Yah, masing-masing kita
rezekinya kan sendiri-sendiri,"

Seperti bandul jam tua yang bergoyang kau lihatlah
kekayaan misterius mau diperiksa, kekayaan tidak jadi
diperiksa, kekayaan mau diperiksa, kekayaan tidak
diperiksa, kekayaan harus diperiksa, kekayaan tidak
jadi diperiksa. Bandul jam tua Westminster, tahun
empat puluh satu diproduksi, capek bergoyang begini,
sampai dia berhenti sendiri,

Kemudian ide baru datang lagi, isi formulir harta
benda sendiri, harus terus terang tapi, dikirimkan pagi-
pagi tertutup rapi, karena ini soal sangat pribadi,

Selepas itu suasana hening sepi lagi, cuma ada bunyi
burung perkutut sekali-sekali,

Seseorang dianggap tak bersalah, sampai dia
dibuktikan hukum bersalah. Di negeri kami,
ungkapan ini terdengar begitu indah. Bagaimana
membuktikan bersalah, kalau kulit tak dapat dijamah.
Menyentuh tak bisa dari jauh, memegang tak dapat
dari dekat,

Karena ilmu kiat, orde datang dan orde berangkat, dia
akan tetap saja selamat,

Kini lihat, di patio rumahnya dengan arsitektur
Mediterania, seraya menghirup teh nasgitel dia duduk
menerima telepon dari isterinya yang sedang tur di
Venezia, sesudah menilai tiga proposal, dua diskusi
panel dan sebuah rencana rapat kerja,

If storms wanted to come, let them come, he would always rise above any flash flood. When others sank and were never seen again, he always said, "Yes, God provides for us all in the way He sees best,"

Like the rhythm of the pendulum of an old clock, the authorities decide to investigate those who somehow have more money than they should, but they don't investigate them, they should investigate them, but they don't, they want to, but they don't. The old Westminster clock was made in 1941, the pendulum grows tired of moving backwards and forwards, and finally stops,

Then the authorities think of a new idea, people should declare their interests by filling in a form, honestly, of course, and submit the details in a sealed envelope, early in the morning, these are private matters after all,

Then everything is silent again, apart from the occasional cooing of a pet pigeon,

A man is considered innocent until the law proves him guilty. This is a beautiful saying we have in this country. How can we prove anyone guilty, if we can't lay a finger on him. If we can't reach out to him from a distance, if we're never allowed to get close to him,

The man is a magician, regimes may come, and regimes may go, but he will always be safe,

Look at him, on the patio of his Mediterranean-style mansion, sipping Javanese herbal tea and talking to his wife on the telephone as she tours Venice, after he has evaluated three proposals, two panel discussions and the recommendations of one working committee,

Sementara itu disimaknya lirik lagu favoritnya My Way,
senandung lama Frank Sinatra yang kemarin baru
meninggal dunia, ditingkah lagu burung perkutut
sepuluh juta dari sangkar tergantung di atas sana dan tak
habis-habisnya di layar kaca jinggel bola Piala Dunia,

Go, go, go, ale ale ale . . .

Ikranegara

Merdeka

belum

While listening to his favorite song, "My Way," an old
song by Frank Sinatra, who has just died, and the
cooing of his ten million rupiah pigeon in its cage over
there, and the jingle of the World Cup endlessly
repeated on his television,

Go, go, go, ale ale ale . . .

1998

IKRANEGARA

Freedom!

no, not yet

May 20, 1998

Notes

Preface

1. "When we speak of literature, we enter the realm of contemplation."
The late Rev. Y. B. Mangunwijaya S.J., "Pemasyarakatan Susastra Dipandang dari Sudut Budaya," in *Menjadi Generasi Pasca-Indonesia,* ed. Sindhunata (Yogyakarta: Kanisius, 1999): 55.

2. Nevertheless, Adam Schwarz notes "some important continuities from the Old Order, and especially from the 1959–65 Guided Democracy period, to the New Order: the Armed Forces' view of its place in society and in government; the president's belief in a powerful presidency; a broadly shared sense of nation; a domineering Java; a divided Muslim community; a resented ethnic Chinese business class; a weak legal system and, closely related, a rich tradition of corruption, nepotism, smuggling and patronage." *A Nation in Waiting* (Sydney: Allen & Unwin, 1999): 3. Harold Crouch has argued that the whole period since Independence has been marked by "a steady movement towards authoritarianism." See his chapter, "The Trend towards Authoritarianism: The Post-1945 Period," in *The Development of Indonesian Society,* ed. H. Aveling (New York: St. Martin's Press, 1980): 166–204.

3. Michael Vatikiotis, *Indonesian Politics under Suharto,* 3rd ed. (London: Routledge, 1998): xv.

4. Following the reformed spelling system of 1972, I have referred to the president as "Suharto" throughout. The name is also written "Soeharto."

5. "Crime, Law and State Authority in Indonesia," in *State and Civil Society in Indonesia,* Monash Papers on Southeast Asia, no. 22, ed. Arief Budiman (Clayton: Monash University, 1990): 195.

6. Arief Budiman, *State and Civil Society in Indonesia,* p. 2.

7. Surveys of the beginnings of the "modern" period can be found in A. Teeuw, *Modern Indonesian Literature* (The Hague: M. Nijhoff, 1967); Burton Raffel, *The Development of Modern Indonesian Poetry* (Albany: State University of New York, 1967); and my *Thematic History of Indonesian Poetry: 1920 to 1974,* Special Report no. 9 (DeKalb: Center for Southeast Asian Studies, Northern Illinois University, 1974).

8. The topic of "generations" is a constant one in the criticism of Indonesian literature. The major papers are collected in *Sumber Terpilih: Sejarah Sastra Indonesia Abad XX,* ed. E. Ulrich Kratz (Jakarta: Kepustakaan Populer Gramedia, 2000). I intend to discuss this matter in depth in a companion study to this anthology, *Finding Words for Secrets: On Translating Indonesian Poetry*. In this anthology, I use the term in a fairly broad sense to describe a group of writers of similar ages and backgrounds, working in similar thematic areas and employing similar literary styles.

9. "Flying a Kite: The Crimes of Pramoedya Ananta Toer," in *Figures of Criminality in Indonesia, the Philippines and Colonial Vietnam,* ed. V. L. Rafael (Ithaca, N.Y.: Southeast Asian Program Publications, Cornell University, 1999): 258. Similarly, Adam Schwarz has also claimed that: "The New Order, almost insistently anti-intellectual, is all but bereft of great plays, books and films," *A Nation in Waiting,* 235.

10. A useful theoretical framework for the consideration of the relationship between literary and socio-political facts can be found in Terry Eagleton, *Criticism and Ideology* (reprint, London: Verso, 1986). I also intend to discuss this topic in depth in *Finding Words for Secrets: On Translating Indonesian Poetry*.

11. See Crouch's essay "Indonesia's Strong State" in *Weak and Strong States in Asia-Pacific Societies,* ed. P. Dauvergne (Canberra: Dept. of International Relations, Australian National University, 1998): 93–113.

12. This term was first used by the late Y. B. Mangunwijaya. See *Menjadi Generasi Pasca-Indonesia* (Becoming the Post-Indonesian Generation).

13. Harry Aveling, "Développements récents: 1966–1990," in *La Littérature Indonésienne: Une introduction,* Cahier d'Archipel 22, ed. H. Chambert-Loir (Paris: Collection Jeanne Cuisinier, 1994): 147. The quotation from Grotowski comes from his book *Towards a Poor Theater* (New York: Simon and Schuster, 1968): 57.

Chapter One

1. The essay, "Angkatan 66, Bangkitnya satu generasi," was first published in *Horison* (Aug. 1966), and is reprinted in Jassin's collection *Angkatan 66, Prosa dan Puisi* (Jakarta: Gunung Agung, 1968): 1–22. The quotation here is from page 5 of the anthology.

2. Tarzie Vittachie, *The Fall of Sukarno* (London: Andre Deutsch, 1967): 80.

3. J. D. Legge, *Sukarno: A Political Biography* (Harmondsworth: Penguin Books, 1973): 398.

4. Legge discusses Sukarno's fascination with titles, slogans, and ritual terminology in *Sukarno,* chapter 13. See also the 1963 essay by Goenawan Mohamad, "Seribu Slogan dan sebuah puisi," reprinted in *Kesusasteraan dan Kekuasaan* (Jakarta: Pustaka Firdaus, 1993).

5. In his joint volume *Tirani dan Benteng* (Jakarta: Yayasan Ananda, 1993): xxv, Taufiq Ismail lists the names of seven "martyrs," killed during the demonstrations: three from Jakarta (Arief Rachman Hakim, Djubaidah, Mohamad Sjafei), two from Jogjakarta (Margono, Arief Ambar Winangun) and one each from Banjarmasin (Hasanuddin Madjedi) and Makassar (Sjarief Alkadri).

6. Raj Vasil, *Governing Indonesia* (Singapore: Butterworth-Heinemann Asia, 1997): 61.

7. Damien Kingsbury, *The Politics of Indonesia* (Melbourne: Oxford University Press, 1998): 64.

8. "Sukarno's Ideal," *Quadrant* (Sept.–Oct. 1969): 91.

9. It has been estimated that two thousand books were banned between 1965 and 1966. See Krishna Sen and David Hill, *Media, Culture and Politics in Indonesia* (Melbourne: Oxford University Press, 2000): 37.

10. Jassin, *Angkatan 66,* p. 11.

11. *Islam Observed* (Chicago: University of Chicago Press, 1968): 86.

12. As is argued in a wider context in R. Robison, *Indonesia, The Rise of Capital* (Sydney: Asian Studies Association of Australia, Allen & Unwin, 1986): 128, n. 12.

13. Goenawan Mohamad, "Njanji Sunji Kedua: Sadjak: sadjak Sapardi Djoko Damono," *Horison* (Feb. 1969): 42.

14. "Sadjak-sadjak perlawanan Taufiq Ismail dan 'Angkatan 66,'" *Bakat Alam dan Intelektualisme* (Jakarta: Pustaka Jaya, 1971): 89–106.

15. See Keith Foulcher, *Social Commitment in Literature and the Arts: The Indonesian "Institute of People's Culture" 1950–1965* (Clayton: Centre of Southeast Asian Studies, Monash University, 1986); also Harry Aveling, "Indonesian Writers and the Left, Before 1965," *RIMA* (Jan.–June 1970): 1–7.

16. R. Robison: *Power and Economy in Suharto's Indonesia* (JCAP, np, nd): 23–24, 41. Despite their apparent removal in 1966, the "communists" were also perceived throughout the whole period as a continuing threat to the stability of Indonesia by the New Order government.

17. Nevertheless, Jassin continued to defend his concept of the "Generation of 1966" well into the early 1970s. See his "Angkatan 66 dan Sajak

Sepi," *Horison* (July 1972): 195, and "Angkatan 66 sudah mampus?" *Horison* (June 1974): 163.

18. A. Teeuw, *Modern Indonesian Literature* (The Hague: M. Nijhoff, 1967): 255.

19. Goenawan Mohamad, "Njanji Sunji Kedua": 42.

20. Taufiq's work appeared in the collection *Manifestasi* (Jakarta: Tintamus, 1963) in 1963, but he does not mention this book in the "bio-data" to *Tirani dan Benteng* (Jakarta: Yayasan Ananda, 1993). The first poem in this work is *"Bukit biru, bukit kelu."*

21. See K. Foulcher, "The Events Surrounding 'Manikebu,'" *BKI* 125:4 (1969): 429–65; and Goenawan Mohamad, "The 'Cultural Manifesto' Affair: Literature and Politics in Indonesia in the 1960s," Working Paper no. 45 (Clayton: Centre of Southeast Asian Studies, Monash University, 1988).

22. See Ajip's essay "Sumbangan Angkatan Tebaru Sastrawan Indonesia kepada Perkembangan Kesusasteraan Indonesia," *Kapankah Kesusastraan Indonesia Lahir* (Jakarta: Bhratara, 1964).

Chapter Two

1. Barbara Hatley, "Cultural Expression," in *Indonesia's New Order*, ed. H. Hill (Sydney: Allen and Unwin, 1994): 222.

2. See Goenawan Mohamad: "Kemerdekaan kreativitas: Sebuah pikiran di sekitar Taman Ismail Marzuki," *Kesusasteraan dan Kekuasaan,* 105–16 (cited in chap. 1, n. 4).

3. See David T. Hill, "The Two Leading Institutions: Taman Ismail Marzuki and *Horison*," in *Culture and Society in New Order Indonesia,* ed. Virginia Matheson Hooker (Kuala Lumpur: Oxford University Press, 1993): 246–62.

4. "Sadjak-sadjak Toeti Heraty," *Horison* (Oct. 1967): 308.

5. On European romanticism, see Rene Wellek, *Concepts of Criticism* (New Haven: Yale University Press, 1963): 161.

6. *The Development of Modern Indonesian Poetry,* 154–55 (cited in preface, n. 7).

7. In English, reference should be made to Goenawan's essays "Contemporary Indonesian Literature," *Solidarity*, Sept. 1968, and "You Can't Go Home Again," *Quadrant*, Sept. 1969.

8. "Sadjak-sadjak Toeti Heraty," 308.

Chapter Three

1. M. Ricklefs, *A History of Modern Indonesia since c. 1300* (London: Macmillan, 1993): 304.

2. See Michael Morfit, "Pancasila: The Indonesian State Ideology ac-

cording to the New Order Government," *Asian Survey* 21:8 (Aug. 1981): 838–51.

3. S. Tiwon, "A Lost Decade: Preliminary Thoughts," a paper submitted to the Conference on Postcoloniality and the Question of Modern Indonesian Literature (University of Sydney, May 1998): 108.

4. Robison, *Indonesia: The Rise of Capital:* 106 (cited in chap. 1, n. 12).

5. Kingsbury, *The Politics of Indonesia:* 70. See also the article by David Reeves, "The Corporitist State: The Case of Golkar," in *State and Civil Society in Indonesia,* ed. Arief Budiman: 151–76 (cited in preface, n. 5).

6. David Jenkin, cited in R. Goodfellow, "*Api dalam Sekam:* The New Order and the Ideology of Anti-Communism," Working Paper no. 95 (Melbourne: Centre of Southeast Asian Studies, Monash University, 1995): 16. See also Oey Hong Lee, *Indonesia Facing the 1980s* (Hull: Europress, 1979): 95.

7. "Wiranto and Habibie: Military-Civilian Relations since May 1998," in *Reformasi, Crisis and Change in Indonesia,* ed. Arief Budiman, Barbara Hatley, and Damien Kingsbury (Melbourne: Monash Asia Institute, 1999): 141.

8. M. Vatikiotis, *Indonesian Politics under Suharto,* 3rd ed. (London: Routledge, 1998): 113.

9. S. Tiwon, "A Lost Decade," 103.

10. Ibid., 108.

11. "Kesusasteraan Indonesia Modern dan Persoalan-persoalan masyarakat," *Horison* 4:2 (1969): 35; cited in Sapardi Djoko Damono, "Kritik Sosial dalam Sastra Indonesia: Lebah Tanpa Sengat," *Politik Ideologi dan Sastra Hibrida* (Jakarta: Pustaka Firdaus, 1999): 87.

12. Quoted by Sapardi Djoko Damono, "Kritik Sosial dalam Sastra Indonesia," 95.

13. *O Amuk Kapak* (Jakarta: Penerbit Sinar Harapan, 1981): 13–14.

14. Savitri Scherer: "Yudhistira Ardi Noegraha: Social Attitudes in the Works of a Popular Writer," *Indonesia* 31 (April 1981): 31.

15. "Whose Left?" rev. ed. Working Paper no. 33 (Melbourne: Centre for Southeast Asian Studies, Monash University, Sept. 1985): 2.

16. "Subversion or Escapism? The Fantastic in Recent Indonesian Fiction," *RIMA* 20:1 (Winter 1986): 51.

17. Ibid., 64.

18. Ibid., 53.

19. Ibid., 64.

20. Ibid., 52.

21. In 1973, for example, the Indonesian parliament affirmed an idea of National Awareness which insisted that "the Indonesian culture is essentially one and its various forms are only a reflection of the cultural wealth of the people." Raj Vasil, *Governing Indonesia,* 122 (cited in chap. 1, n. 76).

22. Marshall Clark, "Monsters and Mayhem: Surrealism in Indonesian Fiction," *Amida* 2:4 (1996): 14.

Chapter Four

1. Schwarz, *A Nation in Waiting,* 33 (cited in Preface, n. 2); see also J. Mackie and Andrew MacIntyre, "Politics" in *Indonesia's New Order,* ed. H. Hill (Sydney: Allen and Unwin, 1994): 13, and Kingsbury: *The Politics of Indonesia,* 104f (cited in chap. 3, n. 5).

2. D. T. Hill, *The Press in New Order Indonesia* (Perth: University of Western Australia Press, 1994): 37.

3. Ibid., 38.

4. Schwarz, *A Nation in Waiting,* 35, citing J. Mackie and A. MacIntyre, "Politics," 14.

5. *Indonesia: The Rise of Capital* (Sydney: Allen & Unwin, 1986): 165.

6. B. Hatley, "Cultural Expression," 228 (cited in chap. 2, n. 1).

7. Schwarz, *A Nation in Waiting,* 36; see also Kingsbury: *The Politics of Indonesia,* 107–8.

8. Mackie and MacIntyre, "Politics," 15.

9. Schwarz, *A Nation in Waiting,* 36; see also Kingsbury, *The Politics of Indonesia,* 107–8, and Vatikiotis, *Indonesian Politics under Suharto,* 18 (cited in chap. 3, n. 8).

10. Kingsbury, *The Politics of Indonesia,* 154.

11. Vatikiotis, *Indonesian Politics under Suharto,* 140.

12. Kingsbury, *The Politics of Indonesia,* 154.

13. Schwarz, *A Nation in Waiting,* 36; see also Vatikiotis, *Indonesian Politics under Suharto,* 105.

14. Vatikiotis, *Indonesian Politics under Suharto,* 236.

15. D. T. Hill, "'The Two Leading Institutions': Taman Ismail Marzuki," in *Culture and Society in New Order Indonesia,* ed. Virginia Matheson Hooker (Kuala Lumpur: Oxford University Press, 1993): 253.

16. The papers are collected in *Pengadilan Puisi,* ed. Pamasuk Eneste (Jakarta: Gunung Agung, 1986).

17. Mangunwijaya, "Sastrawan Religious," in *Menjadi Generasi Pasca-Indonesia,* ed. Sindhunata, 151–52 (cited in preface, n. 1); see also D. T. Hill, "Two Leading Institutions," 253.

18. Sen and Hill, *Media, Culture and Politics,* 27 (cited in chap. 1, n. 9).

19. *The Mastadon and the Condors,* trans. H. Aveling (Calcutta: Writers Workshop, 1981).

20. Brief comments on this play can be found in Hatley, "Cultural Expression," 227.

21. *The Struggle of the Naga Tribe,* trans. Max Lane (St Lucia: University of Queensland Press, 1979).

22. Originally published as *Potret Pembangunan dalam Puisi* (Jakarta: Lembaga Studi Pembangunan, 1980). (*State of Emergency,* trans. Swami Anand Haridas [Sydney: Wild and Woolley, 1980]).

23. Hatley, "Cultural Expression," 228.

24. Haridas, *State of Emergency,* 58–61.

25. For commentary on this poem, see R.W. Connell, *Which Way Is Up? Essays on Class, Sex and Culture* (Sydney: Allen and Unwin, 1983).

26. B. Hatley, "Constructions of 'Tradition' in New Order Indonesian Theatre," in *Culture and Society in New Order Indonesia,* ed. Hooker, 55.

27. "Rendra ditahan, Syafruddin dibebas," *Kompas* (May 5, 1978).

28. Krishna Sen, *Indonesian Cinema: Framing the New Order* (London: Zed Books, 1994): 114.

29. "Sastra, Politik dan Ideologi," *Politik Ideologi dan Sastra Hibrida,* 56 (cited in chap. 3, n. 11).

30. Chapter 15, paragraph 36.

31. Originally published in *Indonesia* (April 1, 1966). Reprinted in Anderson's *Language and Power* (Ithaca, N.Y.: Cornell University Press, 1990): 140.

32. "Analysing Indonesia's New Order State: A Keywords Approach," *RIMA* 20:2 (Summer 1986): 31. See also Virginia Matheson Hooker, "New Order Language in Context," *Culture and Society in New Order Indonesia,* 272–93.

33. "Seribu Slogan dan sebuah puisi," reprinted in *Kesusasteraan dan Kekuasaan* (Jakarta: Pustaka Firdaus, 1993): 76–77.

34. "Goenawan Mohamad," *Kompas* (May 2, 1999): 2. See also Ariel Heryanto, *Language of Development and Development of Language: The Case of Indonesia,* Pacific Linguistics, Series D-86 (Canberra: Dept. of Linguistics, Australian National University, 1995).

Chapter Five

1. Mackie and MacIntyre, "Politics," 17 (cited in chap. 4, n.1).

2. Vatikiotis, *Indonesian Politics under Suharto,* 105 (cited in chap. 3, n. 8).

3. Kingsbury, *The Politics of Indonesia,* 112 (cited in chap. 3, n. 5).

4. Mackie and MacIntyre, "Politics," 46.

5. Ibid., 17.

6. Vatikiotis, *Indonesian Politics under Suharto,* 25, 62. But compare Schwarz, *A Nation in Waiting,* 284.

7. Kingsbury, *The Politics of Indonesia,* 108.

8. W. Frederick and R. L. Worden, eds., *Indonesia: A Country Study* (Washington, D.C.: Federal Research Division, Library of Congress, 1993): 246.

9. Vatikiotis, *Indonesian Politics under Suharto,* 103.

10. Reuven Kahane uses the term "conspicuous" to identify one of the characteristics of Indonesian political symbols. The other characteristics he describes are that the terms are abstract and non-pragmatic; speculative; emphasize unity; are contradictory; and are monopolized by a very small group, often the president himself. *The Problem of Political Legitimacy in an Antagonistic Society: The Indonesian Case,* Sage Research Papers in the Social Sciences, Studies in Comparative Modernization Series, Hebrew University of Jerusalem, vol. 1 (Beverly Hills: Sage Publications, 1973): 23.

11. See R. Goodfellow, "*Api Dalam Sekam:* The New Order and the Ideology of Anti-Communism," Working Paper no. 95 (Clayton: Centre of Southeast Asian Studies, Monash University, 1995).

12. M. C. Ricklefs, *A History of Modern Indonesia since c.1300* (London: Macmillan, 1993): 307.

13. M. van Langenberg, "The New Order State," in *State and Civil Society in Indonesia,* ed. Arief Budiman, 123 (cited in preface, n. 5).

14. Ibid., 133.

15. *Indonesia: A Country Study,* ed. W. Frederick and R. L. Worden, 246. M. C. Ricklefs, *A History of Modern Indonesia since c.1300,* 306.

16. D. Bourchier, "Totalitarianism and the 'National Personality': Recent Controversy about the Philosophical Basis of the Indonesian State," in *Imagining Indonesia: Cultural Politics and Political Culture,* Southeast Asia Series, no. 97, ed. J. Schiller and B. Martin-Schiller (Athens: Ohio University Center for International Studies Monographs in International Studies, 1997): 165.

17. D. Reeve, "The Corporatist State: The Case of Golkar," in *State and Civil Society in Indonesia,* ed. Arief Budiman, 157.

18. Bourchier, "Totalitarianism," 157f.

19. Kingsbury, *The Politics of Indonesia,* 147–48, 195.

20. M. Glasius, *Foreign Policy on Human Rights: Its Influence on Indonesia under Soeharto,* (Antwerp: Intersentia, 1999): 270.

21. Mackie and MacIntyre, "Politics," 28.

22. Vatikiotis, *Indonesian Politics under Suharto,* 140–41; Schwarz, *A Nation in Waiting,* 36; Kingsbury, *The Politics of Indonesia,* 109.

23. Kingsbury, *The Politics of Indonesia,* 114; and Vatikiotis, *A Nation in Waiting,* 127. See also: *Briefing Book: The Petition of 50 Group and the Tanjung Priok Incident* (Lanham-Seabrook, Md.: Indonesian Publications, Oct. 1994).

24. Glasius, *Foreign Policy on Human Rights,* 98.

25. Vatikiotis, *Indonesian Politics under Suharto,* 107.

26. "The Cultural Aspect of State and Society: Introduction," in *State and Civil Society in Indonesia,* ed. Arief Budiman, 294.

27. *Menjadi Generasi Pasca-Indonesia,* 88 (cited in preface, n. 1).

28. Kingsbury, *The Politics of Indonesia,* 154.

29. W. Frederick, "Dreams of Freedom, Moments of Despair: Armijn Pane and the Imagining of Modern Indonesian Culture," in *Imagining Indonesia,* ed. J. Schiller and B. Martin-Schiller, 86, n. 28.

30. Mackie and MacIntyre, "Politics," 52, n. 39.

31. Krishna Sen and David Hill, *Media, Culture and Politics in Indonesia,* 39.

32. These figures are taken from *Media, Culture and Politics,* 37.

33. *A Nation in Waiting,* 245–46.

34. Glasius, *Foreign Policy on Human Rights,* 275.

35. *A Nation in Waiting,* 245.

36. Glasius, *Foreign Policy on Human Rights,* 40.

37. "Indonesia since 1945: Some Problems of Interpretation," in *Contemporary Indonesia: Political Dimensions,* ed. J. Mackie et al. (Clayton: Australian Indonesian Association and Centre of Southeast Asian Studies, Monash University, 1979): 10.

38. Mackie and MacIntyre, "Politics," 17. See also Kingsbury, *The Politics of Indonesia,* 86, and M. Vatikiotis, *Indonesian Politics under Suharto,* 38, 141.

39. Jon Ormur Halldorsson, "State, Class and Regime in Indonesia: Structural Impediments to Democratization," unpublished Ph.D. thesis (University of Kent at Canterbury: Centre of Southeast Asian Studies, 1991): 306.

40. See A. MacIntyre, "State-Society Relations in New Order Indonesia: The Case of Business," in *State and Civil Society in Indonesia,* ed. Arief Budiman, 390, n.31, citing Daniel Lev.

41. R. Goodfellow, *Api Dalam Sekam,* xv-xix.

42. See Suzanne Brenner, "On the Public Intimacy of the New Order: Images of Women in the Popular Indonesian Print Media," *Indonesia* (April 1999): 13–37.

43. Laurie J. Sears, ed., "Introduction," *Fantasizing the Feminine in Indonesia* (Durham, N.C.: Duke University Press): 18.

44. Toril Moi, *Sexual / Textual Politics: Feminist Literary Theory* (New York, Routledge, 1985): 166–67, cited in Sears, *Fantasizing the Feminine,* 19.

45. *Fantasizing the Feminine,* 19.

46. Julia I. Suryakusuma, "The State and Sexuality in New Order Indonesia,"

in *Fantasizing the Feminine in Indonesia,* 92–119. ("*Ibu*" is the Indonesian word for "mother.")

47. Cited in Saraswati Sunindyo, "Murder, Gender and the Media: Sexualizing Politics and Violence," *Fantasizing the Feminine in Indonesia,* 125.

48. Diane L. Wolf, "Javanese Factory Daughter: Gender, the State, and Industrial Capitalism," *Fantasizing the Feminine in Indonesia,* 140–62. See also Aihwa Ong, *Spirits of Resistance and Capitalist Discipline: Factory Women in Malaysia* (Albany, N.Y.: SUNY Press, 1987).

49. Sylvia Tiwon, "Models and Maniacs: Articulating the Female in Indonesia," *Fantasizing the Feminine in Indonesia,* 57–65.

50. Rosalind O'Hanlon, "Recovering the Subject: Subaltern Studies and Histories of Resistance in Colonial South Asia," *Modern Asian Studies* 22:1 (1988): 220, cited in Virginia Matheson Hooker, *Writing a New Society: Social Change through the Novel in Malay* (Sydney: Allen & Unwin, 2000): 8.

51. *Writing a New Society,* 9.

52. On poetry by women, see Korrie Layun Rampan: *Wanita Penyair Indonesia* (Jakarta: Balai Pustaka, 1997). Women's writing tended be more sporadic and less intense than that by men.

53. The Indonesian is more explicit: "*ia rasa tak ada dosa,*" she feels that there is sin (involved in the relationship).

54. See his remarks in the introduction to his volume, *Isteri* (Jakarta, Gramedia, 1997): ix.

55. Barbara Hatley, "Nation, 'Tradition,' and Constructions of the Feminine in Modern Indonesian Literature," in *Imagining Indonesia,* ed. J. Schiller and B. Martin-Schiller, 101.

56. Hatley, "Nation, 'Tradition,' and Constructions of the Feminine," 94.

57. Ibid., 93.

58. Hatley, "Constructions of 'Tradition' in New Order Indonesian Theatre," in *Culture and Society in New Order Indonesia,* ed. Virginia Matheson Hooker, 67, n. 3.

59. Hatley, "Nation, 'Tradition,' and Constructions of the Feminine," 94.

60. Sapardi Djoko Damono: *Sihir Rendra: Permainan Makna* (Jakarta: Pustaka Firdaus, 1999): 17.

61. See Ariel Heryanto, *Language of Development and the Development of Language: The Case of Indonesia,* Pacific Linguistics, Series D-86 (Canberra, Dept. of Linguistics, Australian National University, 1995): 38.

62. Subagio Sastrowardoyo, *Sekilas Soal Sastra dan Budaya* (Jakarta: Balai Pustaka, 1999): 93.

63. An English translation of "No Night Market" can be found in my *Pramoedya Ananta Toer: A Heap of Ashes* (St Lucia: University of Queensland Press, 1975): 107–59.

Chapter Six

1. C. Geertz, *The Religion of Java* (Glencoe: The Free Press, 1960): 12.

2. Ibid., 150.

3. James Peacock, *Muslim Puritans: Reformist Psychology in Southeast Asian Islam* (Berkeley: University of California Press, 1978): 18.

4. *Semasa Kecil di Kampung,* (Jakarta: Balai Pustaka, 1950): 50.

5. C. Geertz, *The Religion of Java,* 5.

6. Ibid., 128.

7. Ibid., 150.

8. The title of a paper given by Zifirdaus Adnan at the Conference on State and Civil Society in Indonesia, held at Monash University, Melbourne, in 1990.

9. Schwarz, *A Nation in Waiting,* 10 (cited in preface, n. 2).

10. Ibid., 12.

11. "Religion and Politics in Indonesia since Independence," in *Religion and Social Ethos in Indonesia,* ed. J. A. C. Mackie, (Clayton: Australia-Indonesia Association and Centre of Southeast Asian Studies, Monash University, 1975): 23. It must be stressed that Anderson does then go on to argue that the aims of the NU should really be evaluated in terms of its religious ends, preserving and extending a religious way of life, and not by purely political criteria.

12. "Priyayi Value Conflict" in *Religion and Social Ethos in Indonesia,* 35.

13. R. Tanter, "The Totalitarian Ambition: Intelligence and Security Agencies in Indonesia," in *State and Civil Society in Indonesia,* ed. Arief Budiman, 250.

14. "The Construction of an Indonesian National Culture, Patterns of Hegemony and Resistance," in *State and Civil Society in Indonesia,* ed. Arief Budiman, 309.

15. See Akbar S. Ahmed, *Postmodernism and Islam* (London: Routledge, 1992). The best studies of the Revivalist movement in Southeast Asian Islam have been done on Malaysia rather than Indonesia. See, for example, Judith Nagata, *The Reflowering of Malaysian Islam* (Vancouver: University of British Columbia, 1984); Chandra Muzaffar, *Islamic Resurgence in Malaysia* (Kuala Lumpur: Fajar Bakti, 1987); and Zainah Anwar, *Islamic Revivalism in Malaysia* (Petaling Jaya: Pelanduk, 1987).

16. "Improvising Political Cultural Change: Three Indonesian Cases," in *Imagining Indonesia,* ed. J. Schiller and B. Martin-Schiller, 27.

17. C. Geertz, *The Religion of Java,* 307.

18. On Amir Hamzah see: H. B. Jassin, *Amir Hamzah: Raja Penyair Pujangga Baru* (Jakarta: Gunung Agung, 1962); A. Teeuw, *Modern Indonesian Literature,* 1:84–103; H. Aveling, *A Thematic History of Indonesian*

Poetry, chapter 2 (see preface, n. 10); and Md. Salleh Yaapar, *Mysticism and Poetry: A Hermeneutical Reading of the Poems of Amir Hamzah* (Kuala Lumpur: Dewan Bahasa dan Pustaka, 1995).

19. See Ahmad Nurullah, "Sufisme dan Puisi Indonesia '80an," and Puji Santosa, "Puisi-puisi 1980an dan kecenderungannya," both papers presented to the Dialog Penyair Jakarta, 7–8 Nov. 1989. The major study is Ungku Maimunah Mohd. Tahir, *Islam in Modern Indonesian Literature 1966–1980s: Some Preliminary Observations* (Singapore: Southeast Asian Studies Program, 1990). On *"sastera Islam"* in Malaysia, see: A. Kamal Abdullah, *Unsur-unsur Islam dalam Puisi Melayu Moden* (Kuala Lumpur: Dewan Bahasa dan Pustaka, 1988); Norazmi Kuntum, *Teori dan Pemikiran Sastera Islam di Malaysia* (Kuala Lampur: Dewan Bahasa dan Pustaka, 1991); and H. Aveling, *Shahnon Ahmad: Islam, Power and Gender* (Bangi: National University of Malaysia Press, 2000).

20. In a letter to Ben Anderson, cited in Anderson's "Rewinding 'Back to the Future,'" a paper presented to the Conference on Indonesian Democracy in the 1950s and 1990s, Monash University (Dec. 1992): 1.

21. Hatley, "Constructions of 'Tradition' in New Order Indonesian Theatre," 57–58.

22. Ibid., 61. The poem was published in 1989 by Yayasan Al-Muhammady, Yogyakarta, and reprinted in 1991 and 1984.

23. *Syair Lautan Jilbab,* v; Hatley, "Constructions of 'Tradition' in New Order Indonesian Theatre," 61.

24. Liddle, "Improvising Political Cultural Change," 37 (cited in chap. 4, n. 26).

25. A number of the poems were reprinted in Ajip Rosidi's anthology *Laut Biru Langit Biru* (Jakarta: Pustaka Jaya, 1977).

26. *Cahaya Maha Cahaya* (Jakarta: Pustaka Firdaus, 1991): xiv.

27. H. Aveling, "Emha Masuki Sumber Keresahan Lain," *Berita Minggu,* Kuala Lumpur (June 21, 1992).

28. An important philosophical study of Emha's work is Budhy Munawar-Racman, "Puisi-puisi perenial Emha Ainun Nadjib dan Pemikiran Islam Indonesia," *Horison* (July 1991): 7–17.

29. "Priyayi Value Conflict," 35.

30. *Islam Observed,* 54 (cited in chap. 1, n. 11).

Chapter Seven

1. Jon Ormur Halldorsson, "State, Class and Regime in Indonesia," 341 (cited in chap. 6, n. 39).

2. H. Crouch, "Democratic Prospects in Indonesia," paper presented to the Conference on Indonesian Democracy in the 1950s and 1990s, Monash University, 9.

3. This sentence mainly follows Ian Chalmers, "Capitalist Development and the Changing Role of Parliament in Contemporary Indonesia," Conference on Indonesian Democracy in the 1950s and 1990s, 13.

4. For example, Hill and Mackie, "Introduction," *Indonesia's New Order,* xix (cited in chap. 2, n. 1).

5. The ease with which scholars refer to a period of "openness" in Indonesian political thought between approximately 1989 and 1994 disguises the difficulty of pinning the term down with any significant precision. A major, although short-term study, is Max Lane, *"Openness," Political Discontent and Succession in Indonesia: Political Developments in Indonesia, 1989–91,* Australia-Asia Papers no. 56 (Brisbane: Centre for the Study of Australia-Asia Relations, Griffith University, 1991).

6. Vatikiotis, *Indonesian Politics under Suharto,* 97 (see chap. 3, n. 5).

7. D. Bourchier, "Totalitarianism and the 'National Personality': Recent Controversy about the Philosophical Basis of the Indonesian State," in *Imagining Indonesia,* 172 (cited in chap. 6, n. 16).

8. R. William Liddle, "Improvising Political Cultural Change: Three Indonesian Cases," in *Imagining Indonesia,* 40 (cited in chap. 5, n. 16).

9. Vatikiotis, *Indonesian Politics under Suharto,* 142 (cited in chap. 3, n. 8). Edward Aspinall, "Student Dissent in Indonesia in the 1980s," Working Paper no. 79 (Clayton Centre of Southeast Asian Studies, Monash University, 1993) is a study of 155 demonstrations between 1987 and 1990; Aspinall accepts that there were far more demonstrations which were never reported.

10. Ibid., 115.

11. P. Eldridge, "Non-government Organizations, the State and Democratization in Indonesia," in *Imagining Indonesia,* 198.

12. Ian Chalmers, "Capitalist Development and the Changing Role of Parliament in Contemporary Indonesia," 13.

13. Lane, *Openness,* 28–30.

14. Vatikiotis, *Indonesian Politics under Suharto,* 116.

15. Kingsbury, *The Politics of Indonesia,* 121 (cited in chap. 3, n. 5).

16. Ariel Heryanto, "Part III: Introduction," in *State and Civil Society in Indonesia,* ed. Arief Budiman, 293 (cited in preface, n. 5).

17. Vatikiotis, *Indonesian Politics under Suharto,* 116.

18. Ibid., 88.

19. Douglas E. Ramage, *Politics in Indonesia* (London: Routledge, 1995): 41.

20. Van Langengerg, "The New Order State," in *State and Civil Society in Indonesia,* ed. Arief Budiman, 137.

21. Vatikiotis, *Indonesian Politics under Suharto,* 194.

22. Ibid., 194.

23. Ibid., 97.

24. Schwarz, *A Nation in Waiting,* 233. Frederick and Worden, *Indonesia,* 249 (cited in preface, n. 2).

25. D. T. Hill, "The Two Leading Institutions," 251–52 (see chap. 4, n. 15).

26. B. Hatley, "Constructions of 'Tradition' in New Order Indonesian Theatre," 55 (cited in chap. 4, n. 26).

27. Schwarz, *A Nation in Waiting,* 231.

28. Liddle, "Improvising Political Cultural Change," 32.

29. Ibid., 32.

30. Benny Subianto, "The Indonesian Middle Class and the Idea of Democracy," Conference on Indonesian Democracy 1950s and 1990s (Melbourne: Monash University, 1992), provides interesting detail on the middle-class audience who attended the final performance and their response to the banning.

31. Frederick, "Dreams of Freedom, Moments of Despair," 74 (cited in chap. 5, n. 16).

32. Hatley, "Cultural Expression," 245 (cited in chap. 2, n. 1).

33. Schwarz, *A Nation in Waiting,* 232. English translations of *Time Bomb* and *Cockroach Opera,* by Barbara Hatley and John McGlynn respectively, were published by The Lontar Foundation, Jakarta, 1992.

34. Schwarz, *A Nation in Waiting,* 234 (cited in preface, n. 2).

35. Kingsbury, *The Politics of Indonesia,* 157.

36. D. T. Hill, *The Press in New Order Indonesia* (1994): 41.

37. Ibid., 12.

38. Korrie Layun Rampan, *Puisi Indonesia Kita: Sebuah Perkenalan* (Yogyakarta: Nur Chaya): 1. Cited in Muhammad Haji Salleh, "Recent Indonesian Poetry, 1975–1985," *Tenggara* no. 24 (1989): 112.

39. Korrie Layun Rampan, *Wanita Penyair Indonesia* (Jakarta: Balai Pustaka, 1997): 488.

40. Sapardi Djoko Damono, "Pembelaan untuk Horison," *Politik, Ideologi dan Sastra Hibrida,* 116–28.

41. "Notes on the Indonesian Literary Scene," *Manoa* 3:1 (Spring 1991): 166.

42. Budi Darma, "Alam Pikiran YB Mangunwijaya," *Kompas* (Feb. 14, 1999): 5.

43. Frederick, "Dreams of Freedom, Moments of Despair," 75.

44. Ibid., 88, n. 45.

45. For an example of the penalties imposed on literary activists, see Will Derks, "*Sastra Perjuangan:* Literary Activism in Present-day Indonesia," *IIAS Yearbook 1995* (Leiden, 1996): 42–52.

46. Harry Aveling, "Développements récents: 1966–1990," 147 (see preface, n. 13).

47. Agus R. Sarjono, "Sastra Indonesia dalam Empat Orde Baru," *Horison* (Aug. 1998): 27.

48. Ariel Heryanto, "What does Post-Modernism Do in Contemporary Indonesia?" *Sojourn* 10:1 (1995): 34–44.

49. Ariel Heryanto, writing in the new periodical *Kalam* in 1994, cited in Michael Bodden, "Satuan-satuan kecil and the Uncomfortable Improvisations in the Late Night of the New Order: Democratization, Postmodernism and Postcoloniality," a paper presented to the International Research Workshop on Postcoloniality and the Question of Modern Indonesian Literature, University of Sydney (May 1998): 250.

50. *Mengenang Kriapur (1959–1987)* (Jakarta: Dewan Kesenian Jakarta, 1988).

51. Puji Santoso, "Puisi-puisi 1980-an dan Kecenderungannya," 9.

52. *Tiang Hitam Belukar Malam* (Bandung: Forum Sastra Bandung, 1996).

53. *Mengenang Kriapur (1959–1987)*, "Kota kota kota," 30; "Sajak buat negaraku," 18.

54. "Menghayati Sajak-sajak Obskurantis-imajisme," *Berita Buana* (July 29, 1986), cited in Wahyu Wibowo, *Konglomerasi Sastra* (Jakarta: Paronpers, 1995): 110.

55. "Apokalipsa dalam Kepenyairan Baru," *Berita Buana* (Dec. 23, 1986), reprinted in *Mengenang Kriapur (1959–1987)*, 12–14.

56. Abdul Hadi W. M., "Mengenal Kriapur: Penyair yang Mati Muda," *Berita Buana* (Mar. 9, 1987), reprinted in *Mengenang Kriapur (1959–1987)*, 5–9.

57. From the Indonesian newsweekly, *Tiras* (May 2, 1996), quoted by Sarah Maxim and Linda Owens in their introduction to "Selected Poems: Afrizal Malna," *Indonesia* no. 62 (1996): 83–89.

58. Second printing published in 1994 by Bentang Intervisi Utama, Yogyakarta.

59. *Asiaweek* (Feb. 5, 1999): 43.

60. Hatley, "Nation, 'Tradition' and Constructions of the Feminine," 100.

Chapter Eight

1. Hill and Mackie, *Indonesia's New Order,* xix. The comparisons made here draw largely on that book, especially pages xxiii–xxvii, and 56 (cited in chap. 4, n. 1).

2. Crouch, "Indonesia's 'Strong' State," 105 (cited in preface, n. 11).

3. *Indonesia's New Order,* xxiv.

4. Peter Reith, "Indonesia's Foreign and Defence Policies," in *Indonesia: Dealing with a Neighbour,* ed. C. Brown (Sydney: Allen and Unwin, 1996): 21.

5. Gareth Evans, "Australia and Indonesia: Neighbours for Half a Century," *Indonesia: Dealing with a Neighbour,* 10.

6. Hall Hill, "The Indonesian Economy: The Strange and Sudden Death of a Tiger," *Canberra Times* (June 7,1998), reprinted in Edward Aspinall, Herb Feith and Gerry van Klinken, *The Last Days of President Suharto* (Clayton: Monash Asia Institute, 1999): 15.

7. "Australia and Indonesia," 10.

8. E. Aspinall, "Opposition and Elite Conflict in the Fall of Suharto," in *The Fall of Soeharto,* ed. G. Forrester and R. J. May (Singapore: Select Books, 1999): 131–32.

9. Schwarz, *A Nation in Waiting,* 311–12 (cited in preface, n. 5).

10. Vatikiotis, *Indonesian Politics under Suharto,* 177 (cited in chap. 3, n. 5).

11. Hill and Mackie, *Indonesia's New Order,* xxiii–xxvii, 56.

12. Schwarz, *A Nation in Waiting,* 312.

13. *The Last Days of President Suharto,* iii–iv.

14. Kingsbury, *The Politics of Indonesia,* 14 (cited in chap. 3, n. 5).

15. Schwarz, *A Nation in Waiting,* 331.

16. Lane, "Mass Politics and Political Change in Indonesia," in *Reformasi: Crisis and Change in Indonesia,* ed. Arief Budiman, Barbara Hatley, and Damien Kingsbury (Clayton, Monash Asia Institute, 1999): 240.

17. *The Last Days of President Suharto,* 1.

18. Hall Hill, *The Indonesian Economy in Crisis* (Sydney: Allen & Unwin, 1999): 7.

19. Ken Young, "The Crisis: Contexts and Prospects," in *The Fall of Soeharto,* 112.

20. Crouch, "Indonesia's 'Strong' State," 93.

21. Hall Hill, "The Indonesian Economy," *The Last Days of President Suharto,* 16.

22. Kingsbury, *The Politics of Indonesia,* 88.

23. Crouch, "Indonesia's 'Strong' State," 94.

24. Crouch, "Indonesia Stagnates from the Top," *Sydney Morning Herald* (Jan. 5, 1998), reprinted in *The Last Days of President Suharto,* 23.

25. Muhammad Chatib Basri, "Indonesia: The Political Economy of Policy Reform," *Reformasi,* 27.

26. Edward Aspinall, Herb Feith, and Gerry van Klinken, *The Last Days of President Suharto,* v.

27. For details of the new cabinet, see David Jenkins, "Suharto Digs in with His All-crony Cabinet," *Sydney Morning Herald* (Mar. 16, 1998), reprinted in *The Last Days of President Suharto,* 31–32.

28. Forrester and May, "Introduction," *The Fall of Soeharto,* 17.

29. Details of Rais's "fall from grace" with Suharto in early 1997 are provided in Marcus Mietzner, "From Soeharto to Habibie: The Indonesian Armed Forces and Political Islam during the Transition," in *Post-Soeharto Indonesia: Renewal or Chaos?* ed. G. Forrester (Bathurst: Crawford House, 1999): 66.

30. Discussions of the characteristics of the students of 1998 can be found in David Jenkins, "Vanishing Regime," *Sydney Morning Herald* (Apr. 18, 1998), reprinted in *The Last Days of President Suharto,* 34–36; and Aspinall, "The Indonesian Student Uprising of 1998," *Reformasi,* 230–32.

31. For discussions of relationships between Wiranto and Prabowo, see Crouch, "Wiranto and Habibie: Military-Civilian Relations since May 1998," *Reformasi,* 128, and Bourchier, "Skeletons, Vigilantes and the Armed Forces' Fall from Grace," *Reformasi,* 150.

32. Ikrar Nusa Bhakti, "Trends in Indonesian Student Movements in 1998," in *The Fall of Soeharto,* 174.

33. Max Lane, "Mass politics and political change in Indonesia," in *Reformasi,* 241.

34. Aspinall, "The Indonesian student uprisings of 1998," in *Reformasi,* 215.

35. Louise Williams, "Business as Usual," *Sydney Morning Herald* (Mar. 14, 1998), reprinted in *The Last Days of Soeharto,* 29.

36. Peter Waldman, Raphel Pura, and Marcus Brauchli, "Changes Put Suharto on the Outside, Looking In," *Asian Wall Street Journal* (May 25, 1998), reprinted in *The Last Days of Soeharto,* 89.

37. See van Klinken, "The May Riots," *The Last Days of Soeharto,* 50–53 for details.

38. Dewi Anggraeni, "Exposing Crimes against Women," *The Age* (Melbourne, June 21, 1998), reprinted in *The Last Days of Soeharto,* 65–66; Don Greenlees, "Heat on Jakartagenerals," *The Australian* (Nov. 4, 1998), reprinted in *The Last Days of Soeharto,* 158, suggests that there were at least 52 confirmed cases of rape and more than 400 cases reported. For a theoretical analysis of this sexual violence, see Ariel Heryanto, "Rape, Race and Reporting," in *Reformasi,* 299–334.

39. Forrester estimates that eventually there may have been as many as 50,000 students at the parliament buildings, "A Jakarta Diary, May 1998," *The Fall of Soeharto,* 42.

40. For examples of this analogy, see Schwarz, *A Nation in Waiting,* 363, where Amien Rais may be quoting military sources, whom he expected to use live ammunition; and David Jenkins, "Vanishing Regime," 37, where an earlier use is attributed to Professor Sadli, a former minister.

41. Forrester, "Introduction," *The Fall of Soeharto,* 22.

42. Aspinall, "Opposition and Elite Conflict in the Fall of Soeharto," in *The Fall of Soeharto,* 139.

43. Mohammad Fajrul Falaakh, "Islam and the Current Transition to Democracy in Indonesia," in *Reformasi,* 218.

44. Details of the roles of the various actors can be found in the sources referred to throughout this chapter.

45. A translation of Suharto's speech is given in *The Fall of Soeharto,* 246–47.

46. The many meanings of this term are discussed in *Reformasi,* ii, 73, and 86.

47. "No More Bloodshed Reformation," *Horison* (June 1998): 4–5.

48. Rendra, "Agenda Reformasi Seorang Penyair," *Horison* (June 1998): 6–7.

49. On Seno's work, see Michael H. Bodden, "Seno Gumira Ajidarma and Fictional Resistance to an Authoritarian State in 1990s Indonesia," *Indonesia* (October 1999): 153–56. Seno's stories on the Dili massacre were published as *Saksi Mata* (Yogyakarta: Yatasan Bentang Budaya, 1994), English translation by Jan Lingard, Bibi Langker, and Suzan Piper, *Eyewitness* (Sydney: ETT Imprint, 1995). Seno discusses the importance of the critical role of literature when journalism is heavily censored in his collection of essays, *Ketika Jurnalisme Dibungkam Sastra Harus Bicara* (Yogyakarta: Bentang, 1997).

50. Keith B. Richburg, "Indonesia's Unintentional Martyrs: Slayings of Four Students Transformed a Nation," *Washington Post* (June 8, 1998), reprinted in *The Last Days of Soeharto,* 45–50, gives details of the death of these students. Aspinall notes in "Opposition and Elite Conflict in the Fall of Soeharto," 143, that one of the four (he does not say which one) had previously carried a placard calling in "a humorous and self-deprecating manner" for reductions in the cost of "photocopying and perfume."

51. *Reformasi,* 74.

52. The openness of "belum" is explored in James Sneddon, *Understanding Indonesian Grammar* (Sydney: Allen and Unwin, 2000): 81.

The Poets

ABDUL HADI W. M. (Abdul Hadi Widji Muthari)
Dr. Abdul Hadi was born in Sumenap, Madura, in 1946. He is a graduate of Gajah Mada University, Yogyakarta, and the Universiti Sains Malaysia, Penang, where until 1997 he lectured in the Literature Program, with a special interest in Muslim Sufi writing. He is the author of *Laut Belum Pasang* (1971), *Cermin* (1975), *Potret Panjang Seorang Pengunjung Pantai Sanur* (1975), *Tergantung Pada Angin* (1977), and the collected volume *Anak Laut Anak Angin* (1983); and scholarly essays on Muslim writing, traditional and modern.

ACEP ZAMZAM NOOR (Muhammad Zamzam Noor)
Born Tasikmalaya, West Java, 1960, Acep was educated at the residential religious school Pondok Pesantren Cipasung, Tasikmalaya, where he currently lives, and in Jakarta. Acep is also a graduate in Fine Arts of the Bandung Institute of Technology (1987), and has studied at the Universita Italiana per Stranieri, Perugia (1991–93). He is author of *Tamparlah Mukaku* (1982), *Aku Kini Doa* (1986), *Kasidah Sunyi* (1989), *Di Luar Kata* (1996), and *Di atas Umbria* (1999).

AFRIZAL MALNA
Afrizal was born in Jakarta in 1957. He has studied briefly at the Sekolah Tinggi Filsafat Driyakara, Jakarta (1981); and worked variously as a building contractor, insurance salesman, and art director. During his extensive travels in Europe in the early eighties, he received a special award from the Radio Netherlands in 1981. Afrizal is the author of *Abad yang berlari* (1984), *Yang Berdiam dalam Mikropon* (1990), both republished in *Arsitektur Hujan* (1995); and *Kalung Dari Teman* (1999).

Ahmadun Yosi Herfanda

Born in Kaliwungun, central Java, in 1956, Ahmadun graduated in Education from the Yogyakarta Teachers' College. Although he now works as a reporter and editor, he also has personal interests in painting and the theater. His published volumes include *Ladang Hujan* (1980), *Sang Matahari* (1984), *Sajak Penari* (1991), and *Sembahyang Rumputan* (1996).

Ajip Rosidi

Ajip Rosidi was born in Jatiwangi, Cirebon, West Java, in 1938. He is the author, in both the Indonesian and Sundanese languages, of many volumes of poetry, fiction, and criticism. A former director of the publishing house Pustaka Jaya, Jakarta; Ajip served until recently as Professor of Indonesian at Osaka Gadai (Osaka University of Foreign Studies). His volumes of poetry in Indonesian include *Pesta* (1956), *Ketemu di jalan* (1956), *Cari muatan* (1959), *Surat Cinta Endaj Rasidin* (1960), *Jeram* (1970), *Ular dan kabut* (1973), *Sajak-sajak anak matahari* (1979), *Nama dan makna* (1988); and the collected volume *Terkenang Topeng Ceribon* (1993).

Arifin C. Noer

Arifin was born in Cirebon, West Java, in 1941 and died in 1995. He was a graduate in Civil Administration from the Universitas Cokroaminoto in Solo, but subsequently worked as a theater director and highly successful film producer. He received the SEA Write Award, Bangkok, in 1990. Arifin's major poetry volumes are *Selamat Pagi Jajang* (1979), and the posthumously collected volume *Nyanyian Sepi* (1995).

Cecep Syamsul Hari

Born in Bandung, West Java, in 1967. Cecep graduated in Civics from the Bandung Teachers' College. He is the author of *Dua Wajah* (with Beni R. Budiman, 1992) and *Kenang-kenangan* (1996).

Darmanto Jatman

Darmanto was born in 1942 in Jakarta. A graduate in Psychology from the Universitas Gajah Mada, Darmanto has long been a lecturer in Social Sciences at the Universitas Diponegoro in Semarang. He is the author of *Bangsat!* (1974), *Sang Darmanto* (1976), *Ki Blakasuta Bla Bla* (1980), *Karto Iya Bilang Mboten,* and the collected volume *Golf untuk Rakyat* (1994). He has also published other volumes on the psychology of communication, literature, and culture.

Dorothea Rose Herliany

Dorothea was born in Magelang, Central Java, in 1963 and studied in the Indonesian Letters department of the Catholic Teachers' College, IKIP Sanata Dharma, in Yogyakarta. She currently resides in Magelang. Although she is best known as the author of a number of volumes of poetry, including *Nyanyian Gaduh* (1987), *Matahari yang mengalir* (1990), *Kempopong Sunyi* (1993), *Nyanyian Rebana* (1993), *Nikah Ilalang* (1995) and *Mimpi Gugur Daun Zaitun* (1999), Dorothea also writes short stories and manages her own small press.

Emha Ainun Nadjib (Mohammad Ainun Nadjib)

Emha was born in Jombang, East Java, in 1953, receiving his education at the Muslim religious school Pondok Pesantren Gontor and, briefly, in the Economics Faculty of Gajah Mada University. Emha travels widely, speaking on Islam, and is particularly popular with students. His poetry volumes include *"M" Frustrasi* (1976), *Sajak-sajak Sepanjang Jalan* (1978), *Nyanyian Gelandangan* (1982), *99 untuk Tuhan* (1983), *Syair Lautan Jilbab* (1989), *Seribu Masjid Satu Jumlahnya* (1990), and *Cahaya Maha Cahaya* (1991). He is also the author of a number of volumes of essays and social commentary.

Goenawan Mohamad (Goenawan Soesatyo Mohamad)

Goenwan was born in Batang, Central Java, in 1944. He studied psychology at the University of Indonesia from 1960, before proceeding to study politics at the Collège d'Europe, Belgium, 1965–66. He is well known as a journalist and was the chief editor of the newsweekly *Tempo* from 1971 until 1994, when it was banned by the Indonesian government. Goenawan is the author of *Pariksit* (1971), *Interlude* (1973), *Misalkan Kita di Sarajevo* (1999), and the collected *Asmaradana* (1992), as well as various volumes of essays.

Ikranegara

Ikranegara was born in Loloan Barat, Bali, in 1943. He is best known as a theater director, and his productions include translations of Ionesco's *The King is Dead* and Shakespeare's *Julius Caesar*. His poems have been published as *Angkat Puisi* (1979) and *Tirai* (1984).

Kriapur (Kristanto Agus Purnomo)

Kriapur was born in Solo, Central Java, in 1959 and unfortunately died in a traffic accident in 1987. A graduate of the Universitas Sebelas Maret, Solo, he served as a teacher, headmaster, and Lecturer in Indonesian Literature at Universitas Sebelas Maret. Poetry from two of his manuscripts,

"Perjalanan Luka" and "Mimpi Buruk Sebuah Dunia," was published in
the posthumous *Tiang Hitam Belukar Malam* (1996).

Linus Suryadi AG (Linus Suryadi Agustinus)

Linus was born in Yogyakarta in 1951 and died in 1999. He undertook
some tertiary education in English but was largely an autodidact, working
on various newspapers and magazines in Jogjakarta. His prose lyric, *Pengakuan Pariyem* (1981), attracted considerable attention for its bold use of
Javanese words and phrases. His other poetry volumes include *Langit
Kelabu* (1980), *Yogya Kotaku* (1997), and *Tirta Kamandanu* (1997).

Rendra (Raden Mas Willibrordus Surendra Rendra Bawana Rendra)

Rendra was born in 1935, in Solo. He was educated at Universitas Gajah
Mada and, in the mid-sixties, at the American Academy of Dramatic Arts
in New York. He founded the extremely innovative Bengkel Theater, a
theater workshop group, in 1967, and was later imprisoned briefly for his
political comments in 1979. He now lives in community with the group in
Depok, outside Jakarta. Rendra is the author of the following volumes of
poetry: *Ballada Orang-Orang Tercinta* (1956), *Empat Kumpulan Sajak* (1961),
Blues Untuk Bonnie (1971), *Sajak-Sajak Sepatu Tua* (1972), *Potret Pembangunan dalam Puisi* (1980), *Orang-Orang Rangkasbitung* (1993), and *Disebabkan oleh Angin* (1993). He has presented many highly successful theatrical
performances as actor and director, and has also published other volumes of
short stories, play translations, and essays on theater. Rendra received the
SEA Write Award in 1996.

Sapardi Djoko Damono

Professor Dr. Sapardi Djoko Damono was born in Solo in 1940, and is a
graduate of Universitas Gajah Mada and the University of Indonesia. He
has taught at various universities and was until recently Dean of the Faculty of Letters, University of Indonesia. Sapardi is the author of *dukaMu
abadi* (1969), *Mata Pisau* (1974), *Akuarium* (1974), *Perahu Kertas* (1983), and
Sihir Hujan 1984); he has also published various volumes of literary criticism, as well as literary translation especially from American writing. He
received the SEA Write Award in 1987.

Sitok Srengenge

Sitok was born in 1965 in desa Dorolegi, Grobogan, Central Java. He is a
graduate of Jakarta Teachers' College and the author of *Persetubuhan Liar*
(1992) and *Anak Jadah* (in press). Sitok's short stories have appeared in the joint

anthology *Para Pembohong* (1996). He currently works as a theater coordinator for the Utan Kayu Arts Complex and is an editor of the magazine *Kalam*.

Sitor Situmorang

Sitor was born 1924, Harianboho, North Sumatra and variously educated in North Sumatra, Jakarta, and in Cinematography at the University of California (1956–57). He was a member of the literary "Generation of 1945," and Chairman of the Lembaga Nasional Indonesia, a committed Sukarnoist literary organization, during the period of Guided Democracy. Sitor has worked as a journalist, administrator, and teacher of Indonesian language. He was imprisoned on political grounds from 1967 to 1975, after the establishment of the "New Order" in 1966. His works include *Surat Kertas Hijau* (1954), *Jalan Mutiara* (1954), *Dalam Sajak* (1955), *Wajah Tak Bernama* (1955), *Zaman Baru* (1962), *Dinding Waktu* (1976), *Danau Toba* (1981), *Angin Danau Toba* (1981), and the two collected volumes *Bunga di atas batu* (1989) and *Rindu Kelana* (1994).

Subagio Sastrowardoyo

Born in 1924, at Madiun, East Java, Subagio studied at Universitas Gajah Mada and Yale University. He taught at various universities in Indonesia and South Australia, before returning in the late seventies to Indonesia to serve in a senior administrative position with the government literary publisher Balai Pustaka. Subagio was the author of *Simphoni* (1957), *Daerah Perbatasan* (1970), *Keroncong Motinggo* (1975), *Hari dan Hara* (1979), and *Simphoni Dua* (1990), and his poetry has been collected as *Dan Kematian Makin Akrab* (1995). He also wrote short stories and literary criticism. Subagio died on July 18, 1995.

Sutardji Calzoum Bachri

Al-Haj Sutardji Calzoum Bachri was born in Riau in 1942, and is a graduate in Civil Administration, from Pajajaran University, Bandung. He has worked as an editor and journalist. His three volumes—*O* (1973), *Amuk* (1977), and *Kapak* (1981)—were published together in 1981 under the joint title *O Amuk Kapak*. He received the SEA Write Award in 1979. After a period of writing very little, he undertook the pilgrimage to Mecca in the late 1980s and this has significantly altered the direction of his writing.

Taufiq Ismail (Taufiq Ismail Abdul Gaffar Ismail)

Taufiq was born in 1937, at Bukit Tinggi, West Sumatra, but raised in Pekalongan, Java. Although he graduated from the Faculty of Veterinary

Science, University of Indonesia in 1962, he has worked extensively as an arts administrator and, most recently, as a public relations officer for a large overseas firm. He is the author of *Tirani* (1966), *Benteng* (1966), *Buku Tamu Musium Perjuangan* (169), *Puisi-Puisi Sepi* (1971), *Kota, Pelabuhan, Ladang, Angin dan Langit* (1971), *Ladang Jagung* (1973), *Puisi-Puisi Langit* (1990), and *Malu (Aku) Menjadi Orang Indonesia* (1998), and a number of commemorative volumes.

TOETI HERATY (Toeti Heraty Noerhadi-Roosseno)
Dr. Toeti Heraty was born in Bandung in 1937. She took a first degree in medicine at the University of Indonesia between 1951 and 1955, then an advanced degree in psychology in 1962 (with a thesis on Simone de Beauvoir); after taking a degree in philosophy at Leiden University in 1974, she finally completed a doctorate, also in philosophy, at the University of Indonesia in 1979 (with a thesis on the Self and Culture). She teaches philosophy at the University of Indonesia and currently serves as the Rector of the Jakarta Institute of the Arts. Author of *Sajak-Sajak 33* (1973) and *Nostalgi = Transendensi* (1995), she has also edited a volume of Dutch and Indonesian poetry, and a collection of poetry by women.

YUDHISTIRA ANM MASSARDI (Ardi Noegroho Moelyono)
Yudhistira was born in 1954 at Subang, West Java, but educated in Yogyakarta. He currently works as a journalist and magazine editor. Author of *Sajak Sikat Gigi* (1983), and a pioneer of the mocking, rebellious poetic movement of the early seventies known as *"sajak mbeling"* (disrespectful poetry), he is equally well-known for his satirical novels based on updated wayang themes, most especially *Arjuna mencari Cinta* (Arjuna looking for love), as well as a number of plays and short stories.

List of Poems by Author